THE STATES AND THE NATION SERIES, of which this volume is a part, is designed to assist the American people in a serious look at the ideals they have espoused and the experiences they have undergone in the history of the nation. The content of every volume represents the scholarship, experience, and opinions of its author. The costs of writing and editing were met mainly by grants from the National Endowment for the Humanities, a federal agency. The project was administered by the American Association for State and Local History, a nonprofit learned society, working with an Editorial Board of distinguished editors, authors, and historians, whose names are listed below.

Oregon

A Bicentennial History

Gordon B. Dodds

W. W. Norton & Company, Inc.
New York

American Association for State and Local History
Nashville

979.5

Library of Congress Cataloguing-in-Publication Data

Dodds, Gordon Barlow, 1932–
   Oregon: a bicentennial history.

   (The States and the Nation series)
   Bibliography: p.
   Includes index.
   1. Oregon—History. I. Title. II. Series.
F876.D6   979.5   77–9080
ISBN 0–393–05632–5

Published and distributed by W.W. Norton & Company, Inc.
500 Fifth Avenue
New York, New York 10036

Printed in the United States of America

1 2 3 4 5 6 7 8 9 0

To

Paul, Ruth, and Jennifer

Contents

Illustrations

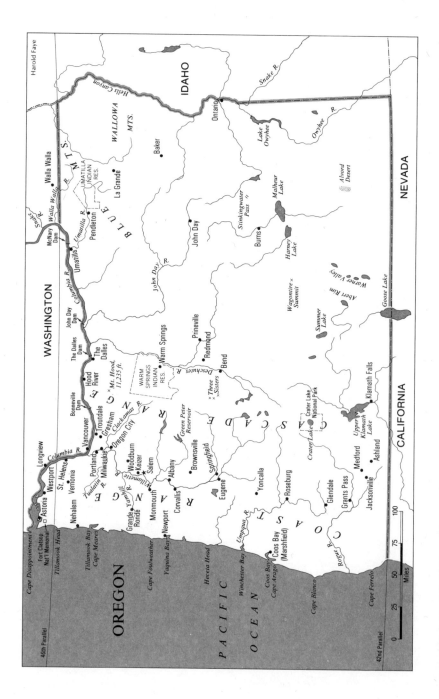

Invitation to the Reader

IN 1807, former President John Adams argued that a complete history of the American Revolution could not be written until the history of change in each state was known, because the principles of the Revolution were as various as the states that went through it. Two hundred years after the Declaration of Independence, the American nation has spread over a continent and beyond. The states have grown in number from thirteen to fifty. And democratic principles have been interpreted differently in every one of them.

We therefore invite you to consider that the history of your state may have more to do with the bicentennial review of the American Revolution than does the story of Bunker Hill or Valley Forge. The Revolution has continued as Americans extended liberty and democracy over a vast territory. John Adams was right: the states are part of that story, and the story is incomplete without an account of their diversity.

The Declaration of Independence stressed life, liberty, and the pursuit of happiness; accordingly, it shattered the notion of holding new territories in the subordinate status of colonies. The Northwest Ordinance of 1787 set forth a procedure for new states to enter the Union on an equal footing with the old. The Federal Constitution shortly confirmed this novel means of building a nation out of equal states. The step-by-step process through which territories have achieved self-government and national representation is among the most important of the Founding Fathers' legacies.

The method of state-making reconciled the ancient conflict between liberty and empire, resulting in what Thomas Jefferson called an empire for liberty. The system has worked and remains unaltered, despite enormous changes that have taken

place in the nation. The country's extent and variety now surpass anything the patriots of '76 could likely have imagined.
The United States has changed from an agrarian republic into a
highly industrial and urban democracy, from a fledgling nation
into a major world power. As Oliver Wendell Holmes remarked
in 1920, the creators of the nation could not have seen com-
pletely how it and its constitution and its states would develop.
Any meaningful review in the bicentennial era must consider
what the country has become, as well as what it was.

The new nation of equal states took as its motto *E Pluribus
Unum*—"out of many, one." But just as many peoples have
become Americans without complete loss of ethnic and cultural
identities, so have the states retained differences of character.
Some have been superficial, expressed in stereotyped images—
big, boastful Texas, "sophisticated" New York, "hillbilly"
Arkansas. Other differences have been more real, sometimes instructively, sometimes amusingly; democracy has embraced
Huey Long's Louisiana, bilingual New Mexico, unicameral Nebraska, and a Texas that once taxed fortunetellers and spawned
politicians called "Woodpecker Republicans" and "Skunk
Democrats." Some differences have been profound, as when
South Carolina secessionists led other states out of the Union in
opposition to abolitionists in Massachusetts and Ohio. The result was a bitter Civil War.

The Revolution's first shots may have sounded in Lexington
and Concord; but fights over what democracy should mean and
who should have independence have erupted from Pennsylvania's Gettysburg to the "Bleeding Kansas" of John Brown,
from the Alamo in Texas to the Indian battles at Montana's
Little Bighorn. Utah Mormons have known the strain of isolation; Hawaiians at Pearl Harbor, the terror of attack; Georgians
during Sherman's march, the sadness of defeat and devastation.
Each state's experience differs instructively; each adds understanding to the whole.

The purpose of this series of books is to make that kind of understanding accessible, in a way that will last in value far
beyond the bicentennial fireworks. The series offers a volume
on every state, plus the District of Columbia—fifty-one, in all.

Each book contains, besides the text, a view of the state through eyes other than the author's—a "photographer's essay," in which a skilled photographer presents his own personal perceptions of the state's contemporary flavor.

We have asked authors not for comprehensive chronicles, nor for research monographs or new data for scholars. Bibliographies and footnotes are minimal. We have asked each author for a summing up—interpretive, sensitive, thoughtful, individual, even personal—of what seems significant about his or her state's history. What distinguishes it? What has mattered about it, to its own people and to the rest of the nation? What has it come to now?

To interpret the states in all their variety, we have sought a variety of backgrounds in authors themselves and have encouraged variety in the approaches they take. They have in common only these things: historical knowledge, writing skill, and strong personal feelings about a particular state. Each has wide latitude for the use of the short space. And if each succeeds, it will be by offering you, in your capacity as a *citizen* of a state *and* of a nation, stimulating insights to test against your own.

James Morton Smith
General Editor

Preface

𝒯HIS book is an attempt to interpret the major themes, political, cultural, and economic, in the history of Oregon since the arrival of the first explorers. It also tries to indicate where the people of the state have most significantly influenced national and international developments and events, and have been affected by them. Although focussed thus upon a region that became a single state, the book does have a further purpose in singling out the experiences that separate Oregon from the other states of the Republic. To do justice in a short work to these large themes requires that much of consequence in the history of the state be omitted. Many important men and women, groups, and topics must be only touched upon or even passed over simply for lack of space. Yet the fact that this volume is the first history of the state published in more than thirty years gives the author hope that future scholarship will remedy its inadequacies, for the documents are rich, the workers few, the opportunities many in writing about almost any aspect of the state's history.

My most important influence in this book, as in my life, is my wife Rosemary. She contributed to the research and read the entire manuscript, portions of it several times. The full manuscript also was scrutinized and significantly improved by the scholarship of Edwin R. Bingham, Vernon Carstensen, Rodman W. Paul, Kent D. Richards, and Craig E. Wollner. Stephen Dow Beckham, Thomas D. Morris, and Robert Peters read portions to my benefit; Professor Beckham and Henry B. Zenk kindly allowed me to examine unpublished manuscripts dealing with the Indians; and Robert Sutton assisted in the research for another section. Robert E. Burke, T. A. Larson, and Wayne Suttles contributed their assistance in various ways. Gerald

xiii

George, the managing editor of the States and the Nation Series, contributed immeasurably in numerous ways to the preparation of this book. Gary W. Hansen was an ideal research assistant.

The format of this series does not allow comprehensive documentation of material derived from secondary authors as required in a scholarly monograph. I would, however, like to acknowledge specifically the contributions to Oregon historiography of several undergraduate and graduate students of Holy Names College (Oakland), Portland State University, Reed College, Santa Clara University, Stanford University, Syracuse University, the University of California (Berkeley), the University of Oregon, and the University of Washington. The seminar papers, theses, or dissertations of these students have been invaluable to my study of regional history and to the writing of this book: Warren Blankenship, Mary Chewning, David Cole, Janice K. Duncan, Christopher H. Edson, John S. Ferrel, Charles F. Gould, Martha Hicks, Daniel C. Hill, Oznathylee A. Hopkins, Robin Huffman, Amy Kesselman, Manly R. Maben, Franz M. Schneider, Philip Silver, Claude Singer, Richard Slatta, Marjorie R. Stearns, Jack E. Triplett, Walter K. Waters, Esther G. Weinstein, and Robert C. Woodward.

No one can write anything about the history of Oregon without employing the unsurpassed resources of the Oregon Historical Center. Thomas J. Vaughan, the director, and many members of his staff have been indispensable sources of information and encouragement, especially Cathy de Lorge, Barbara H. Elkins, Priscilla F. Knuth, Gordon W. Manning, and Arthur C. Spencer.

For a splendid effort in preparing the manuscript for the press I am indebted to Elizabeth L. Berg, Karen S. Birky, Linda C. Owen, Barbara J. Rossman, Sharon D. Swanson, and Shari Vice.

Oregon

1

The Old Oregon Country: The Outer Limits of Rival Empires (1500–1806)

I

A perceptive visitor conversing with residents of the state of Oregon in the bicentennial year, whether in city, small town, countryside, or suburbia, east or west of the Cascade Mountains, from the Columbia valley in the north to the Rogue River in the south, could hardly fail to learn that the men and women of Oregon are intimately dependent upon nature; that this dependence results in a colonial status economically; that colonialism in turn forces citizens into an awareness of national and international developments; and that the people themselves are ethnically and culturally homogeneous. What the visitor might not realize is that these characteristics have persisted since the era of the first settlements.

Oregon's relationship to nature is more noticeable than in most of the fifty states. The commonwealth's most valuable industries today are forest products, agriculture, and tourism. The extractive industries, beginning with the quest for the fur seal and the sea otter, then developing into the beaver trade, lumber milling, wheat raising, and salmon canning, all resting upon the regional waterways, have always been the basis of its economy. The modern tourist, equipped with camper, butane stove, and water skis, wearing hiking boots and packing a nylon tent, is also the heir of the past, of the generations of adventurers, landscape painters, and health seekers who have sought in Oregon's uncluttered spaces opportunities of a nonmaterial nature.

From the beginning the Oregonian has been a colonial. Relying economically upon outside markets, deferring culturally to San Francisco, Chicago, or New York, much of his life has been determined by decision-makers residing far from the borders of the state. But colonialism has not meant isolation. Indeed, however they might try to avoid the demands of world or of nation, Oregonians have been dragooned into recognition of external forces. The Oregon Country was the focus of imperial rivalry among five powers. From this conflict there emerged two final contenders for sovereignty. England ultimately yielded the territory south of the 49th parallel, but the victorious American citizens in the years ahead had to contend with—among a myriad of challenges to the status quo—the California gold rush, congressional attitudes on slavery, Asian immigration, promoters of transcontinental railroads, world wars, the Ku Klux Klan, abstract art, and thousands of outsiders crowding into the state.

Historically, most of these migrants have been similar. Initially, the Caucasian traders, missionaries, and explorers stamped—forcibly or otherwise—their commercial and religious institutions upon the Indian, and later farmers and businessmen continued to bring to their new homes a pervasive racism that has long afflicted the ethnic minorities within the region. The white man's discriminatory cultural values, laws, treaties, and constitutions since the days of the first explorers have been an enduring legacy of his transplanted culture. All of these features of Oregon's life—nature, colonialism, internationalism, and homogeneity—have their roots in the formative era, and in nations thousands of miles from the Pacific slope.

II

Oregon falteringly entered the civilized world as a minor offshoot of the intellectual, economic, and political revolutions reshaping Europe in the three centuries from 1500 to 1800. With the opening of the great frontier of Asia, America, and Africa after the voyages of Columbus, European businessmen and monarchs sought to exploit the natural resources of the undeveloped continents. Organized into proprietary colonies and joint-stock companies, protected by powerful monarchs such as Elizabeth, Ferdinand, and Isabella, equipped with potent arms and ammunition, their consciences secured by the mission of expanding Christianity, the conquerors force-fed the development of Old World mercantile capitalism with the natural resources of the New.

Epochal advances in science and technology accompanied Europe's new affluence. In the seventeenth century Bacon, Galileo, and Descartes attacked the conception of an earth-centered universe where scholars gained truths by means of deductive logic. Now through induction and empiricism they fanned a critical spirit that promised to lay bare the secrets of nature hitherto obscured by reactionary scholasticism. Toward the close of the century and throughout the next the genius of Isaac Newton, revealed in his *Mathematical Principles of Natural Philosophy* (1689), spread from scholars' studies to dilettantes' salons on the wings of innumerable popularizations, until the European world assented to Pope's couplet: "Nature and nature's laws lay hid in night; / God said, 'Let Newton be', and all was light." Newton's three laws of motion seemed to reveal for all time the major outlines, both terrestrial and celestial, of the physical universe. These achievements, it should be noted, were not isolated feats of the scientific great, for they rested upon the solid foundation of the labors of many men who first timidly banded together in obscure discussion clubs and lonely scientific associations, often in fear of secular or religious defenders of the status quo, but who in time gained the patronage of the rich, the noble, and the powerful in forming such great intellectual clearinghouses as the French Academy of Sciences and the British Royal Society that served to keep scholars in touch even across international boundaries.

The triumph of science was the triumph of reason. Churchmen had long welcomed human reason as a divine gift, as a means supplementary to faith to perceive God's truths. In the wake of the discovery of scientific laws, philosophers increasingly regarded reason as a way to discern the laws of politics and society and economics which they believed to be as immutable as the physical laws that the great Newton had revealed. It became a commonplace that everybody, not just the individual genius or the devoutly religious, possessed at least a modicum of reason. Confidence in reason refurbished the ancient belief in natural law, that deposit of virtue in the breast of every person, savage, barbarian, or civilized, that inspired him to moral conduct. And if all are rational, if all are moral, then all too are endowed with natural rights against the power of despotic institutions and personages, however exalted they may be.

The inevitable conclusion from the increasing faith in man's faculties, in humanism, was the ideal of progress. By the eighteenth century most intellectuals in Europe, England, and America felt secure in the belief that all aspects of human endeavor were improving or destined to improve. This era, after all, was the age which gave the word *civilization* its modern connotation of "the triumph of reason"; it was the epoch which condemned the medieval past as the "Dark Ages"; it was the period in which most thinkers proclaimed the present as superior even to the revered antiquity of Greece and Rome; the time when the Marquis de Condorcet proclaimed a century's faith: "It is certain that Man will become perfect."

Europe's trust in progress, even perfection, was not local or parochial, not snobbish or nationalistic. Humanism meant humanity; progress, natural law, and natural rights meant cosmopolitanism, for surely nature was not discriminatory, did not confine its gifts to the European world. Whether because of these philosophic assumptions or because of the discoveries of the sixteenth-century explorers, men and women of the seventeenth and eighteenth centuries turned eagerly for knowledge or diversion to the intriguing worlds of America and the East. What they discovered there was not easy for their countrymen to assimilate, for the titled aristocracy of the salons and courts and the newly leisured middle class of coffeehouses and drawing rooms received confusing signals from the reporters of distant continents. The sources of information were various; some authors had been to the exotic regions, some had not. Furthermore, the literary genres were not uniform since military reports, missionary assessments, and travellers' interpretations competed with realistic and utopian novels for the attention of the curious. Finally, the content of these writings gave the reader a wide choice in his response to the alien worlds.

Cortes and Pizarro, in looting the gold and silver of the Aztec and Inca civilizations, had indubitably found the greatest treasure trove of history. Ponce de Leon knew of the fountain of everlasting life. Everyone had heard of the seven golden cities of Cibola, or the golden man, or the Northwest Passage (the Strait of Anián) through North America to the Pacific, or the undiscovered continent—Terra Australis—created symmetrically to balance the northern hemisphere. Most intriguing of all, somewhere in the unexplored regions was domiciled the noble savage.

Rarely has there been such a compelling misconception. For the man or woman for whom progress and reason and civilization had not produced comparable institutions in Europe, solace came in the belief that in favored places of the globe resided a human being close to nature: generous, orderly, simple, and natural in the best sense of the words, unburdened by the artificialities of dogmatic church or tyrannical state, a being whose life was both mirror and model for the pampered European. Scores of writers drew his primitive and romantic portrait. Most popular of all was Baron de Lahontan, whose *New Voyages to North-America* glorified the Iroquois, and Lahontan was no armchair utopian but one who had himself lived in their bark longhouses.

And yet there was another side to the non-European cultures and their primitive inhabitants. One could not be sure that Baron Lahontan caught the true image of the New World for there were other writers, of equal credentials, who may have found not only wealth in distant places but also danger: mighty storms, threatening forests, insufferable climates. Primitive man, these critics claimed, was indeed savage, but scarcely noble: dirty, treacherous, lustful, backward, he and his culture deserved only the option of destruction or assimilation. But whether one found the undeveloped continents a source of virtue or of vice, of utility or of frustration, fascination with them led to an ever-widening concern with their environment and society, a concern manifested in a proliferation of dangerous ventures to unknown coasts. Among these beckoning regions, the sources of both temptation and trepidation, was the vast domain of the Oregon Country (far larger than the present state of Oregon), extending from the Pacific Ocean to the Rocky Mountains, and from the northern border of California (42°) to the southern boundary of Alaska (54°40′).

III

The opening of the Oregon Country to the Caucasian race was a product of the Anglo-Spanish rivalry of the Renaissance. Beginning from the base in the West Indies secured by Columbus, Spain's *conquistadors* fanned out through Central and South America. From 1492 through 1535 their quest for gold carried them to the great cultural centers of Indian America where they laid tribute the Aztec, Chibcha, and Inca peoples. Buoyed by the treasures of Latin America, Spanish maritime explorers pushed into the Pacific, discovered the Philippine Islands, and first circumnavigated the globe. By 1600 Spain's treasure galleons had linked the Philippines with Acapulco and the Spanish Main with Cadiz. Her monarchs, Charles V (1516–1556) and Philip II (1556–1598), dazzled Europe with their empire's cultural magnificence and political hegemony and their unquenchable liberality in pouring the wealth of the Indies into the wars of religion arising out of the Reformation. The mines of Aztec and Inca, however, were something less than eternal in their supply. Admission of this inescapable fact, coupled with geographic delusions and the maddening blows of

England, turned the attention of Spaniards to their northern borderlands. Shortly after Cortes's conquest of Montezuma, Spain had started her explorations northward to California from Panama and western Mexico, but the Pacific Northwest became desirable only because it represented one of the innumerable European fantasies about America.

The Strait of Anián connecting the Pacific and the Atlantic oceans was, men avowed, not only a geographic fact but a source of mercantile wealth. A short northern passageway, avoiding the dangerous capes to the south, would be worth a fortune in time, logistics, and safety for the fragile vessels of the day. The Pacific Northwest, along with other favored regions of America, promised more than this long-desired waterway. Gold and silver, pearls, precious stones, exotic plants lay there just as they had beckoned men of all nations—Verrazano, Champlain, Raleigh, Gilbert, John Smith, to recount the most familiar—to eastern North America. Private enterprise with the blessing of the crown (secured by a promise of one-tenth of the profits—the same arrangement made by Ferdinand and Isabella with Columbus) was the time-honored instrument at hand. The results were expected to bolster the declining fortunes of Mexico and Peru and sustain Spain's position as the most glorious and most extensive empire of world history.

The confident beginnings of this anticipated renaissance began all across the Spanish borderlands. In the middle of May in 1539 Hernando de Soto sailed from Cuba to plant a colony 600 strong in Florida, a land of elastic boundaries that might well contain the seven golden cities of Cibola. Four years later the survivors, reduced by half, wandered into Mexico City after traversing most of the present southeastern United States and discovering the Mississippi River, which became for De Soto both his glory and his grave. In February 1540 Francisco Vasquez de Coronado left from Compostela for the Seven Cities of Cibola. When he returned two years later to the City of Mexico, Coronado reported the tall grasses, the mercurial climate, and the shaggy buffalo of the Great Plains, but no cities of gold. And farthest west Antonio de Mendozo, the great viceroy of Mexico, dispatched an expedition in 1542 commanded by Juan

Rodriguez Cabrillo, a naval officer, to seek the Strait of Anián by sailing north beyond California. Disease killed the commander, but his lieutenant, Bartolome Ferrelo, carried on and may have become the first white man to catch sight of the coast of Oregon, before wind and fog forced his expedition to turn back just south of the 42nd parallel, the later boundary between California and the Northwest. These three great probes, east, center, west, all ended in failure, but so far as the Northwest coast was concerned, the failure may have been a boon to Spain for, upon reflection, her officialdom decided not to follow Ferrelo's wake in fear that a discovered Anián might become a curse, might benefit the *nouveaux* empires of France or Russia or England more than its nondiscovery would succor Spain. For the same reason it was better to leave, out of sight if not out of mind, the minerals and pearls of the Northwest.

England, however, was painfully visible, to Spanish eyes, for under Queen Elizabeth, the charismatic "Gloriana" of her people, that hitherto insignificant nation had become a world power in arts, commerce, and statecraft. Her gains were Spain's losses in both the diplomacy of continental chancelleries and on the decks of ships of war in the Atlantic, the Caribbean, and the misnamed Pacific. The struggle between English corsair and Spanish galleon is one of the epic themes of maritime history and one not unrelated to the genesis of Caucasian Oregon. It opened in the Pacific with Francis Drake's attacks on the western coasts of South America and his capture of the treasure galleon bound from the Philippines to Acapulco in 1578–1579. On this voyage, hunting for a port to refit, Drake may have reached what became the Oregon line, but the evidence remains unclear. A decade later the English privateer Thomas Cavendish raided Peru, then took a galleon worth one million dollars; the Spanish viceroy feared he had slipped in and out of the Pacific through the Strait of Anián.

Spain's responses to the English assaults fluctuated between rage and hesitation. Some colonial officials favored exploration of the California and Northwest coasts to establish antibuccaneering bases; others, fearful of financial drain and naval overexpansion, cautioned inaction. One final exploratory effort was made just at the beginning of the new century. In 1602–1603 Sebastián Vizcaíno and Martín de Aguilar sailed from Acapulco to chart the coast of northern California. They reached a latitude of 43° before the sea and scurvy defeated them, ending Spain's last thrust towards the Oregon Country for 171 years, and she then settled to a conscious policy of neglect concerning the Pacific Northwest. The Spanish allowed the Strait of Anián again to slip from memory in the hope that no foreign power would reveal it to provide a means of leverage against their possessions. Thus the legacy of Spain's maritime pioneers became one of courage, resourcefulness, and ultimate oblivion, as official policy demanded that their maps, their charts, their logbooks lie concealed, even from other Spaniards.

IV

The year 1774 was one of anguish for the great imperial rivals Britain and Spain. In Philadelphia rebellious colonists met in the First Continental Congress to petition George III for redress of grievances. A continent away Spain, too, was on the defensive. Her colonial governors worried not about rebellious subjects but about Russian entrepreneurs, fur traders hunting sea otter in Alaskan waters who were, so feared the Spanish, ambitious to push down the entire coast of western North America even to California in pursuit of their lucrative aquatic quarry. A more depressing prospect for Spain was a potential by-product of Russian expansion. What if they discovered the Strait of Anián, followed it to the center of the continent, and then struck southward to the core of the Iberian empire, the silver-producing provinces of northern Mexico? Or what if the British followed the same southerly route, perhaps coming through Anián from the east, from Hudson Bay or the Saint Lawrence?

To forestall the Russians, the Spanish had begun at San Diego in 1769 their famous California mission chain. At these imperial outposts they planned to secure the province with a handful of soldiers, a few dedicated friars, and numerous Christian Indians. Farther north, information was the first requirement, and to obtain it Viceroy Antonio Maria de Bucareli, a century and three-quarters after Spain's previous expedition, sent Juan Pérez to the Northwest coast in 1774. Pérez's men reached their farthest north at 55°30', encountered canoe loads of Haida Indians, and discovered a future pivot of international power politics and commercial relations, Nootka Sound on western Vancouver Island. But Pérez did not land nor did he claim possession anywhere in the Northwest.

Spurred on by further warnings from Madrid, Bucareli sent other mariners, Bruno de Heceta and Juan Francisco Bodega y Quadra, north again in the following year to spy upon the Russians, to explore, to take possession, and to assess the trade potential of the Indians. Heceta entrenched himself forever in the history of exploration when, on August 17, he discovered what he took to be the Strait of Anián, but what Robert Gray later rediscovered and named the Columbia River. But Heceta did not investigate the waterway. He found the Indians to be formidable (they killed seven members of a landing party) and he only reached 58°30' north rather than his chosen destination of 65°. His sole success, and that was chimerical, was to claim possession of the country for imperial Spain. The failures of Pérez and Heceta stood in stark, perhaps unfair, contrast to the exploits of the first English explorer of the Pacific Northwest.

In a London salon one April evening in 1776, the diarist James Boswell reflected upon a couple standing across the room: "It was curious to see Cook, a grave steady man, and his wife, a decent plump Englishwoman, and think that he was preparing to sail round the world." [1] Boswell, of course, did not confuse James Cook's appearance with his achievements, for the unprepossessing mariner was one of the greatest explorers who ever lived. The son of a day laborer, Cook had early gone to sea, had risen to command a collier in the north of England, and had served efficiently in the Seven Years War as a naval officer. His reputation as a navigator earned him the command of an expedition to the South Pacific in 1768–1771, sponsored by the Royal Society, when he observed the transit of Venus and

1. Charles Ryskamp and Frederick A. Pottle, *Boswell: The Ominous Years, 1774–1776* (New York: McGraw-Hill, 1963), p. 309.

searched faithfully but fruitlessly for Terra Australis, the unknown continent. He became the first white man to visit New
Zealand in more than a century and he also touched at Tahiti.
The year after his return he began a four-year sweep that carried him to the Antarctic and through many islands of the Central and South Pacific. Returning triumphantly from his second
voyage, Cook personified for Europe the eighteenth-century virtues of cosmopolitanism, humanity, and reason. His navigational skill was legendary, his antiscorbutic measures innovative, and his patrons impressive.

Now Cook was preparing for his third and final voyage, the
only one concerned with North America. His instructions, dated
two days after the proclamation of the Declaration of Independence, were a compendium of the century's aspirations: the Admiralty ordered Cook to find the Northwest Passage, to inven-
tory the natural environment, to take possession of territory
unclaimed by foreign powers, and to deal kindly but firmly with
the natives.

Cook's vessels, *Resolution* and *Discovery,* departed from
Plymouth on July 12, 1776, passed around Cape Horn, and
reached the Northwest coast at Cape Blanco on March 7, 1777,
after passage via New Zealand, Tonga, and Tahiti. Cook then
proceeded northward to Nootka Sound, unwittingly bypassing in
foul weather and in the night two great attractions for the
searcher for the Northwest Passage, the Columbia River and the
Strait of Juan de Fuca. After a stay of a month's duration at
Nootka he sailed north to Alaskan waters, hoping to find a passage to the Arctic Ocean, but he was turned back by ice at his
highest latitude, 70°44'. Cook then retired to winter quarters in
Hawaii, where he was killed in a skirmish with the natives.
Command of the expedition then fell to Capt. Charles Clerke,
and after his death to Capt. John Gore, who finally brought the
ships home on October 4, 1780. Cook's voyage was important
not only for itself but also because its journals, unlike those of
the Spanish discoveries, were published openly for the world to
admire. According to his biographer, J. C. Beaglehole, Cook on
his third voyage settled the general outline of the American
coast from Cape Blanco to Nootka Sound and from a few de-

grees beyond Nootka to Cook Inlet. He firmly placed the general line of the Alaskan Peninsula, discovered the true nature and direction of the Aleutian chain, and also made preliminary surveys of Alaska beyond those islands.

In addition to the geographical record that his biographer rightfully celebrates, impressive as it was, Cook's final voyage had other implications for the Pacific Northwest. The most important concerned the fur trade. For almost forty years there had been a market in north China for the pelts of seals and otters. The Russians had inaugurated this traffic from the rich sealing grounds of Alaska, and later, as we have seen, they threatened to encroach upon Spanish California. Thus it was not surprising in December 1779, when *Resolution* and *Discovery* anchored in Macao on their homeward journey, that their seamen were able to dispose of the skins acquired in casual trade in America. What did amaze them was the rate of exchange. As the official journal put it: "We sold the remainder of our furs to much greater advantage, then [*sic*] at Kamchatka; the Chinese being very eager to purchase them and gave us from 50 to 70 dollars a skin; . . . for what we bought with only a hatchet or a Saw." Lt. James King added, "The rage with which our seamen were possessed to return to Cook's River [Inlet], and, by [*sic*] another cargo of skins, to make their fortunes, at one time, was not far short of mutiny." The result of this momentous discovery, within half a decade of its publication, was to send the first of a multinational flotilla to the Northwest coast with almost incalculable consequences for the North Pacific Indians, for the fortunes of British businessmen, for the economy of the United States, and for Anglo-Spanish relations.[2]

The mariners who rushed to Nootka Sound and Alaska could choose from a variety of impressions offered by several of Cook's men whose logs or journals they had eagerly scanned. Statesmen, natural historians, and armchair travellers also were intrigued by the description of the natural environment and cultural patterns of the area. A composite view of their impressions

2. J. C. Beaglehole, ed., *The Journals of Captain James Cook on His Voyage of Discovery,* 4 vols. (Cambridge: At the University Press, 1955–1967), 3:714.

of Nootka gathered from the Cook expedition documents might run like this: The climate of the Pacific Northwest at this latitude was mild in comparison to the Atlantic Coast, surprisingly so, and indeed was as congenial to farming as to the fur trade. Although the Indians had neither necessity nor desire to practice agriculture, the advanced state of the wild plants early in the season, the size of the trees that testified to the fertility of the soil, and the warmth of the spring temperatures promised a land "fit for cultivation." But Lieutenant King also gave the primitive counterpoint to this pastoral scene: "The high mountains which rise on the back & far inland are many of them bare, & serve to heighten & finish the Picture of as wild & savage a Country as one can well draw in so temperate a climate." [3]

Not surprisingly, Cook's men were also ambivalent about the noble savages of Nootka. They judged them not only against the standard of the European philosopher but also against their experiences with the native peoples of Hawaii and the South Seas. The wisest observers, like King, recognized the difficulties of distinguishing Man from men: "rather few of us are capable seperating [*sic*] the invariable & constant springs by which we are all mov'd, & what depends on education & fashion." [4] Yet the Admiralty's instructions required judgment, and certain broad areas of agreement did emerge.

The Indians were "brave, resolute, and of a good disposition" toward the visitors, although quick to sense and to redress injuries among themselves. They were superb canoemen, fine carvers, and expert manufacturers of wooden boxes and other utensils. They traded furs willingly and sold the favors of their women, who were, once cleansed from paint and ashes, not unattractive if Englishmen "had the Courage & perseverence to attempt the refining of this ore, among which it must be confessed we sometimes found some Jewels that rewarded our trouble, Namely two sparkling black Eyes accompanied with a beautiful Face." [5]

3. Beaglehole, *Cook,* 4:1402–1403.
4. Beaglehole, *Cook,* 4:1406.
5. Beaglehole, *Cook,* 4:1100.

To all the officers the Indians' filthiness was their most repellent aspect. Cook found them to be ''slovenly and dirty to the last degree'' and Clerke, ''the dirtiest set of People I ever yet met with.'' Indian cookery turned the stomachs even of eighteenth-century sailors, especially their art of baking fish, during which the Indians covered the food with ''hot stones & Ashes, & in order to keep the heat they clap on their old greasy habits, that are seen swarming with lice, Old mats & whatever is at hand.'' The Indians stole (although, unlike the South Sea Islanders, less nimbly and only what was valuable—including Cook's gold watch), but perversely were extremely property-conscious themselves, selling not only pelts but trying to drive a bargain for ''the very wood and water we took on board.'' Their music and dances impressed some visitors, repelled others; all were disgusted by reports of Indian cannibalism, a charge later proved to be unfounded. Yet the Indians, however unpleasant in some respects, were redeemed by their furs and by their exotic naturalism, and the Europeans who read about them treasured them as much as they did the primitive peoples of Hawaii or Samoa.[6]

One year after the publication of Captain Cook's *Journals* in 1784 the first of the British fur traders, James Hanna, was on the Northwest coast in a sixty-ton brig to engage in the sea otter commerce. Although very little is known about Hanna, a great deal is clear about the system under which he and the later British traders operated on the coast. The British government continued to adhere to the old policy of mercantilism, although the challenge to it from Adam Smith's *Wealth of Nations* (1776) and other works advocating free trade was beginning to be heard. Mercantilism was a complex theory with many facets. One was the belief that government should allocate exclusive spheres of interest to monopolistic commercial companies, the best-known of which in North America was the Hudson's Bay Company, founded in 1670. Other companies with deceptive names also had a very real interest in the continent. One of them was the South Seas Company, which had title to all British trade

6. Beaglehole, *Cook*, 3:306, 311; 4:1326, 1412.

on the west coast of America and within 300 leagues of it. Another was the East India Company, which had the exclusive right to import goods, including furs, to the China markets. Mercantilism also raised other barriers for British businessmen. One of its tenets was that trade should be in vessels of one's own flag; another was that trading with one's colonies was preferable (for the balance of trade) to trading with a foreign nation. Spain also adhered to these postulates and claimed the sovereignty of the Pacific Northwest by right of the papal bull of 1494 and through the voyages of her explorers. An Englishman contemplating a trading expedition to the Northwest needed both licenses from the two British companies, which were expensive, and the courage to defy the laws of Spain, which might cost one's ship.

The most famous of the capitalists who broke these twin barriers were Richard Cadman Etches and his associates, British businessmen, who had sent two licensed ships to the Northwest in 1786. Their mariners encountered other vessels, including two trading illegally, according to both Spanish and English law, under Portuguese colors, but actually owned by another English syndicate headed by John Meares. Etches's ships traded in the Queen Charlotte Islands and in Alaska before reaching their destination in China in November 1788. To prevent legal difficulties and to reduce competition, the Etches and Meares groups combined in 1788 to form the Associated Merchants Trading to the North West Coast of America. The new company obtained proper licenses and laid plans not only to trade with the Indians but also to plant a trading factory (to be called Fort Pitt) to anchor a chain of posts all along the coast. These prospects were temporarily stymied, however, when the company's ships became the first to encounter Spain's defense of her claims to sovereignty. Gov. Esteban José Martinez seized *Argonaut* and *Princess Royal* in the harbor at Nootka Sound and transported their captain, James Colnett, and the crews to prison in Mexico. After England and Spain approved the Nootka Sound Convention the way was clear for British vessels to voyage to the Northwest coast, and they were the most numerous ships of any nationality until the mid-1790s. Thereafter they yielded primacy to the Americans, who were unhampered by mercantilist regulations either in the Northwest or in China.

The Peace of Paris of 1763 had sealed France's humiliation in the Seven Years War. England had embarrassed her on the high seas, checkmated her on the continent, and ejected her from her vast possessions in North America. To gain revenge upon her rival, France had contributed mightily to the rebellious Thirteen Colonies, but the war that gave America independence brought only financial dislocations to her patron. One of her many trials in these years of struggle was the news of Captain Cook's achievements, news that received plaudits in France despite Cook's nationality, a bittersweet, grudging admiration from the nation that considered herself the intellectual giant of the powers.

France's first response to Cook's accomplishments was the dispatch of Yves-Joseph de Kerguelen-Tremarec to sweep the Pacific in search of the unknown continent of Terra Australis and the trade routes of the Indian Ocean, but his two voyages of 1771–1772 and 1773–1774 were utter fiascoes. To succeed him, France chose a man whose early career bore many similarities to that of Cook, Jean-Francois de Galaud, Comte de La Pérouse. Like Cook, Galaud was not born into the nobility (although his family later purchased him a title); he had gone to sea in his teens, had served with distinction in the Seven Years War, and was recognized as a careful navigator and a humane commander. When Louis XVI and his minister, Claret de Fleurieu, prepared an expedition to redeem Kergulen, Fleurieu remembered La Pérouse as a friend and as a distinguished officer. The government gave him command of two vessels, *Boussole* and *Astrolabe,* and a breathtaking set of orders that added up to a command to explore the Pacific more comprehensively than anyone, even Cook, had ever done. The primary purpose of the voyage was scientific, to make one of the grand eighteenth-century surveys of all the conceivable gifts of nature discernible to a mariner's eye, and it received preparations worthy of its goals. Scholars and scientists from the Academy of Science and the Society of Medicine prepared La Pérouse with a set of questionnaires and checklists to record his data, and the eminent naturalist Buffon, among a host of other notables, contributed suggestions. Sailors stowed an abundance of presents in the holds to pave the way for co-operation with the natives. A secondary objective of the expedition was to canvass the territorial possessions and the military and naval strengths of rival powers. In regard to the Pacific Coast, La Pérouse was to explore it fully from Mount Saint Elias in Alaska to the Spanish capital at Monterey in California. Especially was he to keep before his eyes, as he swept this huge arc of latitude, the great objective of the Northwest Passage.

La Pérouse began his staggering task on July 2, 1785, when *Astrolabe* and *Boussole* departed Le Havre. Almost one year later on June 23 the ships struck the Alaskan Coast in the latitude of 59°. Two weeks later La Pérouse found a spacious bay that he named Frenchmen's Harbor, now known as Lituya Bay, where he landed to refit and to take on wood and water. On a small island within the bay he established an astronomical observatory and then proceeded to examine a large river discharging into the harbor, which he hoped was the outlet of a passage to the Great Lakes. The inevitable disappointment that dashed this hope set the tone for La Pérouse's other disenchantments with the region. During his stay of about five weeks he lost twenty-two of his men in a squall that swamped their two small sounding boats. Although the Indians were willing to sell La Pérouse the observatory island, he found them to be otherwise distasteful, indeed a caricature of the Noble Savage:

> Philosophers may exclaim against this picture if they please. They may write books by their fire-sides, while I have been voyaging for thirty years. I have been witness to the knavery and injustice of these people, whom they depict as good, because they are so little removed from a state of nature; but this nature is sublime only in the great, in the minutiae of things it is negligent. It is impossible to penetrate woods not thinned by the hand of civilized man; to traverse plains filled with stones and rocks, and deluged with impassable morasses; and to associate with the man of nature, because he is savage, deceitful, and malicious.[7]

7. J. F. G de la Pérouse, *A Voyage Round the World,* 2 vols. (London: A. Hamilton, printer, 1799), 1:397–398.

Time and environment both worked against La Pérouse. The coastline was so jagged, so studded with inlets, bays, and rivers, that he realized that to conduct a thorough search for the Northwest Passage would consume months allocated for his more valuable work in the Central Pacific. But when La Pérouse departed for Monterey on July 30 he took with him not only unhappy memories and unfavorable impressions and a sense of mission unfulfilled, but also a belief that even in this depressing area Art could improve Nature. The explorer had found the soil fertile and the vegetation lush; fish and game abounded; the scenery was more awesome and picturesque even than that of the Alps or Pyrenees; and, most useful of all, Frenchmen's Harbor was an ideal trading post for otter skins. Upon leaving Alaskan waters, La Pérouse sailed to California, thence on to Russia, where he sent his journals overland to Paris, and to Australia, where he entrusted more reports to a British naval officer. The prescient wisdom of these precautions became evident when his two ships were lost with all hands in a hurricane on the reefs of the island of Varrikoro in the New Hebrides sometime in 1788.

The Pacific Northwest first came to the world's attention as a source of great international tension in the famous Nootka Sound Affair of 1789. The genesis of this incident was that the Spanish Governor Martinez arrived at Nootka on May 5, 1789, to find two British trading vessels riding in the harbor brazenly defying the Spanish possessory claims to the region. The governor seized these vessels and then in July seized two other English ships commanded by James Colnett, compounding his indiscretion by arresting the commanding officer. Heated arguments broke out between the two officers, with Martinez brandishing the discoveries of Heceta and Pérez and later explorers, while Colnett retaliated with the explorations of Cook. On two occasions after his capture, Colnett, who suffered from a family malady, attempted to commit suicide by plunging into the sea. Although less dramatic, the response of Martinez's superior, Viceroy Revillagigedo in Mexico, was also one of dismay. He knew that Spain's domestic and international situation was already precarious with the ascent to the throne of the new monarch Carlos IV, who was under the domination of his queen

María Luisa and her close adviser Manuel de Godoy. Abroad, Spain's closest ally was plunged into the turmoil of revolution with Louis XVI, a virtual captive of the French National Assembly.

William Pitt the Younger, precocious son of a brilliant sire (described by his admirers as "not a chip off the old block, but the old block himself"), saw and seized Spain's travail as Britain's opportunity. His vision was not confined to redressing grievances of a handful of peltry traders at Nootka Sound. What Pitt wanted to do was to force open the Spanish empire in the New World to British commerce; his instrument was a novel interpretation of the concept of sovereignty. Pitt argued through correspondence and through his minister at Madrid that the Spanish voyages of discovery and proclamations of possession at Nootka and all along the Northwest coast were invalid. Sovereignty, he declared (in contravention of Britain's claims elsewhere on the globe), rested upon colonization and occupation. However inconsistent, even hypocritical, this assertion sounded to the Spanish courtiers, they were in no position to resist it. By the summer of 1790 it was clear to all that Spain's case against England was weakened not only by the transition to the new rulers but also by the fact that she had never publicized the discoveries of Pérez and Heceta.

Pitt's demands that Spain restore the confiscated vessels and abandon her claims to exclusive sovereignty were strengthened by popular passions against Catholic Spain rooted in the days of Philip and the Armada, of Drake and Hawkins. One ballad put the British case most belligerently:

> It's a farce you may make your weak Subjects believe,
> But our right's equal to yours from Adam and Eve.
> Therefore if you don't make us immediate amends
> No longer can we look upon you as Friends[.]
> Should you wish for a War we have got a new race
> Of such brave fighting fellows not the Devil dare face!

More specific interests joined the mob passions: merchants, industrialists, fur traders all had a stake in supporting the prime minister. War seemed imminent and Spain tried to bolster her negotiating position by calling upon her ally France. But France was no help as the revolution accelerated, and the king was reduced to a partner of the National Assembly, whose members were afraid to aid Spain against her enemy.

Pressing his advantages home, Pitt presented an ultimatum in October 1790. The choice for Spain was either to fight or to restore the captured ships and to modify her claims to sovereignty. Carlos IV consulted his advisers, who counselled rejection even at the cost of war, but the king spurned this course and bowed to the British demands. The resultant treaty, the Anglo-Spanish Convention of 1790, permitted the subjects of both nations to carry on commerce freely "north of parts of the Coast already occupied by Spain" prior to April 1789. The date is important because Martinez planted the Spanish colony at Nootka on May 5, 1789.

This concession was an enormous victory for Pitt, for it could thereafter be interpreted as meaning Spain had no rights by occupation north of San Francisco. The whole region to the north was now open to British trade. For Spain the treaty was also epochal; in the words of historian Warren Cook: "The Nootka crisis signals the beginning of the end of the Spanish Empire in America." What she had long feared, effective commercial rivalry in the region between Alaska and California, was now both a reality of business and of power politics.[8]

The Nootka incident affected not only monarchs and empires. Martinez's seizure of British vessels occurred only months after the inauguration of George Washington as first president of the United States, and it produced the initial foreign policy crisis under the Constitution. Washington and his cabinet feared that if war came Britain would seek permission from the neutral United States to march from bases in Canada to strike at the Spanish possessions in Florida and Louisiana. As a small and impotent power, with a total military establishment of fewer than 1,000 men, the United States was faced with the dilemma of offending, even perhaps fighting, one of the two great em-

8. Warren L. Cook, *Flood Tide of Empire: Spain and the Pacific Northwest, 1543–1819* (New Haven: Yale University Press, 1973), p. 241.

pires. Assent to the British request would alienate Spain; refusal could mean another war with the former mother country. The president and cabinet members divided over the issue, but finally resolved upon neutrality and refusal to let Britain pass. Fortunately for the new nation the consequence of this decision was never tested, for the Nootka Sound Convention nullified the need for the feared request. But the United States policy of peacetime neutrality was established.

With the crisis defused, exploration of the Northwest coast continued pacifically. Spain's answer to Cook and La Pérouse was the great Malaspina expedition, which took much of the world within its purview. The expedition, proposed and led by Alejandra Malaspina and José Bustamente y Guerra, sailed on the twin corvettes, *Descubierta* and *Atrevida,* which departed Cadiz in 1789. Although not originally part of the plan of the voyage, the Pacific Northwest was later included so that Malaspina could search for the Northwest Passage. In late June 1791 he first touched the Northwest Coast at Yakutat Bay (59°) and then moved southward to Nootka. Although the members of the expedition remained in the Northwest for only a month, the artists made invaluable sketches of the Indians, and the scientists also accomplished a good deal of work. Malaspina proved to be astute in assessing the weakness of Spain's political position when he argued for the abandonment of mercantilist restrictions in favor of free trade. He predicted that if these changes were made the Spanish would defeat all their competitors in the Chinese market because of the proximity of California to the Northwest, which would assure the traders a supply of food and other goods. But neither Malaspina's scientific labors nor his economic arguments had any influence. Their author, suspected of currying the queen's favor and of seeking to displace her counsellor Godoy, was banished from the country and his reports were never published in his lifetime.

After the Nootka Convention the Spanish attempted to strengthen their slipping grasp upon the Northwest coast. In the very year of the treaty, 1790, Spain sent three expeditions northward from California. Francisco de Eliza re-established the settlement at Nootka, incidentally becoming the first person to practice agriculture in the Pacific Northwest. Salvador Fidalgo was in Alaska to ascertain recent movements of the Russian fur traders. Finally, Manuel Quimper explored the Straits of Juan de Fuca. His voyage was a part of the revised Spanish plan to retain a portion of the Northwest south of Nootka Sound by founding a naval base at the western end of the strait to guard the only passage to the interior (no one at that time knew that Vancouver Island was an island).

Spain also leaned upon diplomacy. The key to this effort came in the exchanges between the Spaniard Bodega and the Englishman Vancouver in 1792 and 1793, as representatives of their respective governments, when they debated what exactly the Nootka Convention required to be returned to England and the implications of this restoration. Both men were true gentlemen, with a great respect for social amenities and for each other, and they refused to allow their political disagreements to poison their personal relationships. The disagreements arose over the two diplomats' differing readings of the convention and the instructions from their governments. Bodega asserted that he had to restore only the small tract of land Meares had acquired before April 1789; that Spanish sovereignty over the rest of Nootka (and the entire area north of California) was unimpaired by the convention; and that he and Vancouver should make a boundary settlement between the two nations at the Strait of Juan de Fuca. Vancouver contended that he must receive back the entire territory of the port of Nootka and that—most important of all—the British had the right to trade anywhere on the Pacific Coast north of San Francisco. His instructions, he continually avowed, afforded him no room for maneuver. After many lengthy sessions, characterized by courtesy and good faith, Bodega and Vancouver gave up, and referred their problems to their capitals. Then followed another treaty in 1793 which granted Meares $210,000 for his property and a final one in 1794 that officially sealed Spain's abandonment of exclusive sovereignty, thereby opening the Nootka region to England and other nations as well. Further consequences of this impasse for Spain were the abandonment of Neah Bay, since a boundary could not be obtained, the rejection by the Spanish government of a Bodega plan (reminiscent of that of Malaspina) to control the Northwest through trade goods from Mexico, and the final departure of Spain from Nootka in 1795.

George Vancouver's importance in Northwest history goes beyond that of his unsuccessful diplomacy. This great explorer had joined the British navy as a youth and had served in various stations, including that of midshipman on Cook's third voyage. He could have had no better model than that master of command and navigation, although his own judgment and courage were exemplary, in spite of his chronic complaint of a hyperthyroid condition. On March 8, 1791, the officers of the Admiralty issued Vancouver instructions for an expedition that would put all his qualities to the test. Vancouver was ordered to receive back the English lands and buildings confiscated by Martinez, and to explore the Pacific Coast from latitude 60° north to 30° north, concentrating upon the Northwest Passage and upon the number of early European settlements in the area.

In the three summer seasons from 1792 to 1794, in work involving some danger, much hardship, and a great deal of tedium, the crews of Vancouver's vessels, *Discovery* and *Chatham,* patiently searched the Northwest coast. During his first season Vancouver carefully traced the shoreline from 39°5′ (in modern California) to 52°18′ (in present British Columbia). The highlights of this year—in addition to the cordial if unfruitful negotiations with Bodega—were the discovery, parallel to that of Spanish vessels under Quimper, that Vancouver Island was indeed insular and that the shoreline south of Whidbey's Island had great agricultural potential. Illustrative of the last, he envisioned this future for the area about Restoration Point:

> The serenity of the climate, the innumerable pleasing landscapes, and the abundant fertility that unassisted nature puts forth, require only to be enriched by the industry of man with villages, mansions, cottages, and other buildings, to render it the most lovely country that can be imagined; whilst the labour of the inhabitants would be amply rewarded, in the bounties which nature seems ready to bestow on cultivation.

He noted, however, that north of Point Atkinson the country becomes desolate and devoid of animal life. The nadir of the year, as every schoolchild knows, is that Vancouver failed to rediscover the Columbia River (and also missed the Fraser). Off Cape Disappointment on April 27, 1792, he noticed the "river colored water," but "Not considering the opening worthy of more attention, I continued our pursuit to the N.W." Two weeks later Gray found the river and courteously passed the information on to Vancouver. Vancouver ordered his Lt. William R. Broughton to explore it with *Chatham.* Broughton cruised along the Columbia almost to the union with the Willamette and made the usual observations of the Indians and of nature. Although he considered that the river would be useless for shipping, Broughton, unlike Gray, did take formal possession of it, arguing that his claim was superior to that of Gray in that the American did not enter the river.[9]

In 1793 and 1794 Vancouver returned to the Northwest after wintering in Hawaii. In these years he carefully charted the coastline as far north as Alaska, interviewed the Russian traders there (and was impressed by their understanding of the Indians), and continued his biological and ethnological work. His most enduring accomplishments were his surveys and his cartography, and within them his most interesting immediate conclusion was to destroy the idea of the Northwest Passage. Not the Strait of Juan de Fuca, not Lynn Canal (which Vancouver named for his birthplace), not Cook Inlet, not any other promising bay or river from 30°N to 56°N could ever again be claimed as the long-sought Anián. On August 16, 1794, the crews met to celebrate the completion of the survey of the last bit of shoreline and "In the course of the evening no small portion of facetious mirth passed amongst the seamen, in consequence of our having sailed from old England on the *first of April,* for the purpose of discovering a north-west passage." [10]

In spite of his "failure" concerning the quest for the

9. George Vancouver, *A Voyage of Discovery to the North Pacific Ocean and Round the World,* 3 vols. (London: G. G. and J. Robinson, 1798), 1:210, 259.

10. Vancouver, *Voyage,* 3:285.

Northwest Passage that began on April Fool's Day, George Vancouver was a magnificent eighteenth-century scientist and gentleman. He was cosmopolitan, generous to rival mariners, and sympathetic to the aboriginal peoples. He believed in progress and was proud of the achievements of his country and of his age. Courageously writing the report of his voyages while awaiting death at the age of forty, Vancouver glorified (on the first page of his great report) the mariners of all nations who had participated in the discoveries:

> In contemplating the rapid progress of improvement in the sciences, and the general diffusion of knowledge, since the commencement of the eighteenth century, we are unavoidably led to observe, with admiration, that active spirit of discovery, by means of which the remotest regions of the earth have been explored; a friendly communication opened with their inhabitants; and various commodities, of a most valuable nature, contributing either to relieve their necessities, or augment their comforts, introduced among the less-enlightened part of our species. A mutual intercourse has been also established, in many instances, on the solid basis of a reciprocity of benefits; and the productive labor of the civilized world has found new markets for the disposal of its manufactures. Nor has the balance of trade been wholly against the people of the newly-discovered countries; for, whilst some have been enabled to supply their visitors with an abundance of food, and the most valuable refreshments, in exchange for iron, copper, useful implements, and articles of ornament; the industry of others has been stimulated to procure the skins of animals, and other articles of a commercial nature; which they have found to be eagerly sought for by the traders who now resort to their shores from Europe, Asia, and the eastern side of North America.[11]

V

Private enterprise, not the Admiralty, was responsible for the last of the eighteenth-century British explorations, but the goal of the Northwest Passage remained. The North West Company, an organization of Canadian fur merchants formed to combat the

11. Vancouver, *Voyage,* 1:i.

Hudson's Bay Company in central Canada, sent Alexander Mackenzie in 1789 to search for a water route to the Pacific. Instead Mackenzie reached the Arctic along the great river that now carries his name. Four years later, with a party of ten men (eight whites and two Indians) Mackenzie tried again, beginning his journey from Fort Chipewyan on May 9, 1793. His route was along the Peace and Parsnip rivers across the Rockies and then to the Fraser River, which he unknowingly discovered but mistook for the Columbia. Knowing that the Columbia flowed into the Pacific far to the south, he struck overland and finally reached the Pacific by descending the Bella Coola River. Near its mouth he found a large rock on which he painted the famous inscription: "Alexander Mackenzie, from Canada, by land, the twenty-second of July, one thousand seven hundred and ninety-three." He was the first man of record to cross the continent by land.[12]

The journey in both directions was a testimony to Mackenzie's genius as a leader. On many occasions, mishaps disheartened the party, and both Indians and whites frequently begged the leader to return home. Sand flies, rain, white water, indifferent or threatening Indians, portages through thickets that tore one's clothes to ribbons were varied and frequent trials. The nadir was a twenty-four-hour disaster on James Creek, which Mackenzie named Bad River, when the canoe overturned in the rapids with the loss of all the bullets and much of the equipment. The entire party effected what Mackenzie called "a miraculous escape" from drowning and his men then hoped that nothing would prevail upon the leader to go on, but he ordered them to dry the remaining supplies, passed out food and rum, and exhorted them to continue. One additional miracle was required to permit the party to proceed to the Pacific, for one of the men, carelessly smoking his pipe, was observed walking unscathed across eighty pounds of drying gunpowder: "I need not add [as Mackenzie understated in his journal] that one spark might have put a period to all my anxiety and ambition."[13]

12. W. Kaye Lamb, ed., *The Journals and Letters of Sir Alexander Mackenzie* (Cambridge: At the University Press, 1970), p. 378.

13. Lamb, *Mackenzie,* p. 300.

Mackenzie's journey had remarkable consequences. He was convinced that there was no single Northwest Passage, but he was also convinced that his trip opened up vast possibilities for British power and British commerce. He broached the scheme in its formative version the year after his return and continued to urge it upon government officials for the next sixteen years. Mackenzie's plan was based upon the assumption that the territory of the Pacific Northwest lacked the potential for agriculture; it would thus be secure for the fur trade indefinitely. He wanted government to foster the commercial possibilities derived from this fact by creating the merger of the Hudson's Bay and the North West companies. This corporation would then be free to import through Hudson Bay (formerly closed to all but the monopolistic HBC) goods which would be distributed to Indians all along the beaver and otter country of the Northwest. The pelts collected, through arrangement with the East India Company, would then be sent to China. In sum, Mackenzie proposed a single company to control the fur trade of British North America, but his grand scheme was taken to be grandiose, not only by the government and the rival HBC, but by the majority of his own company. Its attempted execution fell later to American hands.

Whoever might follow Mackenzie's plans or footsteps in the future would have to reckon with the compelling impressions of his journal. Like the other eighteenth-century explorers, regardless of nationality, Mackenzie was intrigued by the Indians. His interest, although primarily commercial, also partook somewhat of the disinterested ethnologist. Mackenzie was impressed by the Indians as canoemen, even rating them superior to his voyageurs: "the Canadians who accompanied me were the most expert canoe-men in the world, but they are very inferior to these people." He was amazed that these "children of Nature" were adept in art; as he walked among the Bella Coola people "near the house of the chief I observed several oblong squares, of about twenty feet by eight. They were made of thick cedar boards, which were joined with so much neatness, that I at first thought they were one piece. They were painted with hieroglyphics, and figures of different animals, and with a degree of correctness that was not to be expected from such an uncultivated people." The environment of the Northwest would have delighted a contemporary romantic aesthete as this observation, recorded four days out on the return journey, confirms:

> Nor was it possible to be in this situation without contemplating the wonders of it. Such was the depth of the precipices below, and the height of the mountains above, with the rude and wild magnificence of the scenery around, that I shall not attempt to describe such an astonishing and awful combination of objects; of which, indeed, no description can convey an adequate idea.[14]

VI

About two weeks after the delegates fixed their signatures to the new constitution at Philadelphia, a convivial gathering was in progress aboard the ship *Columbia,* riding in Nantanskit Roads off Boston harbor. "The evening was spent in murth [*sic*] and glee," wrote one of the participants, "the highest flow of spirits animating the whole Company Jovial songs and animating sentiments passed the last evening we spent on [the Atlantic] side of the Continent." *Columbia* would depart the next day, October 1, 1787, for the Pacific Northwest, the first American vessel to enter the maritime fur trade.[15] Cook's *Journals* and the British Etches group's successes had inspired the Boston merchant Joseph Barrell to fit out *Columbia,* under the command of John Kendrick, and her consort *Lady Washington,* with Robert Gray as captain, for the Oregon Country. As commander of the expedition, Kendrick was instructed to conduct himself scrupulously in the new territory, to treat the Indians well, and to respect the claims and citizens of other nations.

The outward voyage was marred by the separation of the two ships off Cape Horn on April 1, 1788, and by the suicide of the astronomer, John Nutting, who threw himself overboard, but Gray's *Washington* raised the Pacific Coast of northern California on August 2, 1788, and the ship worked north searching for

14. Lamb, *Mackenzie,* pp. 364, 367, 395.

15. Frederic W. Howay, ed., *Voyages of the "Columbia" to the Northwest Coast 1787–1790 and 1790–1793* (Boston: Massachusetts Historical Society, 1941), p. 4.

a good harbor to take on wood, water, and antiscorbutics. Southern Oregon "was beautyfully divercified with forists and green verdent launs," and at a spacious bay which they took to be the opening of the River of the West, Gray sent a party ashore. One of its members, the captain's cabin boy, a black youth named Marcus Lopius, left his cutlass behind as the party withdrew to the ship. An Indian saw his opportunity, and stole the weapon; Lopius pursued him and wrenched the sword away, but before his shipmates could intervene the Indians "drenched there knives and spears with savage feury in the boddy of the unfortunate youth. He quited his hold and stumbled but rose again and stagered towards us but having a flight of arrows thrown into his back and he fell . . . and instantly expiered while they mangled his lifeless corse." Gray christened the bay Murderer's Harbor (now Tillamook Bay), but did not retaliate against the Indians.[16]

Washington pushed on to Nootka Sound to find *Columbia* and Meares's ships, *Felice* and *Iphigenia*. The British traders tried to scare off the American competition by "fabricating and rehursing vague and improvable tales relative to the coast of the vast danger attending its navigation [and] of the Monsterous Savage disposition of its inhabitants," but the two ships continued to trade along the coast until Gray, who had exchanged ships with Kendrick, took *Columbia* to China where he traded the furs for Bohea tea while Kendrick remained on the Northwest coast. Gray's vessel ultimately reached Boston on August 9, 1790, after a voyage of 48,889 miles, the first American ship to circumnavigate the globe. Ironically, in spite of the plaudits of New England, the voyage was unprofitable for the owners, since the tea, which was damaged at sea on the return voyage, sold at a low price. In other respects Gray's endeavor was of national significance. *Columbia* and *Lady Washington* had not only shown the flag where it had not been seen before, but they had acquired and disposed of a cargo of skins in competition with seasoned British traders; they had established good relations with the Indians despite some provocations; and they

16. Howay, *"Columbia,"* pp. 30, 38.

had claimed to have seen the western end of the Northwest Passage (probably at either Clarence Strait or Dixon Entrance) while cruising in Alaskan waters. They had also in passing written off the land of British Columbia for farming as "indeed the trees are every where of so enormious a sise that it would be attended with emence labour to Clear the Land." [17]

Joseph Barrell and his associates were not farmers, and they were not discouraged with their first trading venture, for the 250-ton *Columbia,* manned by fifty officers and men and carrying a cargo of blue cloth, copper, and iron, was again on the Northwest Coast in August 1791. This time the vessel worked for several months southward from Alaska, acquiring furs, and paying for them not only in trade goods but also in the usual mishaps of a trading voyage: scurvy, an Indian plot to capture the ship, and deadening routine in the rainy weather. On May 12, 1792, Gray's men immortalized themselves not by the discovery of the river they named for their ship (which Heceta had accomplished), but by running into its mouth and "at five, P.M., came to in five fathoms water, sandy bottom, in a safe harbor, well sheltered from the sea by long sand-bars and spits." During the next few days the ship probed the mouth of the Columbia River and traded with the Indians whom they found friendly and attractive: "The Men at Columbia's River are strait limb'd, fine looking fellows, and the women are very pretty. They are all in a state of Nature, except the females, who wear a leaf Apron (perhaps *'twas* a fig leaf)." The courtesy of the Indians and the fish, game, and fertile soil made the Columbia's mouth an ideal place for a trading post, which, in conjunction with one in the Queen Charlotte Islands, would monopolize the trade of the Northwest coast. But the momentous significance of the rediscovery of the great river and the two weeks that Gray's men spent upon it was not for commerce but for politics. Although neither Gray nor his owners thought the event important enough to preserve the log, it later passed into other hands who altered it to contend that he had formally taken possession of the river for the United States. Again and again until the final settlement with England in 1846, American diplomats would assert

17. Howay, *"Columbia,"* pp. 49, 59.

their country's claim to the vast Columbia watershed on the basis of Gray's exploration of its mouth.[18]

But that development lay in the long future. At the time, what was valuable about Gray's two voyages for the postrevolutionary generation of Americans was that they led to a rush of American maritime traders to the Northwest. The work of these seamen was of enormous significance for the national economy of the United States, as the Americans, now restricted in the markets of the British Empire after independence, had to find substitutes for the West Indies, Asia, and the mother country to ensure a favorable balance of payments. The sea otter was the commodity that helped tide the country over its postwar depression and into the recovery of the 1790s. And by the turn of the century Americans dominated the sea otter trade.

The genesis of the most famous of all American expeditions to the Oregon Country, that of Meriwether Lewis and William Clark, is a composite of many concerns, commercial, political, and scientific. Gray and Kendrick had initiated several successors into the profits of the maritime trade. Alexander Mackenzie had crossed the continent overland, and his reports were read in the United States as well as in the British Empire. An American who had served with Captain Cook, John Ledyard, had actually attempted to go on foot eastward across Siberia and the Aleutian chain to reach the Pacific Northwest. He reached Yakutsk before being turned back by Russian authorities. As early as the 1760s some of Thomas Jefferson's neighbors were discussing an expedition to explore the Missouri and Columbia watersheds, but the immediate precedent for the Lewis and Clark expedition was the employment in 1793 of a French botanist, André Michaux, by the American Philosophical Society to lead a western expedition. Thomas Jefferson, secretary of state and a member of the society, was the moving spirit in the enterprise, which was "to find the shortest & most convenient route of communication between the U.S. & the Pacific ocean." [19] Comprehensive reports of flora, fauna, and Indians were required. Mi-

18. Howay, *"Columbia,"* pp. 435, 399.

19. Donald Jackson, ed., *Letters of the Lewis and Clark Expedition with Related Documents, 1783–1854* (Urbana: University of Illinois Press, 1962), p. 669.

chaux got underway, reached Kentucky, but then was exposed as a French agent trying to organize an attack upon Spanish Louisiana and was recalled. The Michaux fiasco, however, did not kill Jefferson's interest in western exploration, for as president of the United States he revived the project a decade later.

In the fall of 1802 Jefferson first made known his plans to send off a western expedition and on the following January 18 he proclaimed his intentions to the Congress. He requested the sum of $2,500 to dispatch an exploring party through Spanish Louisiana and the Oregon Country to the Pacific. Jefferson told the members of the Senate and the House that the expedition would have commercial value in that it could produce treaties with the Indians of the plains and Rockies whereby they would abandon their alliances with British traders of the Great Lakes and the Saint Lawrence in favor of the continuous navigation of the Missouri River to American territory. Furthermore, since Jefferson, along with other contemporary geographers, believed that there was only a single easy portage between the Missouri and the Columbia, the whole watershed of that river would be opened for American commerce. The expedition promised to furnish incalculable amounts of scientific data and, although Jefferson did not say so publicly, would strengthen the American political claim to the valley of the Columbia, the mouth of which had been first entered by Robert Gray. The international political scene altered, in fact, while Jefferson was laying his plans, as Napoleon sold the entire Louisiana Territory (bounded roughly by the 49th parallel, the Rocky Mountains, the Mississippi, and the Gulf of Mexico) to the United States in April 1803. Now much of the labor of what came to be called the Corps of Discovery would be to inventory American rather than French territory. The magnificent purchase of course did not include any of the disputed Oregon Country.

Under the leadership of two of Jefferson's former Virginia neighbors, both experienced military men and practiced woodsmen, the Lewis and Clark expedition traversed a distance of 3,555 miles round trip from May 14, 1804, to September 26, 1806. Instructions from the president included the main objective (as in the case of the Michaux venture) of following the Missouri to the watershed of whatever river flowing into the Pacific promised "the most direct & practicable water communication across this continent for the purposes of commerce." Furthermore, the Indians were to be cultivated and investigated, and finally the flora, fauna, and mineral resources were to be recorded. Only one special point of inquiry concerned the Pacific Northwest, and that was to discover if the furs of the Pacific Coast might be shipped to market by the Missouri outlet rather than from Nootka.[20]

Departing from a site near Saint Louis, the expedition pushed up the Missouri River to its first winter quarters, the Mandan villages, near present Bismarck, North Dakota. Here were acquired a French-Canadian hunter, Charbonneau, and his Indian wife Sacajawea. When their investigations promised travel free from snow, the expedition departed winter quarters, leaving on April 7, 1805. The corps ascended the Missouri River to the Great Falls and then to its threefold source of the Jefferson, Madison, and Gallatin rivers. Lewis and Clark led their party across the Rockies to the watershed of the Columbia, down the Clearwater to the Snake, and along that river toward the distant ocean. In the evening of October 16, 1805, the members of the Corps of Discovery proceeded in their canoes down the last seven miles of the Snake to its junction with the Columbia, the Great River of the West, to become the first Americans to strike its waters since Gray's men thirteen years earlier had crossed its dangerous bar. For the next day and one-half various members of the party explored six miles up the Columbia, assured the neighboring Indians in council of their peaceful intentions, and, disgusted by the putrid fish they were proffered, purchased forty dogs from them as a food supply.

At four o'clock on the afternoon of the eighteenth they began their descent of the Columbia that carried the expedition into what became the state of Oregon, and it thus becomes appropriate to follow them more closely. During the next four days the party's progress to the rapids at Celilo was uneventful except for

20. Jackson, *Letters of Lewis and Clark Expedition,* p. 61.

the annoyance of lack of fuel, remedied in part by the Indians, and by the attempt of their Indian guides to return home. Fleas were a minor problem and the hair seals in the river a novelty. The explorers had their initial glimpse of Mount Adams and noted the first wooden houses of the Indians since they had left the Illinois country.

The next few days were among the most arduous of the expedition. At Celilo and The Dalles the men had to master the rapids and chutes of the Columbia forcing its way through narrow gorges between towering basaltic walls. The Great Chute of the Columbia made an indelible impression upon Clark "with the water of this great river compressed within the space of 150 paces in which there is great numbers of both large and Small rocks, water passing with great velocity forming [foaming] & boiling in a most horriable manner." Celilo, as the common fishing grounds for the tribes of the Columbia, had a long tradition of Indian economic use, and since the precontact era The Dalles had been a trade emporium between the Indians of the lower river and those of the Columbia Plateau. Clark noted white man's clothing, kettles, and a musket and sword obviously originating from the maritime traders. He reported on the Indians' bargaining skills and their declaration that "the white people below give great prices for every thing &c." [21]

On November 2 Lewis and Clark left The Dalles for the final stage of their journey to the sea, a thirteen-day trip to the end of waterway navigation. This portion of the trip was a generally pleasant interlude marked by the first sight of Mount Hood and by their joy at the pastoral scenes along the river. From their camp on the Sandy River sixty miles westward, the valley

> extends a great Distance to the right & left, rich thickly covered
> with tall timber, with a fiew Small Praries bordering on the river
> and on the Islands; Some fiew standing Ponds & Several Small
> Streams of running water on either Side of the river; This is
> certainly a fertill and a handsom valley, at this time crouded with
> Indians. [22]

21. Reuben Gold Thwaites, ed., *Original Journals of the Lewis and Clark Expedition, 1804–1806*, 8 vols. (New York: Dodd, Mead and Co., 1904–1905), 3:180, 186.
22. Thwaites, *Journals of Lewis and Clark,* 3:202.

The mouth of the Columbia, long desired, proved at first to be disappointing. It was difficult to beat through the high winds, and the canoes had to be abandoned in favor of an overland march to the ocean. The Chinook Indians, because of the ravages of venereal disease, did not present an initial favorable impression. The supply of game seemed insufficient for the support of the party while in winter quarters. It was then decided to take counsel from the members of the expedition as to their next step. Lewis and Clark polled everyone, including York, Clark's black slave, and Sacajawea, and the overwhelming consensus was to move to the south side of the river to investigate the temper of the Indians there, to seek better hunting grounds, to see if salt were available, and to have a chance to encounter a trading vessel that might carry them home. Physical activity in itself would offer a release from the elements summed up in Clark's outcry in his journal: "O! how disagreeable is our Situation dureing this dreadfull weather." After a search of a few days the corps moved to the site of its winter quarters on December 7 and in three weeks' time erected the buildings and named the post Fort Clatsop. Here, inside a stockade fifty feet square, they constructed two rows of rooms (three on the north side, four on the south) separated by a parade ground. This small structure was the expedition members' home for the next few months.[23]

Most readers who perused the *Journals* of Lewis and Clark found the Oregon Country disenchanting. The weather was depressing with only six clear days during the entire winter, and a day without much precipitation called for a special entry: "only three Showers dureing this whole day." Wet weather was not only tedious, but was injurious to health, destructive of gun powder, and dangerous to preserved meat.[24] Life at Fort Clatsop was tiresome in other respects. The men spent hours boiling sea water to make the indispensable preservative salt for the return journey. Their clothing had torn or rotted on the outward journey, but now, with plenty of time and an abundance of elk skins, there developed a shortage of animal brains used for tan-

23. Thwaites, *Journals of Lewis and Clark,* 3:255.
24. Thwaites, *Journals of Lewis and Clark,* 3:299.

ning, nor was there soap for a substitute, nor lye from which to make soap, for the evergreens left insufficient ashes for lye-making. Disease and injuries were troublesome; dysentery, back problems, venereal disease, influenza, and dislocated joints all required special treatment. The Indians were interesting, honest, and helpful for the most part, but their ways were often incomprehensible across the cultural gulf. On one occasion, moreover, violence flared as a member of a small salt-making party narrowly escaped murder by a Tillamook Indian. The diet of elk meat soon became monotonous; Lewis noted in February an "excellent supper it consisted of a marrowbone a piece and a brisket of boiled Elk that had the appearance of a little fat on it. this for Fort Clatsop is living in high stile." With these memories none regretted the day of departure, March 27, 1806, although all could look back on a productive winter quarters: reports were written, astronomical observations somehow made in spite of bad weather, and clothes, salt, and food were laid by.[25]

The return trip through the Columbia valley was relatively uneventful except for the discovery of the Willamette River, which the explorers had missed the previous autumn. Significantly, at The Dalles, Lewis welcomed the dry air and the green grass "after having been so long imprisoned in mountains and those almost inpenetrably thick forrests of the seacoast." After a delay of several weeks waiting for the snows to clear, the expedition members crossed the Rockies and descended the Missouri to Saint Louis, where they were heartily acclaimed. The expedition was one of the notable achievements of exploration and its results were numerous and significant, although their totality was not revealed at once. Only in 1814 was an incomplete account of the journey published and not until 1904–1905 were the full journals of Lewis and Clark given to the public. Historian William Goetzmann concludes that the most significant result of the expedition was to make the American West "an object of desire" to the American people. If this estimate be accurate, what specifically was desirable about the Oregon Coun-

25. Thwaites, *Journals of Lewis and Clark,* 4:49.

try? In Lewis's first report to Jefferson (intended for public consumption and published in the press) he testified to the fur trading potential of the Columbia watershed which, although not as lucrative as the Missouri, "yet it is by no means despicable in this rispect." In contrast to Jefferson's original hope, however, the explorers reported that these furs, and those of the Canadian plains if Britain agreed, should be shipped down the Columbia (not thc Missouri) to the markets of the East Indies. Although Lewis and Clark believed that the route they discovered was the best to connect the two great western rivers, they admitted that the 340-mile mountainous portage between them precluded as many goods being sent from Asia over this route as on the traditional one about Cape Horn. The explorers praised the Willamette Valley as a place of future agricultural settlement. And, as Jefferson had anticipated, the political gains to the nation, which would ensure the benefits of the fur trade and farming, were substantial. The Indians of the Columbia and of the coast, although not uniformly friendly, were not formidable enemies. On the negative side, the contemporary scientist, unlike the trader and statesman, was not to benefit from the work of Lewis and Clark, for the detailed botanical and zoological reports were not published until the twentieth century.[26]

With the return of the Corps of Discovery, the last of the great surveys of the Oregon Country was concluded. What Ferrelo and Cabrillo had falteringly begun in their frail vessels Lewis and Clark had completed. The Northwest Passage was chimera, not fact. The noble savage was nonexistent, except for Lewis and Clark's favorable estimate of the Nez Percé tribe. Yet equally intriguing possibilities were spread before the eyes of men of the Caucasian race, men not of the Latin nations but of England and the United States, who were now on the threshold of the final struggle for regional sovereignty. But their conflicts were not over unpopulated territory. The tragedy of the

26. Thwaites, *Journals of Lewis and Clark,* 4:290; William H. Goetzmann, *Exploration and Empire: The Explorer and the Scientist in the Winning of the American West* (New York: Alfred A. Knopf, 1966), p. 4; Jackson, *Letters of Lewis and Clark Expedition,* p. 322.

white man's advance was that he had predecessors in this abundant country.

The native peoples of the Oregon Country comprised an astonishingly varied mosaic of languages and cultures. Although white men frequently denigrated them as primitive or uncivilized, these observers, apostles of the doctrine of progress, mistook the stability of the Indian ways for simplicity. In actuality the Oregon Indians had very complex cultures, attuned to the rhythms of the changing seasons, and furnished with a rich artistic and cultural life. In the largest sense the Indians of Oregon may be divided, with some exceptions, into four peoples: those of the coast and the lower Columbia; the Columbia Plateau; the south central regions; and the southeast. What united them was not geographic locale, neither was it language or politics, but an intimate dependence upon nature and the compelling necessity to master it.

Nature contributed the salmon, other finned fish, bivalves, whales, and mammalian fauna for the food of the coastal peoples and those of the lower Columbia. On the plateau salmon was supplemented in the diet by mammals, fruits, bulbs, and nuts, and in south central Oregon the Klamath and Modoc relied upon marshes and streams for ducks and geese, fish, and mollusks. In the southeast sustenance came from a variety of natural objects, principally wild seeds, which were at times augmented by deer, rabbits, antelope, and fish.

Nature provided shelter in the form of split plank dwellings, huts, or pit houses. It contributed cooking utensils, weapons, canoes, and storage containers that the Indians made from cedar, willow, and hazel trees, bear grass, spruce root, ferns, and hides. Clothing, too, was its gift. In the realm of the mind and spirit the Indian's animistic religion expressed a desire to control nature for the sake of a rich material life. This animism was marked by rituals ranging from the young Indian's search for a guiding spirit to elaborate ceremonies at the time of spring's first salmon runs. Throughout the long evenings in the winter lodgings, skilled actors dramatized the traditional legends that explained cosmology and cosmogony and reinforced the people's collective virtues in the minds and hearts of young and old.

The political organization of the Oregon Indians ranged from small villages to loose band alliances to tribes. Underlying the leadership of these entities, which the whites found to be distressingly lacking in their concept of political sovereignty, were the two principles of competence and voluntarism. The most adept man would become leader, religious, political, or military, not necessarily through inheritance or wealth. Furthermore, leaders would be followed, not obeyed, as each individual participated in warfare or the hunt on an individual basis, and if a man decided to return home he suffered no stigma for deserting the cause. So far as the Caucasian newcomers went, the Indian attitudes toward nature, in all their ramifications, and their seeming lack of political discipline, were at best exotically quaint and at worst distressingly incomprehensible. Out of these cultural differences, in the heyday of the beaver traders, arose the first manifestations of one of Oregon's oldest social phenomena, the white man's belief in his racial superiority.

2

The Pursuit of Furs, Souls, and the Good Life

I

*T*HE earliest result of the Lewis and Clark expedition was to interest United States businessmen in the beaver trade of the Trans-Mississippi West. Manuel Lisa, the Saint Louis entrepreneur, led a trading party up the Missouri in 1807, the year after the return of Lewis and Clark. But the first American fur trader interested in the Oregon Country was an even greater businessman, a man who was one of the wealthiest Americans of his time. John Jacob Astor, like many Americans, was an immigrant; unlike most, he had emigrated twice. Born the son of a butcher in Germany in 1763, he had joined his elder brother, a manufacturer of musical instruments, in England when sixteen years old. Astor's first experience with America came in 1783–1784, when he journeyed to the New World to visit another brother living in New York City. Conversations with fellow passengers on his ship stirred his interest in the fur trade, and after arriving at Baltimore with a total competence of five guineas and seven flutes, Astor travelled to New York City and, after a brief return to England, settled into the North American beaver trade.

By the year 1808—when he founded the first great United

States corporation, the American Fur Company—Astor dominated the fur business. He had connections with Canadian businessmen, he had agents abroad, and his United States territory extended from New York to the Mississippi. The American Fur Company was designed to consolidate his rule over the Great Lakes country, but his allied organization, the Pacific Fur Company, first brought an American settlement to the Oregon Country.

The genesis of this company, formed in 1810, was Mackenzie's plan to unite the territorial beaver trade with that of the North Pacific into a single corporation. Astor hoped to send a party of men from New York City via ship to anchor the Pacific Fur Company operations by erecting a post at the mouth of the Columbia River. The post was to serve as a base to collect furs gathered in the watersheds of the Columbia and Snake rivers and in Canada both by field parties and by coastal vessels. A second party of men was to be sent overland from Saint Louis to the mouth of the Columbia. Astor hoped to work out a reciprocal division of territory with the Russians in Alaska and the North West Company, but these negotiations failed, and he was forced into a competitive rather than a co-operative relationship with these firms. He anticipated the markets for his furs to be international: China, the eastern cities of the United States, Britain, and Europe. Astor would never have become a millionaire businessman without possessing a sense of timing, good fortune, and the ability to select able subordinates, but ironically all of these qualities failed him in his Oregon venture, and international conflicts and a series of misjudgments converted it from an imperial scheme into a humiliating failure, part tragedy, part comic opera.

Astor gathered his maritime expedition at New York City in 1810, bringing many of its members from Canada and down the Hudson by birchbark canoe to the amazement of the New Yorkers, who gaped from the wharves at the voyageurs bobbing in their unusual craft. His ship, *Tonquin,* was commanded by Capt. Jonathan Thorn, a professional naval officer on leave of absence. The commander of the fur company party, which numbered thirty-three men, was Duncan McDougall, a Canadian like most of the party. Thorn and the landsmen never understood one another; the captain rigorously enforced naval discipline, even abandoning a landing party that missed the ship in the Falkland Islands, until he was forced to return at the point of a pistol. The Canadians rebelled against Thorn's discipline by harassing him in a variety of minor ways, including speaking only the French language when in his presence. The climax of ill-feeling came at the culmination of the voyage when Thorn lost the lives of eight seamen crossing the Columbia bar. Once ashore, however, the spirits of the fur traders rose as they landed in an Edenic world: "The weather was magnificent," a clerk wrote, "and all Nature smiled. . . . The forests looked like pleasant groves and the leaves like flowers." [1]

Although the arduous task of clearing timber to make the fort, named for Astor, showed nature in another dimension, the post was built and preparations for trading were begun. During construction Thorn embarked on a trading voyage to the north, became enbroiled with the Indians on Vancouver Island, and was attacked by them. Taken by surprise, *Tonquin's* crew was overwhelmed, and the survivors abandoned ship (but were later killed by the Indians), except for one wounded sailor who touched off the powder magazine, destroying self, ship, and captors. The overland party, dispatched in 1811, also suffered gravely. Astor's leader, Wilson Price Hunt, became lost along the Snake River, the party separated, and several almost perished before they reached Astoria.

In spite of these troubles Astor's men began trading, placing their posts in competition to those of the North West Company. The rivalry was strong and life often dangerous or lonely, as described by the lone employee at Fort Okanogan: "Only picture to yourself, gentle reader, how I must have felt, alone in this unhallowed wilderness, without friend or white man within hundreds of miles of me, and surrounded by savages who had never seen a white man before. Every day seemed a week, every night a month." [2]

1. Gabriel Franchère, *Journal of a Voyage on the North West Coast of North America*, ed. W. Kaye Lamb (Toronto: Champlain Society, 1969), p. 77.

2. Alexander Ross, *Adventures of the First Settlers on the Oregon or Columbia River*, ed. Milo Milton Quaife (Chicago: R. R. Donnelley, 1923), p. 158.

Competition between the Pacific Fur Company and the North West Company was soon caught up in international strife, the War of 1812. When war was declared the British company persuaded the Royal Navy to send a warship to the Columbia to capture the rival post. The captain of *Raccoon,* finding upon arrival at Astoria that the fort had already changed hands, captured it anyway for good measure. McDougall and the other officers, their position gravely weakened by the loss of *Tonquin* and the failure of the annual supply ship of 1812 to arrive, had sold Astor's interests to the British firm in the fall of 1813. Since the Treaty of Ghent, approved in 1815, ended the war and provided that property captured during the conflict must be restored, and although Astoria was considered to have fallen under this provision, Astor decided not to resume operations. He could not count upon American naval protection, and his competitors had proved more aggressive than anticipated. The Astoria venture was a failure, not because it was ill-conceived, but because of poor personnel decisions, bad luck, and war. Its significance lay in the realm of foreign affairs, for it provided, as a site of permanent occupation, a useful claim to the Columbia watershed on behalf of the United States when the question of the sovereignty of the Oregon Country was decided. But this decision lay in the long future. What British and American diplomats accomplished in the aftermath of the War of 1812 was agreement on the treaty of joint occupation in 1818 that deferred the question of sovereignty until the indefinite future, while it assured the nationals of both countries free access to the entire region. Both parties were content to renew the agreement in 1827 so that time would enable them to strengthen their respective spheres of interest. In reality, however, after the collapse of Astoria, it was the British fur companies that were the sole source of power in the Oregon Country.

II

The heirs to maritime fur traders, to the territorial explorations of Alexander Mackenzie and Lewis and Clark, and to John Jacob Astor were two great British corporations, the North West Company and the Hudson's Bay Company. The roots of the North Westers lie in the arrangements developed by Montreal businessmen for the fur trade north of the Great Lakes and east of the Rockies beginning in the 1770s. To forestall competition in this wilderness, the various supply houses pooled their trading goods at the interior posts and divided their profits at the end of the season. The system frequently broke down because of avarice or personality conflicts, but the North West Company, reorganized several times over the years since 1779, had by 1804 absorbed or defeated most of its Canadian rivals.

One foe could not be intimidated. This was the venerable and potent Hudson's Bay Company (its antiquity certified by the popular tag for its initials, "Here Before Christ") which, in return for an annual rent of two elk and two black beaver, had received from Charles II in 1670 the entire drainage basin of Hudson Bay as its exclusive preserve. No other subject or firm could lawfully set foot upon this magnificent domain of a million and one-half square miles, but the Scotsmen who directed the North West Company were not deterred by their formidable rival, and under the leadership of William McGillivray they developed a two-pronged response to it. One move was to invade the Hudson's Bay region itself in defiance of British law and the employees of the HBC. Until 1821 guerrilla warfare, marked by price-cutting, indiscriminate use of liquor among the Indians, taking of hostages, and even murder, raged throughout the northern wilderness.

The other strategy was to seek new and uncontested beaver country. From Fort William on Lake Superior the North Westers trapped westward along the watersheds of the Saskatchewan and Athabasca rivers toward the Rockies to outflank the HBC from the south. As it enlarged its territory, however, the North West Company found it increasingly difficult to supply economically its traders from Montreal. Accordingly, in 1806 its directors ordered Simon Fraser to locate the Columbia River from the central plains and to trace it to the ocean in the hope that this river might prove to be an efficient logistical route from the Pacific Coast to the interior posts. Finally in 1808 Fraser's party of twenty-four men embarked on a thirty-six-day outward journey to the Pacific along the river that now carries his name. Fraser had as many challenges as Mackenzie: unknown and enormously difficult terrain, the uncertain responses of the Indians, the murmurings of the men. But his leadership was of impeccable stoutheartedness and exemplified that of the trader of all nations. "Our situation is critical and highly unpleasant," he wrote on one occasion, "however we shall endeavour to make the best of it; what cannot be cured, must be endured." And, on another, "while we have a salmon remaining, bad as they are, there will be nothing impossible for us to do." Yet his intrepedity came to naught, for the Fraser proved to be neither the Columbia nor a navigable substitute for it. The Columbia itself was first traced from source to mouth by another great North Wester, David Thompson, explorer, cartographer, Christian—as well as fur trader—who in a series of journeys from 1807 to 1811 finally reached the ocean at Astoria.[3]

Thompson, who had learned the fur business as an employee of the HBC before he switched to its aggressive rival, had a superb knowledge of wilderness ways, knew several Indian languages, and possessed marvellous skills as a surveyor and cartographer. His multiple talents opened up many of the beaver regions of the Oregon Country. In 1810 his company decided to send him the length of the Columbia River to establish a trading post at the mouth in order to beat Astor's men to this strategic point of exchange and to claim the river's watershed for Britain. Although he was unable to gain the primary objective of his great journey, for he did not reach the river's outlet until after the founding of Astoria, his maps were notable contributions to geographic knowledge, and his Columbia River journey was referred to subsequently by British diplomats in negotiations over the Oregon boundary.

After the acquisition of Astoria the North West Company seemingly had a limitless future. Its only rival was gone, Fraser and Thompson had opened a large beaver country, and the company had posts along the main course of the Columbia and in the Rockies. But there were several problems that awaited reso-

3. W. Kaye Lamb, ed., *The Letters and Journals of Simon Fraser, 1806–1808* (Toronto: Macmillan, 1960), pp. 82, 145.

lution before success could be assured. One of these, as historical geographer Donald W. Meinig has pointed out, was the different natural environment of the beaver trade west of the Rockies compared to that of central Canada. In this new country the terrain was rugged and not always penetrable by waterways; the beaver, because of a relative scarcity of its favorite food, was in short supply and the milder winters made its coat less luxurious. The bison, the staple of the plains, appeared infrequently, forcing the men to substitute horse meat as their basic food; this reliance in turn meant a dependence on the Indians who, because of their relative affluence, were not eager to sell horses or to trap furs for the whites. The North Westers also had trouble in finding a suitable headquarters post adjacent both to beaver and friendly Indians and they had difficulty marketing their furs in China because of the monopoly of that market by the East India Company.

In spite of these obstacles the North West Company enjoyed a brief renaissance in the Oregon Country after 1816 under the leadership of the charismatic and corpulent Donald McKenzie. McKenzie selected Fort Nez Perce, at the confluence of the Walla Walla and the Columbia, to be company headquarters. From this base he devised the fur brigade, mobile parties of horsemen, who penetrated deep into the central Rockies and through the Snake River watershed. Profits from the Oregon Country appreciated as knowledge of the virgin beaver territory increased, but even McKenzie's genius could not save the company, for the North Westers were undone by forces and events thousands of miles from the Pacific Northwest.

In 1821 the British government, appalled by the devastation caused by the lawless trade war in central Canada, forced the merger of the North West Company and Hudson's Bay Company. This union brought the HBC to the Pacific Northwest in force for the first time for, as far as British law was concerned, the company was granted exclusive trading privileges and original civil and criminal jurisdiction in the entire region west of the Rockies from the Columbia River North to 54°40', the southern boundary of Russian Alaska. Presented with this domain, the

governing council of the company had to make a series of decisions to develop it.

The London headquarters was initially dubious about the potential of the Columbia River watershed. Some directors wanted to write it off as a field of operations, arguing that it would be unprofitable. Others believed that at least the south bank of the river should be abandoned. To settle the point, the directors ordered their North American governor, George Simpson, to make a field inspection of the Columbia country in the fall and winter of 1824–1825. Simpson, like so many British officers of the fur trading companies, was a Scotsman seeking advancement in the dynamic society of the new world. Astute, courageous, literate, a discerning judge of men and motives, Simpson soon earned the encomium of his superiors as having "acquired a more perfect knowledge of the Indian Trade than perhaps was ever possessed by any one Individual or even by any body of Men who have been engaged in it." [4]

In a series of bold recommendations, persuasively argued, Simpson got the council to consent to retain and nurture the Columbia region, and in the years after the mid-twenties the company ultimately established thirteen posts throughout the Oregon Country, based on its new headquarters, Fort Vancouver, at the junction of the Columbia and the Willamette rivers. Although the company's chief business was furs, HBC employees also sent farm products to Alaska to supply the Russian-American Company posts, established a shipyard at Fort Vancouver, and tried to find outlets for lumber and salmon in Hawaii, South America, and California. Distance, varying demand, and uncertain quality of products, however, made these activities an inferior source of profits compared to those of the vast fur trade empire. The direction of all these endeavors was placed in the hands of Dr. John McLoughlin, chief factor of the company operations west of the Rockies. McLoughlin, a huge man of generous temperament and enormous charisma, fore-

4. Frederick Merk, ed., *Fur Trade and Empire: George Simpson's Journal,* rev. ed. (Cambridge, Mass.: Harvard University Press, 1968), p. 286.

stalled American competition on both land and sea by price competition and by ordering his trapping brigades literally to denude the Snake River area of beaver to make it a barrier against the advance of the Saint Louis fur men. For almost fifteen years, until the late 1830s, HBC competition was obliterated, and the company—through McLoughlin—ruled the Northwest.

Hudson's Bay's success was anchored in developments other than the intrepedity and business acumen of McLoughlin and his traders and trappers. The joint occupation treaties of 1818 and 1827 negotiated between the governments of Britain and the United States postponed the Oregon sovereignty question and left a clear field to the entrepreneurs of both nations. But British trade goods were better and cheaper than those of their rivals, and the capital resources of the bay company were larger and more efficiently focussed. In the underdeveloped colonial region of the Northwest the power of the HBC reflected the advantages enjoyed by a concern representing a nation with a long headstart over its former colony in the industrial, commercial, and financial revolutions. But the British concentrated their efforts upon the fur business and, even there, operated through the medium of a single monopolistic corporation. When challenged by other economic interests, with concomitant political authority, Great Britain's dependence on the fur trade proved fatal.

III

Yet for years before this weakness became apparent the HBC was a source of emulation as well as envy for Americans. Revival of American interest in Oregon occurred in the late 1820s, a decade and a half after Astor's failure in the Northwest, and it took a somewhat different form from the purposes of the Pacific Fur Company. Astor, like Simpson and McLoughlin, was primarily a fur trader; Hall J. Kelley and Nathaniel Wyeth, his countrymen, combined colonization with economic exploitation.

Hall Kelley, a college graduate and a Boston school teacher, was a romantic visionary inflamed from early youth with a passion for chronicles of distant places and voyages of discovery. Although he had never approached closer to Oregon than a con-

tinent's width, he knew the work and writings of Lewis and Clark, Vancouver, Gray, and other explorers, and in his conception of the future of Oregon he synthesized several disparate dreams into a compelling vision. In 1829 Kelley organized an American Society for Encouraging the Settlement of the Oregon Territory, frankly modelled on the pattern of the Hudson's Bay Company. Thereafter in various prospectuses and petitions Kelley asked Congress for aid; he wanted a land grant and military assistance to make his plan attractive to New England investors and to induce settlers to join the venture.

In return for governmental assistance and private capital Kelley promised several advantages to his countrymen. In Oregon he would add to the national wealth through agriculture, fishing, and whaling. He pledged to develop a lucrative trade with the teeming population of the East Indies. Unemployed urban workers would find profitable labor in healthful Oregon. Politically, too, the United States would gain as Kelley's colonists pressured England out of the Northwest and secured the friendship of the Indians. The resources of Oregon were not only beneficial but indeed providential; "these paramount advantages," Kelley wrote, "are indications, that the God of nature has designed it for the great purposes and operations of heaven-born man." The Indian residents of the region, too, were appealing, for they combined military weakness with a character, when treated justly, that was "courteous and kind to strangers; amiable and obliging to one another." [5]

Kelley, for all his effort, was never able to transfer his enthusiasm for Oregon into a practical instrument to people it. His organizational skill was limited and the opposition of the HBC and the Saint Louis fur traders, who circulated accounts denigrating the economic opportunities of the Pacific Northwest, destroyed his plans. Although Kelley was not himself a colonizer, his ideas were influential in publicizing the Oregon Country, nowhere more effectively than in the mind of his Cambridge neighbor, Nathaniel Wyeth.

5. Fred Wilbur Powell, *Hall J. Kelley on Oregon* (Princeton: Princeton University Press, 1932), pp. 35, 60.

Wyeth had gotten his start as a businessman working for Frederick Tudor, the refrigeration entrepreneur, who was engaged in the novel and lucrative pursuit of collecting ice from the farm ponds of Massachusetts and shipping it to Central America. First intrigued, then disgusted, with Kelley and his plan, Wyeth decided to venture his own Oregon settlement in 1832. Wyeth's models were the HBC and the Pacific Fur Company as well as Kelley's dreams. He projected land and maritime expeditions to build a base of operations on the lower Columbia, and from this nucleus he planned to collect furs, preserve salmon, and make lumber in addition to founding an agricultural settlement. The ship would transport the heavy equipment, and Wyeth himself led the overland party of employees and colonists. In spite of careful planning, the fate of Wyeth's expedition of 1832 paralleled Astor's endeavor in that the supply ship was lost and the venture failed. Stranded at Fort Vancouver, Wyeth received the generous hospitality of Dr. McLoughlin, which helped him retain his perspective after his disaster: ''I am now afloat on the great sea of life without stay or support but in good hands i.e. myself and providence and a few of the H. B. Co. who are perfect gentlemen.'' [6]

Upon returning to the East, Wyeth determined to try his luck again in the Oregon Country. He entered into arrangements with the Saint Louis-based Rocky Mountain Fur Company to transport its trading goods to the annual fur traders rendezvous in the Rockies. The profits from this venture were earmarked for the operations on the Columbia, which were again to be established by the men of maritime and overland expeditions. Nathaniel Wyeth's second expedition, led again by himself, was made up of diverse elements. In his party of 1834 he included not only his own men, but also the first Protestant missionaries to follow the trail to Oregon, Jason and Daniel Lee and their small party, and two scientists, botanist Thomas Nuttall and ornithologist John K. Townsend.

Again his preparations were thorough and again Wyeth met

6. F. G. Young, ed., *The Correspondence and Journals of Captain Nathaniel J. Wyeth, 1831–6* (Eugene, Ore.: University Press, 1899), p. 178.

disaster. This time the trouble came from the land, not the sea, for his supply ship crossed the dangerous Columbia bar in safety, but the men were to receive news that the Rocky Mountain Fur Company had decided not to accept Wyeth's trading goods at the rendezvous, asserting that straitened business conditions required them to reduce their operations. This perfectly lawful, although totally unexpected, decision, in some ways comparable to the sale of Astoria to the North Westers, enraged Wyeth, but he fought back against his ill luck by opening a post he named Fort Hall (in present Idaho) and began operations on the lower Columbia. By the fall of 1835, faced at both posts with the opposition of the HBC, which systematically undercut him in their competition for furs, Wyeth lamented his decision to leave safer ventures in a letter to his uncle: "I am surrounded with difficulties beyond any former period of my life and without the health [he was suffering from "bilious fever"] and spirit requisite to support them. In this scituation [*sic*] you can judge if memory brings to me the warnings of those (wiser and older) who advised a course which must at least have resulted in quietness. Yes memory lends its powers for torment." [7]

In 1836 Wyeth gave up, sold out to the HBC, and returned to Massachusetts. There he was re-employed by Tudor and became a man of wealth, while his erstwhile colleague Kelley died a failure. Kelley had actually reached Fort Vancouver in 1834, but instead of leading a prosperous colony, he went as a member of a party of fur traders, travelling north from California in the company of suspected horse thieves, to find a chilling reception from Dr. McLoughlin. He spent much of the balance of his life (he died in 1874) trying to obtain a government pension for publicizing Oregon to the American people.

There was a good deal of truth in his claim. Kelley had stimulated Wyeth's interest and Wyeth had caught the imagination of important elements within the public: in politics, in science, in business and among the restless, unsettled class of American pioneer farmers. Although Wyeth failed because his plans did not arouse sufficient interest in commercial and governmental

7. Young, *Correspondence of Wyeth*, p. 152.

circles in the 1830s to make him competitive with the HBC, he was a magnet for those who came in the next decade to stay. Townsend, his expedition's chronicler, recorded from personal experience what Kelley had merely asserted and what the frontiersman desired, that the land of Oregon was incredibly rich; above all, at Fort Vancouver, he wrote "Wheat thrives astonishingly; I never saw better in any country, and the various culinary vegetables . . . are in great profusion, and of the first quality." And of the Indian guardians of the land, Townsend predicted, "in a very few years the race must, in the nature of things, become extinct; and the time is probably not far distant, when the little trinkets and toys of this people will be picked up . . . as mementoes of a nation passed away for ever from the face of the earth." [8]

IV

Townsend's melancholy conclusion was not shared by contemporary Christian clergy. The interest of the churches in the souls of the American Indians originated at the beginnings of the conquest of the New World, and Spanish, French, and English missionaries, more or less zealous and effectual, were numbered frequently among the frontiersmen of the colonial period. Early in the history of the United States, in 1819, Congress established a policy of subsidizing missionary activity, educational and agricultural as well as religious, among the Indian tribes, but this concern was desultory until the emergence of one of the great religious and social crusades of the nineteenth century, the "Great Revival" of the 1820s and 1830s.

Beginning in western New York state, then spreading across the Union, Protestant ministers began to place a new emphasis in their exhortations to the "unsaved." No longer could a person who had "gained Christ" rest on the certainty of individual salvation, but Christian men and women had an obligation to

8. John Kirk Townsend, *Narrative of a Journey Across the Rocky Mountains to the Columbia River* in Reuben Gold Thwaites, ed., *Early Western Travels, 1748–1846,* 32 vols. (Cleveland: Arthur H. Clark, 1904–1907), 21:298, 333.

reform the social environment so as to make it as congenial as possible to the practice of the Christian faith, particularly the cultivation of pious habits. This powerful conviction underlay the reform movements of the day: the causes of prison reform, abolition of slavery, teaching of the deaf and dumb, Sabbath observance, and the bringing of American civilization and Christianity to the pagan peoples, not the least of which was the American Indian.

In the Oregon Country, Christianity already had some fragile roots. There were chaplains aboard the government exploring vessels. Some of the trappers and traders, both Indian and white, were Christians. Divine services were conducted at Fort Vancouver from time to time, and the HBC, under pressure from its London office, educated and Christianized two young men from the mountain tribes at its American headquarters at the Red River. Consistent with these diverse contacts were reports of a visit by four Nez Percé Indians to Saint Louis in 1831 in search of further knowledge of the Christian faith. This quest was interpreted to mean a desire for the missionary presence in the Oregon Country, and the Board of Missions of the Methodist Episcopal Church was the first to respond to it.

Jason and Daniel Lee and three laymen thus found themselves in Nathaniel Wyeth's caravan on the trail to Oregon in 1834 as a result of multiple causes. Jason Lee, born a Canadian, was a strong preacher, knowledgeable about the world as well as the church, courageous, and tenacious, but—as would become all too evident—ill-equipped to deal with his distant bureaucratic superiors because of his inadequacy as a cost accountant and his disinclination for correspondence.

For ten years Lee's mission labored in Oregon. Although he had abandoned his original plan to work among the Nez Percé (a decision reinforced by McLoughlin, who asserted they were too mobile and fierce for his labors), Lee planted his mission headquarters in the Willamette Valley thirteen miles by river north of the present city of Salem. In the next few years he sent other missionaries to the Indian settlements at Salem, The Dalles, Clatsop Plains, Nisqually, and Oregon City. Three times his people were numerically reinforced, twice in 1837 and again in 1840, and the mission group became for a brief period the most influential of the Americans in Oregon. Yet in 1844 the mission board in New York abandoned its Oregon Indian mission. In understanding the Methodist missionary experience, its successes and failures, its ideology and techniques, its origins and its demise, it is necessary to underscore the pervasive influences of traditional ideals and structures upon its men and women.

With its emphasis upon scriptural understanding, Protestantism demanded literacy. Morality demanded clothing. Contemporary political economy required that farming and trades be taught, since those who labored in the fields or crafts were closer to Nature and to Nature's God than either extreme of hunter or industrial worker. The teachings of Christ required feeding the hungry and healing the sick, and most Indians—ravaged by the white man's economy and diseases—were in desperate need of succour. Far less theoretically, the inadequate financial support from the East forced the missionaries to expend a great deal of time producing their own food, shelter, and clothing. The missionary became a school teacher, an agricultural agent, a physician, and a manual arts instructor.

A particular aspect of eastern civilization that affected the Methodist missionaries was the virulent and pervasive denominationalism of the antebellum era. It affected all religions and denominations. Protestants, for many reasons, found Roman Catholics to be abhorrent. They were believed to be willing tools of the pope and his subordinates in both government and politics. They were identified with the waves of "uncouth" immigrants swarming to American shores. Lurid stories of escaped nuns fleeing from lecherous priests abounded in books, pamphlets, and public platforms. Catholics were synonymous with foreign foes: with Spain, or Mexico, or England (at least in Oregon where most of the HBC employees were Catholics). Roman Catholic clergy counterattacked with verve and vigor, and such internecine conflict doubtless not only confused the Indians about Christian doctrine but appalled them at its clerical application. Illustrative of the missionary rivalry was the creation of competing mission stations at the Clackamas River. Here the Indians were visited from time to time by the Method-

ist clergyman Alvan F. Waller and the Catholic priest Francois
Blanchet. Waller described one confrontation between the two:

> Immediately however he [Blanchet] set up his high claims to
> "apostolic succession" that he was sent to preach the gospel to all
> the world &c. I also professed to be sent to preach the gospel.
> Whence he indignantly replied *"You sent to preach? You the
> successor of the apostles?"* "Yes, said I, I yield nothing to you in
> this respect. I profess to be sent to preach the gospel."

Blanchet's description of this meeting ran as follows:

> After the mass and instruction, while I was surrounded by many
> natives, I saw the minister Waller enter. . . . He gave evidence of
> his displeasure that I came, as an intruder, he said, to preach to the
> natives of his jurisdiction, whom he was accustomed to teach every
> Sunday. My answer was that my mission on the Columbia did not
> except any part of the country; that, not considering him as a true
> messenger, my duty was to disabuse the natives of the false
> doctrines that he was teaching them.[9]

The work of the missionaries was also weakened by the criticism of their "secular" activities by the mission board. As a
great frontier religion Methodism's success—organizationally—
had been based on circuit riders who moved about the frontier
and who were supported originally by the mission board until
sufficient settlement permitted them to be maintained by the
local congregations they served. In Oregon, of course, local
support was not possible (until 1849, and even thereafter board
contributions continued) and to help themselves, as well as the
Indians, the missionaries labored long hours in field and mill.
The practice of self-support, a necessity for the Oregonians,
indeed a virtue, seemed to the eastern officialdom an un-Chris-
tian "worldliness" that endangered the true missionary function
of teaching the Word of God. The major charge against Jason
Lee was this secular emphasis, and his replacement, George
Gary, at the orders of the mission board, quickly closed down

9. Diary of Alvan F. Waller, August 25, 1841, Waller Papers, Oregon Historical Society. Waller quote from the Manuscript Collections of the Oregon Historical Society
and used with permission. Blanchet quote from Carl Landerholm, ed., *Notices &
Voyages of the Famed Quebec Mission to the Pacific Northwest* (Portland: Oregon Historical Society, 1956), p. 85.

the economic facets of the mission after his arrival in the Willamette Valley in 1844.

A nondoctrinal reason for this tack was the increase in the numbers of white pioneers who migrated to Oregon in the early 1840s. The presence of these settlers became the increasing concern of the missionaries, especially as they saw the social situation: "The hopes of the mission [declared the board in 1845], for the future, depend principally upon the success of the Gospel among the emigrants. The Indians are comparatively few in number and rapidly wasting away." The growing numbers of white settlers forced the Methodists to develop institutional responses to their needs, responses that were as conservative as those of the mission era.[10]

These traditional patterns were those that had worked well on other frontiers, from the circuit riders of the Middle West to those of the Pacific Coast. The organization and style of worship at Sunday services, prayer meetings, and camp meetings were identical to those of eastern Methodism. The local class and local congregation were carried to Oregon and they were assembled, as elsewhere, into an annual conference (de facto for a time it is true). The church members also organized themselves into Sunday schools, temperance societies, and missionary societies, as did their brothers and sisters in the East. In doctrine, too, what was true for the pioneer era had been true for the missionary period: "There was a fundamental doctrinal unity in Methodism extending from England to Oregon." [11]

The aspirations, challenges, and failures of the Methodist missionaries were often akin to those of other faiths. The opportunities of the Oregon Country that drew the Lee party in 1834 also brought, in the following year, the veteran clergyman, Samuel Parker, fifty-six years of age, who made a remarkable lone investigation of the Indians of the Rockies on behalf of the

10. Charles Henry Carey, ed., "Methodist Annual Reports Relating to the Willamette Mission (1834–1848)," *Oregon Historical Quarterly* [hereafter cited *OHQ*] 23 (December 1922): 334.

11. Robert N. Peters, "From Sect to Church: A Study of the Permutation of Methodism on the Oregon Frontier" (Ph.D. diss., University of Washington, 1973), p. 164. Used with permission.

American Board of Commissioners for Foreign Missions, an ecumenical endeavor of Presbyterians, Congregationalists, and Dutch Reformed. The year following his favorable report the board dispatched the party led by Dr. Marcus Whitman. This small expedition included three missionary wives, an exceptionally literate and dedicated group, the first white women to cross overland to the Rocky Mountains. From 1836 to 1847 these missionaries and their reinforcements planted several mission stations among the tribes of central and eastern Washington and western Idaho.

Here, among Cayuse, Walla Walla, Nez Percé, and allied tribes the Whitman party engaged in the attempt to evangelize and civilize the Indians and to turn them into sedentary people who would abandon the annual migrations required by the hunting-fishing-gathering cultures. Initially receptive to the gospel, the Indians soon became disillusioned by the failure of the missionaries consistently to improve their material wealth and physical health, to provide, in other words, the advantages implied in acquiring American culture. The missionaries came to represent America not only in terms of their own work, but they also became identified with the approach of white settlers to take the Indians' land. The Whitman Massacre in 1847 was the tragic culmination of the accumulating Indian outrage.

By the summer of this year Indian apprehensions had turned to hatred. A frightening epidemic of measles had broken out among the tribes that Dr. Whitman's medical skills could not check. The Indians nursed their grievances and recalled their ancient practice of taking the life of an unsuccessful medicine man. Others circulated a rumor that Whitman was poisoning his charges to make way for the whites. A part-Indian, Joe Lewis, became the leader of an enraged minority of the Cayuse which attacked the main mission station at Waiilatpu (near present Walla Walla) on November 29, 1847. Of the seventy-five people present that day at Waiilatpu, the Indians murdered fourteen, including Marcus and Narcissa Whitman, and three children died in captivity. Forty-seven captives were taken, and the remainder either escaped or were released at the time of the attack.

The first Catholic priests in Oregon, Francois Blanchet and Modeste Demers, arrived in the fall of 1838 to minister to the employees of the HBC. In 1840 Pierre-Jean de Smet, the pioneer American Catholic Indian missionary, reached the Rockies. Catholic priests, like Protestant ministers, fought each other as well as labored with the Indians and shared the discouragement of Indian tasks. In the end all missionaries came to see their effort with the Indians as insignificant compared to their labor with the whites. Disease and encroachment depleted the tribes; those who survived were tenacious in retaining their religions. The final resolution for many missionaries was to share John Townsend's conclusion. As the Jesuit missionary, Father de Smet, expressed it: the "poor Indians of Oregon . . . who, after having lived peaceably by hunting and fishing, during several generations, will finally disappear, victims of vice and malady, under the rapacious influence of modern civilization." [12] Although poor consolation, some saw the replacement of Indian by white as the workings of the Divine Plan to reward a superior race.

Interdenominational rivalry, personality conflicts, secular attractions, misunderstanding in the East, the coming of the white settler, and the indifference of the Indians destroyed the missionary efforts. Their influence was persuasive, however, in drawing white migrants who knew in their bones that the agricultural land that supported and tempted the missionaries, and that the Indians were so reluctant to plow, was God's gracious gift to American frontiersmen.

V

To the America of the 1840s Oregon's past seemed doubly dated. Not only were the vocations of the maritime explorer, the scientist, the missionary, and the fur trader a part of history—however colorful and valuable they once may have been—but they had no place in the envisioned future. The prospective

12. P. J. de Smet, *Oregon Missions and Travels over the Rocky Mountains,* in Reuben Gold Thwaites, *Early Western Travels 1748–1846,* 29:194.

Oregonians of the decade, the agricultural settlers, left their homes for many reasons and, for a variety of motives, chose the valley of the broad Willamette in preference to unsettled regions of California or Texas or the Middle West. What united these men and women, for the most part residents of the valleys of the Ohio, Mississippi, and Missouri, was the conservatism of their occupation and of their quest for new frontiers to solve their problems.

Pioneers interested in the Oregon Country were a product of earlier frontiers. Into the Middle West, particularly in the southern third of Ohio, Indiana, and Illinois along the north bank of the Ohio River; into Kentucky; and into Missouri had come representatives of pioneer families stretching back in time and place to the southern piedmont, to the tidewater country, and ultimately to England, Scotland, and Ireland. These people were apt to be illiterate, poor, and insular. They were evangelical Protestants in religion, if anything, the supporters of the circuit rider and the camp meeting. Adherents of Jacksonian Democracy in politics, haters of both slavery and free blacks, they championed democracy and equality for whites. Their society, immortalized in Edward Eggleston's *Hoosier Schoolmaster,* contrasted with that of the Yankee culture in the northern part of the Middle West, which was wealthier, better educated, more favorable to the Whig party than that of the southern uplanders. But the southern and New England elements coexisted, although in tension, for both peoples had the underlying similarities, for better or worse, of a common Protestant religion; of the vicissitudes of the family-sized farm; and pride in national and racial achievements. All in all they made excellent material for colonizers and in the years ahead would expel the Mormons from Illinois, drive the Mexicans from Texas and California, and pressure the HBC in the Oregon Country.

This destiny in the late 1830s was unclear, for discouragement hung over the river valleys of the Middle West. Economic depression, the worst in history, flattened the whole country. Farmers and businessmen lost their markets. Local and state governments went bankrupt as hard times destroyed their elaborate schemes for internal improvements. Land sales and agricultural prices slid. Economic depression magnified personal difficulties such as marital troubles, generational conflicts, and the pervasive health problems of a fever-infested lowland country. In the traditional manner, sanctioned by two centuries of success, many citizens restlessly began to consider another move.

Oregon's specific attraction to the discontented was manifold. In the economic realm the region's great appeal was that it promised certain success without changing one's customary methods of farming. Tradition, not innovation, was required. More than a score of actual observers, of different nations and interests, had revealed to the American public the fertility of the soil of the Willamette Valley, its ample rainfall and temperate climate, its waterways communications, its millsites, and its groves of trees dotted throughout the level prairies. For a farming family, necessarily conservative, Oregon represented not a totally new life but a better old one; if not quite a garden of Eden, at least a mightily improved Missouri.

Oregon's pioneers were not all materialistic in their motivation. Crossing the trail for some was an act of patriotism, a chance to participate in saving the country from Britain and the Hudson's Bay Company. For English institutions: the established Anglican church; the system of economic monopoly; a hereditary aristocracy; and a dynastic monarchy conveyed to the American a picture of Britain, although not entirely an accurate one, as a society both antithetical and menacing to the dynamic and pluralistic America of the Age of Jackson. And, in the course of time, if an American territory were created in Oregon following the departure of Britain, an added bonus for the politically ambitious would be the host of offices available to aspiring statesmen.

The pioneers of the 1840s were thus a conservative and nationalistic people. They were largely members of families—unlike those Americans who went in that decade to the mines of California. Most had some money, because the cost of equipment, food, and supplies for the trail was high, and farming in the new country would also require capital until the first crops found a market. And although the pioneer generation was conservative, its members were not staid or unadventuresome. After all, most people in the Middle West stayed home. The pioneers were those who, when weighing the necessity to move and the desire to remain, came down on the side of change, but change for the sake of duplicating the old ways in an environment that was itself, paradoxically, both novel and familiar.

The emigrants' conservatism was amply displayed in the organization of their wagon trains. Stable people, desirous of protecting life and property, the pioneers formed written codes to regulate their behavior on the overland march both through and toward regions without American government. In this respect they reached back to the *Mayflower* pilgrims who, finding themselves outside the boundaries of their intended destination, drew up in 1620 their famous compact to create a government. To command the party and to enforce the regulations, the settlers, as in choosing contemporay militia officers, elected their own leaders from captain to council members. If tradition were not followed there would be protest. When it was proposed within one group to give the captain temporary veto power over the acts of the council, one observer noted that [he] "heard Dumbarton denounce it, as 'an absurd innovation upon a conservative system, and a most gross violation of a cardinal principle of political jurisprudence.' " [13]

Once organized politically and equipped according to the guidebooks, which proliferated with the years, the wagons began their 2000-mile, four-to-six-month journey to the Willamette. As one old settler reminisced: "Our long journey thus began in sunshine and song, in anecdote and laughter; but these all vanished before we reached its termination." Another old timer remembered it differently, for he recalled "the journey that followed as one of the pleasantest incidents of his life. It was a long picnic, the changing scenes of the journey . . . just about sufficed to keep up the interest, and formed a sort of men-

13. George Wilkes, *History of Oregon, Geographical and Political* (New York: William H. Colyer, 1845), p. 71.

tal culture that the world has rarely offered.'' Most people who wrote of the Oregon Trail fell somewhere between these two, finding the journey neither wearisome nor joyous.[14]

There were real dangers on the trail, but probably the most dreaded was the least likely—the attack by Indians. Indian assaults did occur, but they were only upon isolated parties, not upon the organized caravans. The Indians traded with the whites, provided an interesting change of scene, and were targets for the missionaries, but they were not dangerous. Indeed the Indians were often a welcome sight for the pioneers for they provided portage service, served as paddlers and oarsmen, supplied food, furnished guide services, and even gave defense against hostile Indians. Cholera, accidents, boredom, personality conflicts, and politics produced more tension than did the Indians.

A people uprooted from their homes, casting off for a distant country, suffering from heat and thirst on the plains and cold and lack of supplies in the mountains, were easy prey for abrasive conflict. The loss of fixed work routine was particularly hard for the women, for their usual activities of cooking, washing, and child care were almost totally disrupted by mobility, lack of fuel, the high altitudes of the Rockies, muddy streams, and the need to guard their children against falling under the heavy wagons, against rattlesnake bites, and against wandering. Although men missed the security of plowing and harvesting, their driving, scouting, and hunting activities were closer to their normal outdoor pursuits than those of the women. Of course not all women were disconcerted by the migration. Elizabeth Wood, a youthful Illinoisian, writing to her hometown newspaper three days after passing Fort Hall, declared: ''After experiencing so many hardships, you doubtless will think I regret taking this long and tiresome trip, and would rather go back than proceed to the end of my journey. But, no, I have a great desire to see Oregon, and, besides, there are many things we

14. Peter Burnett, ''Recollections and Opinions of an Old Pioneer,'' *OHQ* 5 (March 1904): 67–68; H. S. Lyman, ed., ''Reminiscences of Hugh Cosgrove,'' *OHQ* 1 (September 1900): p. 257.

meet with . . . to compensate us for the hardships and mishaps we encounter." [15]

Tensions burst out in several forms. A well-known conflict was whether or not to allow dogs to accompany the party. On at least two wagon trains a move was made to kill them, since they consumed food and stampeded the cattle. Captains were voted out of office and sundered the train when their followers stayed loyal rather than accompanying the new leader. One leader resigned in disgust over protests against his direction of a buffalo hunt that resulted in a wasteful slaughter of the animals. Parties split, literally or figuratively, over trials of men accused of crime, over whether to wait for slow-moving wagons, over the problems of delays caused by the owners of cattle.

In the end, however, for most settlers it was the cohesive rather than the divisive factors that prevailed. There were a few murders, more assaults, much bickering, and a great deal of nostalgia and homesickness. One young migrant, Agnes Stewart, may have been thinking of the human condition as she stopped on a Sunday under a rocky outcropping: "Away up in the rocks under a projection I saw a hundred little bird nests made of moss and mud. It looked so pretty to see so many little creatures living together so happy." [16] Yet the settlers, like the *Mayflower* pilgrims, demanded and obtained the security of order and routine, even on the Oregon Trail. Laws were written and largely obeyed. When insurmountable policy clashes occurred, votes were taken and leaders changed. Trials were held and judgments rendered.

Joel Palmer, a sensitive and literate observer, caught the persistence of civilization, not the advent of anarchy, as he described a day's rest during the migration of 1845. "Of the women," he wrote,

> some were washing, some ironing, some baking. At two of the tents the fiddle was employed in uttering its unaccustomed voice among

15. Elizabeth Wood, "Journal of a Trip to Oregon, 1851," *OHQ* 27 (March 1926): 199.

16. Claire Warner Churchill, "The Journey to Oregon—A Pioneer Girl's Diary," *OHQ* 29 (March 1928): 88.

the solitudes of the Platte; at one tent I heard singing; at others the occupants were engaged in reading, some the Bible, others poring over novels. While all this was going on, that nothing might be wanting to complete the harmony of the scene, a Campbellite preacher, named Foster, was reading a hymn, preparatory to religious worship. The fiddles were silenced, and those who had been occupied with that amusement, betook themselves to cards. Such is but a miniature of the great world we had left behind us, when we crossed the line that separates civilized man from the wilderness. But even here the variety of occupation, the active exercise of body and mind, either in labor or pleasure, the commingling of evil and good, show that the likeness is a true one.[17]

However one responded to the experiences of the trail as he or she rode, or walked, or floated, or swam from the Missouri along the Platte, the North Platte, the Bear, the Snake—over the Rockies and across the Blues—and then along the Columbia to The Dalles, where the decision was made to travel either by boat to Fort Vancouver or by road around the base of Mount Hood to the falls of the Willamette, the goal was the same: participation in the transit of civilization. At the end of the terrible journey on the Barlow Road around Mount Hood, Philemon V. Crawford discovered the first house of the settlements in the Willamette Valley: "Here we find all of the conveniences of civilized life and we are able for the first time to appreciate them." James Nesmith's terse diary entry encapsulated the goals of the white migrants: "Friday, October 27.—arrived at Oregon City at the falls of the Willamette. Saturday, October 28.—Went to work."[18]

VI

Although he typified many Oregon pioneers, James Nesmith did not represent all of them. There were those who came who

17. Joel Palmer, *Journal of Travels over the Rocky Mountains,* in Thwaites, *Early Western Travels,* 30:53–54.

18. P. V. Crawford, "Journal of A Trip Across the Plains, 1851," *OHQ* 25 (June 1924): 169; James W. Nesmith, "Diary of the Emigration of 1843," *OHQ* 7 (December 1906): 359.

were not white, and who did not enjoy the full economic and social opportunities of the region. Although small in numbers, several non-Caucasian groups were present in early Oregon. One of the earliest ethnic minorities represented was the Hawaiian. In the island nation, King Kamahameha, claiming the throne in 1810 after an internal power struggle, attempted to forge a united kingdom out of competing groups. He decided upon an outward-looking policy to cushion his country against foreigners by absorbing the European's economy and Christianity. The heart of this policy was to send out young men to learn western techniques and values through practical experience. One place they migrated to was the Oregon Country, where Hawaiians had been in the crews of merchant vessels as early as 1788. In the nineteenth century the Hawaiians, also known as Kanakas or "Blue Men" (because they turned that color in the winter drizzles of the Pacific Northwest), soon became a vital labor supply in the fur trade. Captain Thorn brought Hawaiians to the region in *Tonquin* and twelve perished in the destruction of his ship. After the demise of the Pacific Fur Company the Kanakas were welcomed into the ranks of the North West Company. Loyal and docile, asking only food and clothing for compensation, the Hawaiians on one occasion saved Donald McKenzie from a surprise attack at Fort Walla Walla at the hands of his discontented Indian trappers.

The Hudson's Bay Company and Nathaniel Wyeth also found the Kanakas most valuable as laborers, canoe men, sailors, gardeners, herders, and domestic servants, among other pursuits. The missionaries, too, admired the islanders. The Methodists used them as blacksmiths, farm laborers, and kitchen help, and the Lees at one time proposed to import Hawaiian Christians as missionaries to their countrymen. At the Whitman mission the Kanakas were also well received, and they worked in a variety of pursuits. Both Methodist and American board workers found the Kanakas to be in all respects preferable to their Indian charges. The Indians, in missionary eyes, were slow in emulating American agriculture and domestic science, but the Hawaiians were adaptable and hard working. The Indians were suspect when they sought baptism and the sacraments; they were accused of desiring the material advantages of Christian civilization, but when a Kanaka presented himself at the baptismal font his sincerity went unchallenged. Perhaps their lengthier exposure to the West in their homeland or their voluntary search for white civilization in the Northwest made the Kanakas, in contrast to the Indians, more willing to attempt the process of assimilation. If eagerness to adopt American culture was a guarantee of equal treatment, the Hawaiian was secure in his new home.

But racial prejudice came in the baggage of the white agricultural settlers who had feared blacks in the Middle West because of economic competition, miscegenation, and the migration of idle free Negroes from the South. When the provisional government was organized in the early 1840s, the racism of the pioneers was quickly institutionalized in antiblack and anti-Asian laws that limited land ownership to free males who could vote, and then gave the vote to whites only. Employers of Hawaiian labor were taxed three dollars for those islanders already residents and five dollars for those who were to be introduced in the future. After the organic law of 1848 created the territory of Oregon, Kanakas on several occasions applied for American citizenship. The final blow came in the passage of the Oregon Donation Land Act of 1850, which gave to the emigrants 160 to 320 acres of free land (depending on their time of arrival), but which, at the insistence of Territorial Delegate Samuel R. Thurston, excluded from its terms blacks and Hawaiians, although not part-Indians. Thurston feared that the settling of these two groups would result in their unification with the Indians into a racial combination against the dominant ethnic group. After this rebuff most of the Kanakas returned to the Islands, more fortunate than other ethnic minorities, who had no place to go. In the end, in spite of the Hawaiians' efforts to accommodate, racism had conquered assimilation.

Black people were among the first visitors to the Pacific Northwest. Although various legends persist of shipwrecked black men who integrated with the coastal Indians, the first authenticated case of a black visitor was Marcus Lopius, Gray's cabin boy, who lost his life in the scuffle at Murderer's Harbor. York, William Clark's slave, was a stalwart member of the great expedition, and George Winslow accompanied the mountain man Ewing Young to Oregon in 1834. Several blacks crossed the Oregon Trail in the pioneer era, some as slaves, some as free persons.

The most notable of these was George Washington Bush, a free man of means who waged a remarkable fight against legal and social prejudice. Bush had fought against the British under Andrew Jackson at the Battle of New Orleans. Although free blacks were not permitted to live in his home state of Missouri, Bush was so popular that a special act of the state legislature was passed to allow him to remain. In time he caught the Oregon fever and financed a racially integrated overland party to the Northwest in 1844. At the end of the trail he hoped to settle at The Dalles, but racial prejudice drove him to the country around modern Olympia where he became the town father of the Bush Prairie community and a long-lived and much respected citizen.

In Oregon, as in Missouri, Bush's status was exceptional, for most black people met the legal and social hostility of white persons nurtured in the racism of the Middle West. The organic law of the provisional government in 1843 had prohibited slavery, and in 1844 at the behest of Peter Burnett, the leader of the overland migration of 1843 and future governor of California, the legislature of the provisional government passed two statutes regarding blacks. One again prohibited slavery in Oregon; the other forbade the residence of free blacks. The immediate causes of this legislation were Burnett's fear that white women would be sexually endangered by the presence of black males and the threat of James Saules, a black man, to raise an Indian war against the white community. Although the residence law was never officially enforced, and slaves also continued to remain in Oregon, the significance of the antiblack legislation is that it was repeated under the territorial government and under the state constitution until destroyed by amendments to the federal Constitution after the Civil War.

By the Civil War, indeed, there were few nonwhite pioneers in Oregon. Hawaiians, blacks, and the very small number of Chinese and Japanese immigrants were all victimized by enduring prejudice. Although their goal for coming—improving one's status—was the same as the principal objective of the whites, members of minority groups with rare exceptions never were allowed to rise to the level of white persons, whether in social, economic, or political affairs.

3

Roots of a Conservative Commonwealth

I

ᴿEGARDLESS of race, the Oregon migrants of the early years faced a period of economic frustration. With uncertain supplies and the sole and undependable market provided by the Hudson's Bay Company, life in the Oregon Country seemed more like a struggle for subsistence than a means to an abundant life. What changed these primitive economic conditions into something far more dynamic began with a foreman's short stroll along a millrace several hundred miles from Portland early in 1848. As James Marshall described it: "One morning in January,—it was a clear, cold morning; I shall never forget that morning,—as I was taking my usual walk along the race after shutting off the water, my eye was caught with the glimpse of something shining in the bottom of the ditch." [1] Twelve months after Marshall's gold discovery at Sutter's mill, 80,000 people from literally all over the world rushed to California. This heterogeneous group of argonauts wasted no time in producing the necessities of life but acquired their sustenance and shelter from

1. Charles B. Gillespie, ed., "Marshall's Own Account of the Gold Discovery," *Century Magazine* 51 (February 1891): 538.

whatever source was available. Oregon largely filled their demands, for the territory was full of flour and wheat, rich in lumber, and reasonably proximate to San Francisco. It is true that Oregon was temporarily denuded of a labor supply by the lure of gold, as farmers left their fields and migrants rerouted themselves to the Sierras, but many soon learned the lesson of the far greater profits to be made in "mining the miners."

In a general sense this impact of "California gold enabled Oregon to overcome the pressing economic problems which plagued the Willamette community during the 1840s" by permitting the flow of Oregon products into a larger Pacific Coast market and by freeing the region from its servitude to the uncertain market of the HBC.[2] What occurred on January 24, 1848, provided the pioneers with the economic opportunity and social mobility for which they had endured the agonies of the decision to leave home and the discomforts of the Oregon Trail. More specifically, the foothills of the Sierras furnished, in exchange for wheat and lumber, the gold dust that became the first reliable medium of exchange in Oregon and the capital for transportation and urban developments in the territory. Although the fields and forests of California by 1851 were providing for the needs of that state, and causing a brief depression in Oregon, the gold rush to the central and western sections of the Rogue River valley in southern Oregon in 1853 took up the slack, and by the time the strikes there played out the economy was on a plateau that lasted until the end of the decade.

Quickening economic life not only invigorated farmers but it accelerated urbanization. Merchants, land speculators, professional people, editors, all boomed their respective towns, real or projected, in the hope that they would become the successor to Fort Vancouver as the economic metropolis of the Oregon Country. In this competition the residents of Oregon City in the late 1840s clearly possessed certain advantages. They had the prestige of living in the largest town in the area between California and Alaska. They lived in the territorial capital. Most im-

2. Arthur L. Throckmorton, *Oregon Argonauts: Merchant Adventurers on the Western Frontier* (Portland: Oregon Historical Society, 1961), p. 106.

portantly, the falls of the Willamette River guaranteed them not only a source of water power for milling but also provided a break-of-bulk point where goods had to be unloaded for transshipment around the falls. No one elsewhere conceded these advantages. While denigrating the resources of Oregon City, people in Oregon's Milwaukie boasted of their location as superior in terms of deepwater navigation. Portland and Linn City boomers made the same claim, and Saint Helens businessmen talked of their geographical advantage in cutting travel time for vessels from the mouth of the Columbia; indeed their town was chosen as the terminal of the Pacific Mail Steamship Company in 1851.

The victory of Portland in this interurban warfare came at a single stroke. For Portlanders gained an objective that was never efficiently realized by their competitors, the linking of the Willamette-Columbia water route with Oregon's major wheat belt, the 460,000 acres of the Tualatin Plains. Saint Helens interests promoted a road over the Tualatin Hills through the Cornelius Pass from Sauvie Island to the Yamhill River. Linnton businessmen attempted to upgrade a trail to the plains that had been opened up by Peter Burnett and Morton M. McCarver from their community and adjacent Springville and that was known as the Germantown Road. From the Willamette, Oregon City and Milwaukie reached to the Tualatin Plains from the east.

The best route from the rivers to the plains lay through the canyon of Tanner Creek that joined the Willamette at Portland. A rudimentary trail had been grubbed out by Francis Pettygrove, the cofounder of Portland, but it had sharp curves and steep grades. To supplement it a road had been laid out through the Tanner Creek Canyon as early as 1849, but the natural springs of the canyon kept it a morass. To rectify this situation the Portland business community obtained a charter in 1851 from the territorial legislature for the Portland and Valley Plank Road Company. In the same year grading was begun and the first plank was laid on September 27, 1851. Two months later funds were exhausted and construction ceased after ten miles of plank road had been laid. Although the company was reorganized thereafter several times, the road was never very suitable until the 1880s. Still it was passable enough to determine Portland's commercial supremacy over her rivals.

The last half of the 1850s was a period of steady and sustained growth for the most part, although not as spectacular as the California gold rush era. There were flurries of hope that the Indian wars of the mid-decade would stimulate the economy through government purchases, but those who sold supplies or equipment to the federal commissary officers were the losers, since the United States paid in scrip redeemable at the pleasure of Congress. Congress ultimately paid off in 1861 but in depreciated paper money, the famous greenbacks that rose and fell in proportion to the success of the Union armies, armies which were winning no victories in the first year of the war.

By 1860 the economy, because the California market had dried up, was in danger of stagnation, but for the third time gold came to the rescue of the Oregonians. Although the strikes in Idaho, Montana, and eastern Oregon in 1860 and 1861 were neither as valuable nor became as legendary as those of the Forty-Niners, they were of enormous significance to Oregonians and especially Portlanders. The prize of controlling the trade of these mining districts did not fall into Portland's hands without competition, however, for her rivals, although far away, were formidable. San Francisco, metropolis of the Pacific Coast, reached for the miners' gold dust along the overland route eastward to Nevada and then north to the mining fields. Saint Louis, the metropolis of the midcontinent, had an even longer grasp up the Missouri to the Great Falls, which were first reached by steamboat in 1858, and then over the Rockies to the diggings.

To hold their own in this competition, Portland businessmen had to develop an efficient mode of transportation into the interior. The Oregon Steam Navigation Company, the most famous corporation in the state's early history, was formed in 1860 to reach the Inland Empire mine fields. The leading figure of the OSNC was John C. Ainsworth, who headed a concern originally capitalized at $172,000, all of which was raised in Oregon, a tribute to the economic development of the state in the previous decade. The success of the corporation was phenomenal, a success grounded on a policy of moderate dividends

with profits being plowed into improvements, and on the abso-
lute monopoly of the key portages of the Columbia at The
Dalles and the Cascades, which strangled competition. One employee reminisced: "It makes my head swim now, as memory
carries me back to those wonderful rushing days, when the constant fall of chinking coin into the coffers of the company was
almost like the flow of a dashing torrent. The Oregon Steam
Navigation Company had become a millionaire-making machine." [3] All along the Columbia and the Snake ran the economic writ of the OSNC and Portland, commanding the gold
dust of the miners in return for their food and shelter and supplies. The decade of the sixties thus saw the city of Portland develop an east-west axis that supplemented the earlier flow of
Willamette Valley products to Portland, and the city continued
to enjoy its position as export-import hub of the San Francisco
market. Indeed, Portland became the principal urban center of
the entire Pacific Northwest until it lost its supremacy to Seattle
after the turn of the century.

The OSNC monopoly is a remarkable story of private profit
that had public significance. The company laid the basis for the
creation or increase of Portland fortunes that helped to shape the
cultural life of the city. Many of its investors became wealthy,
and Ainsworths, Reeds, and others were moving spirits, sometimes for several decades ahead, in not only the formation of a
wealthy social elite, but in the rise of cultural institutions such
as the opera, symphony, art museum, and library. The powerful
magnates of the OSNC and their families helped develop the
northeastern strain in Portland life which balanced the middle-
western character of the rest of the Willamette Valley. This
Yankee cultural heritage emphasized thrift and prudence and
helped perpetuate the blending within the state's borders of the
North-South mixture that was transplanted to Oregon by the pioneer farmers from the Ohio and Mississippi valleys.

The mining rush to the Inland Empire also fostered the development of railroading and communications. In 1868 Oregon's

3. F. A. Shaver, comp., *Illustrated History of Central Oregon* (Spokane: Western
Historical Publishing Co., 1905), pp. 114–115.

real railroad era began when the great western transportation magnate Ben Holladay began the construction of a line to San Francisco, although it was not to be completed for another twenty years. Two years previously Congress had passed a statute granting land for the construction of a railroad from Sacramento to Portland. In this measure, because of the lobbying of William W. Chapman and Jesse Applegate, a provision was inserted requiring that the state legislature designate an Oregon corporation to receive the land grant and to build the road through the state. A company called the Oregon Central Railroad, and headed by Joseph Gaston, later a historian of the state, received the blessing of the legislature to run a line along the west side of the Willamette. When Holladay appeared in 1868, with a national reputation as an entrepreneur and lobbyist (''the Napoleon of the West''), he got the legislature to transfer the land grant to his east side corporation that was reorganized in 1870 as the Oregon and California Railroad Company. Both companies continued to build until 1874, when Holladay's line acquired its west side rival, but the completion of the line to California was long delayed by the national depression of the 1870s. Meanwhile, the Willamette Valley lines expanded the hinterland of Portland and eased the penetration of Oregon's wheat into national markets.

The discovery of gold in Idaho and Montana brought not only the development of transportation and communication in Oregon but also the beginning of manufacturing. Perhaps of all the enterprises that began in the prosperous decade of the 1860s the highest hopes were attached to wool. The Civil War, which touched Oregon perhaps the lightest of all the states in terms of blood and treasure, did create a demand for the production of wool and for the manufacture of woolens. Both enterprises were rooted in the previous decades, for in 1848 Joseph Watt had brought the first herd of high-grade sheep over the Oregon Trail. Eight years after this venture Watt became the moving spirit in organizing the Willamette Woolen Manufacturing Company, which opened its factory at Salem in the following year. Capital was local, as was the labor source (girls from Salem); machinery and technical management were imported from New

England and the manager, L. E. Pratt, secured the mill equipment from his home state of Massachusetts. The mill manufactured blankets and exchanged them for its wool supply as a device to popularize its line among the state's merchants, a successful stratagem until 1863, when the company fell into the doldrums after the Yankee Pratt was dismissed by the pro-Confederate ownership. Rival firms posed a further challenge to the recovery of the mill when Linn County interests subscribed $24,000 to start a mill at Brownsville in 1863, with supervisory employees brought from New Jersey, and two years later the mill of the Oregon City Woolen Manufacturing Company came into production. These and other pioneer woolens enterprises, in the words of Alfred Lomax, "infused into the pioneer Willamette Valley, not only the technology of an older order of industry, but that of managerial capacity as well." [4]

In spite of these promising beginnings, the woolen mills suffered from serious problems, some indigenous to any frontier area. Fires took their toll, local demand was sporadic, and racial and labor conflicts emerged. The mill at Oregon City in 1869 was the first to employ Chinese laborers, men who had learned the weaving art in California. This change in employment practices, designed to cut costs, also produced an anti-Chinese labor organization, the White Laborers Association, that carried out an unsuccessful protest strike in July. Racism continued underground until the mill burned in 1872 under suspicious circumstances: the watchman's dog was poisoned and the rope to the fire alarm bell was cut. Other mills in time sprang up from Ashland to The Dalles, but by 1881 the state had only four of the twenty-eight woolen mills on the Pacific Coast, a testimony to the problems of Oregon entrepreneurship.

Papermaking began in Oregon in 1866 when William W. Buck organized the Pioneer Paper Manufacturing Company at Oregon City with a combination of local capital and a loan from the Bank of British Columbia. The mill began producing its first

4. Alfred L. Lomax, *Pioneer Woolen Mills in Oregon: History of Wool and the Woolen Textile Industry in Oregon, 1811–1875* (Portland: Binfords and Mort, 1941), p. 183.

product, brown wrapping paper, in January 1867 after a rather embarrassing grand opening ceremony, complete with brass band and dancing, during which the machinery stopped and no one in the assembled crowd—employees, dignitaries, or ordinary guests—could get it restarted. The company collapsed later in the year, but Buck, in conjunction with Henry L. Pittock, the publisher of the Portland *Oregonian,* started a second mill in 1868 on the Clackamas River a mile and one-half north of Oregon City. The labor force was Chinese and the uncertain supply of rags for the wide variety of paper products manufactured was gathered from local farm wives and from as far away as China.

In the allied enterprise of lumbering, Oregonians also made their start in the years before 1880. As in the case of wholesaling, agriculture, papermaking, woolens manufacture, and salmon canning, the forest products enterprise was strongly influenced, as a colonial extractive industry, by nonregional developments. The first sawmill in what became the state of Oregon was started by John McLoughlin at the falls of the Willamette River. Other mills were organized by American businessmen there and on the lower Columbia, and the California gold rush guaranteed a thriving export market for the first time. In 1849–1850 the California market influence was seen in Oregon in the creation of four water-powered mills and the first steam-powered mill in the Pacific Northwest. The miners' demands created a boom in Oregon, population consequently increased, and local urban markets arose that became far more valuable than those formerly supplied by the local farming community. As the years wore on until statehood, which was secured in 1859, lumbering became the most valuable industry in Oregon.

During the next quarter-century, however, lumbering declined in importance as a result of the collapse of the mining booms in California and Idaho. Although replacement markets were sought by the millmen of the Willamette, Columbia, and Coos Bay (where Asa Mead Simpson began his empire in 1856), Oregon lost her supremacy in the Northwest lumber trade to Washington Territory. The terrible perils of the bar of

the Columbia River contrasted unfavorably with the deep and
sheltered harbors of Puget Sound. Nature had also favored the
north with thick stands of timber growing to the water's edge in
contrast to the scattered and inaccessible forests of the lower
Columbia and Coos Bay regions. In the end the lumber industry
of Oregon, as historian Thomas Cox has pointed out, became a
creature of California since the major markets, source of investment capital, and center of entrepreneurial activities were almost all in that state.

California was also the residence of the men who established
the Oregon salmon canning industry. These were the four
brothers of the Hume clan, men from Maine who had first gone
to California to hunt for gold and then had turned to their ancestral pursuit of salmon fishing. In 1864 they, in co-operation with
the tinsmith Andrew Hapgood, began on the Sacramento River
the laborious process of canning salmon and were the first on
the Pacific Coast to do so. The work was entirely one of trial
and error, and the vicissitudes of canmaking, cooking, and marketing were frequent and vexatious. Before the first pack of
2,000 cases was sold, many cans had exploded, and William
Hume had suffered numerous rebuffs from the suspicious housewives of Sacramento when he tried to market the red cans from
door to door. No sooner had these problems been at least partly
overcome than the partners faced new difficulties in the pollution of the Sacramento by hydraulic mining, which threatened to
destroy their supply of fish.

In this crisis the Humes remembered their journey northward
to the British Columbia gold rush of 1859, recalling not their
failure in the mining camps, but the abundant supply of salmon
in the Columbia River. In 1867 they established the first cannery on the Columbia River—on the Washington side—and in
the next year John West, a Scotsman and a disappointed homesteader, established Oregon's pioneer cannery at a place he
named Westport between Astoria and Portland. During the next
dozen years many canneries began operations on both banks of
the Columbia and also along Oregon's coastal rivers. In this
critical period for the industry several precedents were set. Although the great majority of the American public spurned

canned fish in favor of its customary beef and pork diet, salmon penetrated foreign markets from Australia to China to Latin America, and most of it found its outlet in the sooty, industrialized "Black Counties" of central England. Capital for the business came from California or local sources, and labor was divided between white men—local residents or migratory workers from California—who did the fishing, and Chinese, whom social prejudice consigned to the messy butchering and filling tasks in the canneries.

In two areas the Oregon frontier produced major innovations in the fishing business, contrary to what one would expect from an underdeveloped area. In the fall of 1877 in his cannery at Gold Beach at the mouth of the Rogue River, R. D. Hume began the first efforts of private enterprise to propagate artificially the salmon of the Pacific Coast. Although he had numerous trials in this precarious science and was long unable to convince either the public or the Columbia canners of the value of his work, Hume's labor did bear fruit at the turn of the century. There were important technological innovations also, as seine and drift nets were improved (a Portland mechanic invented a machine to make them in 1877), and the first fish wheel was constructed in 1878 at The Dalles.

The extractive industries and manufacturing captured the imagination of Oregonians, but agriculture was the principal economic concern of the region. In both natural and social aspects the setting for the immigrants coming after 1840 was appealing. The Willamette Valley in particular seemed to promise the Edenic setting that most writers had described since Kelley's time. The landscape was varied and appealing. Not only did the natural prairies promise easy plowing, but the forests, spaced among the prairies, along the river banks, and on the hillsides of the Coast Range, furnished building material, fuel supplies, and fencing. The soil, covered with red and white clover, beautiful wild flowers, and tall grasses, had already been proved rich by missionary and retired fur trapper. Buttes, hills, and the more distant mountains of the Cascade and Coast ranges stimulated the eye. Rainfall was ample, and the Willamette and Columbia and their tributaries promised easy access to markets. Winters were mild by midwestern standards. Indeed, measured either by the old home or by the hazardous or tedious environment of the overland trail, western Oregon gave the pioneers rich promise of a radiant future.

This hope was grounded upon the acquisition of agricultural land, the most precious of all natural resources during the pioneer era. But land had not only to be available, it had also to be secured. In order to guarantee the acquisition of land, Oregon's first American government, the provisional government of 1843, wrote into its organic law a provision to register and protect the land claims of the pioneers. Another government, that of the United States, also had a major impact upon the pioneers' quest for land. As early as 1842 the Senate had discussed a bill introduced by Sen. Lewis Linn of Missouri to reward with grants of free land those Americans who moved to Oregon. In the same year Congress had passed its first free land statute, for residents of Florida Territory, giving 160 acres to settlers who would serve as a buffer against warring Seminole Indians. This military measure came to be considered as a precedent for Oregon, where the settlers regarded themselves, as many in Congress agreed, to be performing a similar role in the national defense against the British. Throughout the balance of the decade Oregonians counted on the national government to redeem the implicit promise of these two measures. For four years, however, there was considerable nervousness in Oregon about congressional intentions. The first step to relieve this apprehension occurred in 1846 when a treaty with Great Britain apportioned to the United States the Oregon Country south of the 49th parallel except for the tip of Vancouver Island. Yet when Congress, after a two-year delay, organized the territory of Oregon, it left intact all the laws of the provisional government except the most important ones, those concerning land. Thus the paramount duty of the first territorial delegate, Samuel R. Thurston, was to obtain a homestead law. Employing the reward-for-settlement argument, combined with an appeal that an Oregon homestead law would set a precedent for a national act, Thurston succeeded in obtaining the Oregon Donation Land Act in 1850. This important measure gave 320 acres of land to a male homesteader, with another 320 to his wife in her own name, who settled in Oregon prior to 1853; 160 acres, with an equal amount to wives, went to those who came between 1853 and 1855. Although the Donation Land Act did not engender a rush of settlement to Oregon, it did at last provide the basis for lawful title to the soil.

Those who took up land employed no new means in farming it, relying on the traditional techniques of tillage and harvesting. Crop selection, also, followed the pattern of the Middle West, modified by the knowledge gained from the agricultural operations of the HBC; its subsidiary, the Puget's Sound Agricultural Company; and their retired employees. Wheat, oats, fruit, and vegetables were the major products of the soil. The keenest disappointment to each wave of settlers was the failure of corn as a major crop, for the Willamette Valley lacked a sufficient number of hot days and humid nights to enable this basic frontier plant to flourish. The settlers were willing to experiment with a great variety of plants brought from their homes, ranging from flax to pumpkins, but many of these attempts to reproduce their old crops in Oregon failed.

One successful effort laid the basis for the orchard industry in Oregon. Although the HBC had introduced fruit trees, the founder of the state's commercial pomology was Henderson Luelling, who brought over the trail from the Middle West in 1847 two boxes of 700 vines, shrubs, and fruit trees that he used to found a nursery at Milwaukie with his brother Seth, who developed the Black Republican cherry and the Bing cherry, the latter named for his Chinese foreman. The business flourished since there was a demand for fresh fruit both locally and, until the 1870s, in California. Natural conditions in western and southern Oregon were ideal, particularly the absence of destructive insects and pests, until they were introduced from California in the 1870s. Luelling had many competitors, although his success as a businessman and plant breeder made him wealthy, compensating for his labor in protecting his first shipment: ''a dollar a drop for the sweat I lost in getting the necessary water to keep them alive while we crossed the desert; and their lus-

OREGON

A photographer's essay by Bob Peterson

Photographs in sequence

cious fruit repaid me many times over for the jeers, ridicule and contentions of my comrades.'' [5]

Stock raising also grew from the successful efforts of the HBC and those of the missionaries who brought cattle and sheep from overseas and from California. Sheep raising was an important enterprise in western Oregon until the early 1860s, when the population pressure of farmers displaced it in favor of wheat culture. Beef cattle, too, were significant in the life of farmers in the Willamette Valley who exported them to the gold fields of British Columbia and Washington in the Civil War years. After the war the pioneers who opened central and eastern Oregon to settlement introduced sheep raising and cattle ranching there.

These sections of the state were held in low repute by the early explorers and settlers who passed through them en route to the Willamette Valley. James Nesmith in 1843 expressed his disappointment at the country around the mouth of the Walla Walla River: ''If this is a fair specimen of Oregon, it falls far below the conceptions which I formed of the country. . . . The whole country looks poverty stricken.'' [6] White settlers first came to the area east of the Cascades in the 1850s when they settled the region around The Dalles, a military post, taking up land under the donation act. The legislature created Wasco County in 1854 and settlement increased slowly until the Inland Empire gold rush in the early 1860s. The Dalles then became the major interior shipping point for the mines. In the years ahead Wasco County was subdivided many times as population increased to the east and south.

At different times in the period between 1859 and 1880 three enduring occupations developed in the vast area between the Cascades and the Idaho line. Central and southern Oregon was excellent cattle country because the flat land, the bunchgrass,

5. Joseph W. Ellison, "The Beginnings of the Apple Industry in Oregon," *Agricultural History* 11 (October 1937): 327.

6. James W. Nesmith, "Diary of the Emigration of 1843," *OHQ* 7 (December 1906): 355.

and the scarcity of farmers in the 1850s and 1860s gave the stock raisers a clear field. Sheepmen were numerous in the late 1860s and the 1870s south of The Dalles, between the John Day and Deschutes rivers, and in the Umatilla country. Wheat farmers appeared in the river valleys in the 1860s, and they discovered in the next decade, to their surprise, that the high benchlands above the Columbia could also grow fine crops of wheat. Towns such as Linkville, later called Klamath Falls, Pendleton, Umatilla City, and Prineville sprang up to join The Dalles as market and supply centers for the surrounding country. The store, saloon, and blacksmith shop–livery stable, the early urban mainstays, soon were supplemented by the school, social club, and church as the family succeeded the single male as the basic social unit, although the clergy had the most difficult time in socializing the crude and lawless inhabitants of the first frontier. In The Dalles, for example, the Congregationalists leased a room in the courthouse over the jail: "during religious worship," a settler recalled, "vaporings of profanity and villainous songs mingled with the sacred exhortations from the minister's desk, and during the season of prayer the mocking 'amens' would be heard from the inmates below." [7] But persistence, courage, and wealth produced more than a semblance of order by the late 1870s in the towns east of the Cascades.

II

The coming of American colonists to the Oregon Country, whether as missionaries or farmers, created a demand for a government to represent their interests. Although the HBC had served, since the merger with the NWC, as the virtual sovereign in Oregon, few Americans would acknowledge its supremacy. Indeed, Americans themselves were not of a single mind in their approach to governmental needs or political forms, for by 1840 there were several interests among the small population of Oregon.

The HBC was the dominant force. Its able leader, Chief Fac-

7. Shaver, *Illustrated History of Central Oregon,* p. 150.

tor McLoughlin, was concerned to hold as much territory as possible for the company in the face of Anglophobe American pressures. The company's strength depended not only upon its employees, but upon its retired French-Canadian servants farming in the French Prairie region of the Willamette Valley. Its indispensable allies were the Catholic priests, Blanchet and Demers, whose transportation expenses to Oregon had been subsidized by the company. Employment with the company was more appealing, it was thought, when priests of the Canadians' religious faith were provided.

Among the Americans the Methodist missionaries were the most powerful interest. Led by Jason Lee, they had developed by 1840 extensive agricultural and milling holdings around Champoeg, Clatsop Plains, The Dalles, and Oregon City. American citizens also numbered retired mountain men, most prominent of whom were Joseph Meek and Robert Newell, who had gone into farming after the beaver had played out, and a small number of farmers whose strength would increase dramatically in the next five years.

The political and social issues that preoccupied these diverse groups were fundamental, some inherent in the nature of society, some indigenous to the frontier. The basic question was who would control the political life of the community. Other questions followed. How would the dominant group or groups use their authority to protect life and property? A fundamental issue in a formative commonwealth was the establishment of a community that would appeal to the "right kind" of future migrants and discourage those deemed undesirable. Issues of race relations were also important.

Until the late 1830s the various interests had co-existed amicably and had solved two major problems, both concerning the ex-mountain man, Ewing Young. Young in 1836 planned to erect a distillery, a project offensive to the Methodists on moral grounds and repugnant to the HBC as destructive of friendly relations with the Indians. After their protests, Young yielded gracefully to the wishes of Lee and McLoughlin and abandoned his venture. In the next year co-operation continued among the three men as Lee and McLoughlin helped finance Young in a drive of cattle from California to the Willamette Valley, the genesis of that industry in Oregon.

The origin of an American government in Oregon was contained in a petition Jason Lee carried with him to the East in 1838 on his journey to reinforce the mission strength. This Methodist request to Congress begged that the national government establish a territory in Oregon in order to protect property, and to ensure, in so doing, that solid, moral, civic-minded people would find Oregon appealing rather than "the Botany Bay refugee; . . . the renegade of civilization from the Rocky Mountains; . . . the profligate deserted seaman from Polynesia; and the unprincipled sharpers from Spanish America." [8] When the first overland party, that of Thomas Farnham, arrived in 1839, its members were told of an increase in the number of crimes, and Farnham advised residents to send another petition to Congress seeking territorial status. Neither of these requests bore fruit, and the missionaries, now involved in a number of "secular" interests, but without federal aid, had to move themselves to form a government to protect them against the company, its "heretical" employees, and the unstable adventurers. Their opportunity devolved from Ewing Young, who was as important in death as in life to the political history of Oregon. When he died in 1841 without known heirs, some method had to be devised to dispose of his property. The Methodists took the lead in pushing not for an informal mode of disposing of Young's effects, but for a formal political structure. From February to June 1841, a series of three meetings was held at Champoeg. Although the French Canadians participated in these meetings, they refused to sanction a written constitution and a formal government. The only institutional result was the appointment of a missionary, Ira Babcock, to exercise probate powers under the laws of New York, not under any innovative code.

During the next two years the missionaries and the HBC had to confront new threats to the status quo. Elijah White, who had

8. Quoted in Dorothy O. Johansen and Charles M. Gates, *Empire of the Columbia: A History of the Pacific Northwest,* 2d ed. (New York: Harper and Row, 1967), p. 181.

abandoned the Methodist mission two years earlier, returned to Oregon as a member of the overland party of 1842, bearing with him the honor of presidential appointment as United States Indian agent and the disgrace of having been deposed as leader of the wagon train for his advocacy of killing the dogs in the party. White's obvious political ambitions were a danger to the established interests. So, too, were the new emigrants who were unsympathetic to the missionaries for claiming large amounts of good arable land and for engrossing the excellent millsite at the falls of the Willamette River. The new Americans were also nationalistic, consciously asserting that one of their purposes in coming to Oregon was to drive out the British. To divert the opposition of the new settlers, the Methodists circulated another petition to Congress seeking protection against the machinations of the HBC. Out of these conflicting interests and personalities came the Oregon Provisional Government.

At a meeting at Champoeg held on March 6, 1843, attended by French Canadians and independent (nonmission) Americans, the settlers decided to coalesce into a government. A committee of organization was formed. This committee, now joined by the Methodists, met on March 17 and reported on May 2 to a meeting of about 100 adult males that the residents of the Willamette Valley "organize themselves into a civil community, and provide themselves with the protection, secured by the enforcement of law and order." [9] This report was carried by a slender majority and the dissenters, almost all French Canadians, retired, fearful that organization would lead to incorporation into an American territory.

The most striking thing about the structure of the provisional government is its unoriginality. The preamble stating the need for government was another illustration of the long reach of John Locke, the seventeenth-century English philosopher, whose thought underlay the ideology of the American Revolution, the formation of the Constitution, and the creation of the Bill of Rights. At the May 2 meeting a legislative committee

9. Quoted in John A. Hussey, *Champoeg: Place of Transition, A Disputed History* (Portland: Oregon Historical Society, 1967), p. 152.

composed of nine members was elected. Later in the month and in June the committee met under the chairmanship of Robert Moore, who had been a member of the legislature of Missouri. Another member of the committee possessed a copy of the laws of the Iowa Territory, which also contained the Declaration of Independence, the Constitution, the Northwest Ordinance, and the organic laws of Iowa. Drawing from this experience and tradition the committee report creating the organic law was a blend of Lockean compact theory, a constitution, and statutory law. The governmental form partook of the usual separation of powers, although the executive branch was a committee, rather than a single governor. The most important law gave each settler a land claim one mile square and the Methodist mission a townsite six miles square. But there was no provision for taxation, no process for amendment of the organic law, and no bill of rights. On July 5, a few weeks after the large overland migration was setting out across the plains, the organic law was adopted at a mass meeting sprinkled with a few French Canadians but attended by no representatives of the HBC.

The immigrants of 1843, upon arrival, gave Oregon not only more than 800 new souls, but also a political leader, Peter Burnett of Missouri, who soon became the strongest figure in the legislature. The influence of the newcomers was felt in the legislative elections of 1844 when they chose Burnett and others of their group. This new legislature enacted a tax and removed the Methodist mission's right to hold its townsite. In the following year the organic law was again altered by the legislature to include a bill of rights and to establish the office of governor. Of equal importance, the interests of the HBC were taken into account by the Americans at this time.

For McLoughlin now realized that the company needed to cooperate with the government because the increased population, inflamed with an anti-British spirit of Manifest Destiny, threatened not only the company's property, but also the moral stability represented by the Methodists. Under the leadership of Jesse Applegate and McLoughlin, the Americans and the company agreed that it was desirable to work together to protect land claims; that the company would pay taxes on all goods brought to Oregon for resale; and that the HBC would have control of the appointments for judge and sheriff in the county organized north of the Columbia River. George Abernethy, formerly business manager of the mission, was elected first governor.

The adjustments of 1845 established a governmental framework that survived until 1848. The record and popularity of the provisional government, in the years both before and after its reorganization, were mixed. Historian Walter Woodward has accurately assessed its statutory achievements: "the colonists were conservative in the amount and kind of legislation enacted." [10] Insofar as any extralegal government could do so, land was protected, although the newcomers of the mid-1840s resented the efforts of earlier arrivals to maintain their large claims. The first settlers, in turn, tried to stave off attempts to limit their holdings by forming claims clubs, as was done on earlier frontiers, to secure their property.

Concerning race relations, the settlers translated their border state attitudes into two laws of 1844 prohibiting slavery and forbidding the residence of free black persons. In the minds of white people the Indians were more threatening than the blacks, and frequent rumors of uprisings attained awful reality in the murder of Marcus and Narcissa Whitman at their mission station near Walla Walla in 1847. The attempt of the militia of the provisional government to free the hostages and capture the murderers (the Cayuse War) was a complete fiasco because of desertions and indecisiveness of leadership. The Americans, who had ceaselessly denigrated the HBC, now were placed in the humiliating position of asking the company to rescue the hostages, which Peter Skene Ogden accomplished without loss of life and without charging the Americans for the ransom the HBC paid to retrieve the survivors.

Far more gratifying to Oregonians was the settlement of the Oregon question. The decision as to how sovereignty would be divided between Great Britain and the United States in the Pacific Northwest was finally reached in the Anglo-American

---

10. Walter C. Woodward, *The Rise and Early History of Political Parties in Oregon, 1843–1868* (Portland: J. K. Gill Company, 1913), p. 27.

Treaty of 1846. This goal that had eluded diplomats since the era of the War of 1812 was attained through the resolution of competing interests and ideals in the Oregon Country, in the eastern parts of the United States, and in Britain.

In Oregon the years following the renewal of the joint occupation agreement in 1827 saw the slow deterioration of British power, a process evident at the time but one the British were powerless to arrest. As American interests developed, as Jason Lee and Marcus Whitman and Pierre-Jean de Smet succeeded Nathaniel Wyeth, and as the pioneers in turn replaced them, the accretion of American power in the Northwest took the shape of the formation of the provisional government and the establishment of American economic enterprise. By the mid-1840s the Americans numbered about 5,000 souls, with all but a handful of residents in the Willamette Valley, while the British subjects were scattered throughout Oregon both north and south of the Columbia River, with by far the bulk of them north of the river. Although two Americans did stake out a claim to the grounds of Fort Vancouver itself and the provisional government did organize a county north of the Columbia, men of good will of both nations resolved these issues. Dr. McLoughlin evicted the squatters, who had little support among their fellow Americans, and the provisional government, after negotiations, allowed the company in effect to run its northern county.

Thus, so far as an American presence in Oregon was concerned, it was confined to the region south of the Columbia. Its threat to the status quo lay in two directions: its potential to expand northward, and its influence of propaganda and filial affection upon fellow countrymen living in the United States, who, as voters, would have a far greater influence upon the national government than Oregonians could ever hope to exercise. The interest of the American public in Oregon, ordinary citizens, interest groups, and politicians alike, was sporadic and uncertain until the late 1830s or early 1840s. A great deal had been published about Oregon, most of it complimentary, but few who read Kelley or Townsend or William Slacum (a naval officer whom President Jackson had sent to Oregon in 1836) envisioned themselves, their friends, or relatives migrating to Oregon.

In the early 1840s, however, the issue of the Oregon boundary became both nationalized and sectionalized. Protestants, particularly northerners, read with interest the Methodist mission's petition to Congress asking that it organize a territory in Oregon. Urban northerners dreamed of a settlement that would ensure the ports of Puget Sound as terminals of railroads that would connect with ocean vessels exchanging the goods of America with the "limitless markets of Asia." Middle westerners, crushed by the depression of 1837, caught the "Oregon Fever" that promised a new start in a new country. Nationalists of all sections, although less fervidly anti-British than in the 1820s, would welcome the limitation of Britain's power in Oregon. Northern Democratic party strategists saw favorable settlement of the Oregon question as complementary to the acquisition of Texas for the benefit of its southern wing. All of these people could take comfort in the decree of God or fate or nature that it was America's "Manifest Destiny" to expand to the Pacific slope.

In Britain, Oregon was of far less concern. The sole economic interest in Oregon was the Hudson's Bay Company. Neither the company nor its predecessor, the North West Company, nor British explorers, had established strong territorial claims south of the Columbia. If the literate public thought at all of the HBC it was as a monopolistic anachronism. What did interest the public and the government was a fair settlement of the boundary that—for reason of national honor—would not sacrifice the interests of the Empire by yielding unnecessary concessions.

In 1842, as Britain and the United States proposed to clear away all the outstanding disputes between the two nations, the time seemed appropriate to come to an agreement over the Oregon boundary issue. To resolve these problems the British chose a distinguished diplomat, Lord Ashburton, who was personally friendly to the United States, a man who found Daniel Webster, the secretary of state, also amenable to resolving issues. Quickly the two men came to an agreement on the Maine boundary and on the slave trade, but the solution to the Oregon question evaded them. Lord Ashburton was hamstrung by instructions that permitted him to make as his ultimate offer the old line of the 49th parallel–Columbia River boundary. Although Webster countered with a proposal that Britain might have the line Ashburton proposed (with the Puget Sound harbors) if Mexico could be persuaded to sell the port of San Francisco to the United States, this proposal proved not to be feasible.

The failure to resolve the Oregon boundary question in 1842 was a serious missed opportunity, for it left the matter to be decided in a far more emotional atmosphere. In 1843 occurred a large migration over the Oregon Trail which added some 800 or 900 Americans to the Willamette Valley. In the same year these pioneers reorganized the provisional government established by their predecessors in what could be regarded as a first step toward permanent American occupation. And 1844 was a presidential election year, one of the most interesting of the antebellum years. The Whig party nominated Henry Clay for the third time. The Democrats selected James K. Polk as their candidate. The foreign policy issues in the campaign were significant and revolved about the issues of expansionism. One question was whether the United States should assent to the desire of the independent, slaveholding Republic of Texas to be admitted to the Union as a state in defiance of the wishes of Mexico, its former owner. This addition to the nation was favored by the South and by certain elements in the North. The second question was the settlement of the Oregon boundary. In his campaign Clay advocated a careful, noncontroversial policy toward both Texas and Oregon. He cautioned against exacerbating both issues for fear of creating a crisis, or even war, with Mexico or Britain or both.

The Democrats and their candidate seemingly had no such qualms. The party platform asserted that the United States claim to Oregon (presumably everything west of the Rockies from 42° to 54°40′) was "clear and unquestionable" and that the region should be "re-occupied" by Americans. Convention and candidate also called forthrightly for the annexation of Texas. A bargain was made between northern and southern wings of the party so that the nation would balance a free Oregon with a slave Texas. The tactics worked, and Polk won a sweeping victory in the electoral college, although he soon forgot that his margin among the popular votes was slender.

In spite of his strong position during the campaign, Polk in the summer of 1845 proposed to Richard Pakenham, the British minister, that the two nations settle the boundary on the basis of the 49th parallel. Pakenham inexplicably rejected this offer out of hand and Polk, angered by this rebuff, determined to force the issue. The president decided to ask Congress to advise him to terminate the joint occupation treaty with England by giving the required one-year notice. Then, he implied, either the British would surrender the entire region to 54°40' or the Americans would use force to displace them. Polk at this time, in December 1845, asserted in a public message that the Monroe Doctrine required the abandonment of all British territorial claims in the Oregon Country. Until the late spring of 1846 the Senate debated Polk's request to give notice to Britain and finally authorized him to do so, but in a conciliatory manner that invited the British to reopen the negotiations. Once this opportunity was presented the British speedily accepted it.

The forces and personalities that effected not only the defeat of Polk's confrontation tactics but also the British willingness to decide the boundary question had many similarities on both sides of the Atlantic. These peace forces included the reciprocal relationship between British textile manufacturers and southern cotton planters that would be disturbed in case of war. International bankers, merchants, and shipping interests in both countries also favored peace, as did their spokesmen in Parliament and Congress. The informed public in Britain and America realized that division at the 49th parallel was an equitable one based upon the respective explorations and settlements of the two countries. Cultural exchanges also made for peace, since people who read Scott and Dickens, Whittier and Longfellow, felt a strong and abiding kinship. In the end even the politics of the situation worked toward a peaceful settlement. British parties faced the grave problems, far more important than Oregon, of crop failures and unrest in Ireland, coupled with agitation to remove the agricultural tariff. Polk, a southerner, was satisfied with the incorporation of Texas and saw no need, with a war with Mexico looming over that issue, to risk splitting his party and the nation over a claim to a 54°40' settlement. By 1846 each side knew that they would pay a heavy price for neglecting other problems to remain at loggerheads over the Oregon boundary.

Once Oregonians received the news of the Anglo-American treaty of 1846 there no longer seemed a need for a provisional government, and few desired its continuance. But the manner of its replacement by an organized American territorial government was controversial and proved to be the last effort of the Methodists to influence Oregon politics. Early in 1847 Governor Abernethy sent J. Quinn Thornton to Congress as an official delegate of the provisional government. Thornton, a member of the mission party, was not authorized by the legislature as a delegate, but was sent personally by the governor to represent the Methodist interests in securing their land claim at Willamette Falls and in obtaining appointment of Methodists to the offices of the territorial government. To counter Abernethy's action, the legislature sent to Washington Joe Meek, the grandiloquent ex-mountain man and a distant relative of President Polk, as its advocate of territorial status. The legislators instructed Meek, who styled himself as "Envoy Extraordinary and Minister Plenipotentiary from the Republic of Oregon to the Court of the United States," to obtain a free homestead act and to secure capable officeholders regardless of their religious or political preferences. Meek's hand was strengthened by his bearing news of the Whitman Massacre, a persuasive argument for immediate granting of territorial status.

Oregon's case in Congress was enormously complicated by the emotional era in which it was presented. The late 1840s were the most divisive years in domestic politics since the struggle over the Missouri Compromise (1819–1821), as Congress debated the issue of the Wilmot Proviso: whether or not it could or should close to slavery the territory to be acquired from Mexico at the close of the war then raging. Although not a part of this domain, Oregon was subsumed within the debate, for its future would affect the sectional balance. If it were a free territory it would presumably become a free state and if a slave territory it would possibly become a slave state. Both the apostles of slavery expansion and slavery containment had a stake in scrutinizing the Oregon bill, but it was finally adopted and territorial status achieved on August 14, 1848.

As residents of a territory Oregonians became participants in an old, quasi-colonial form of government that dated to the Northwest Ordinance of 1787. The voters elected the territorial legislature and a nonvoting delegate to Congress; the president of the United States, with the consent of the Senate, appointed the territorial governor, secretary, judges, and council. (Abraham Lincoln, then a lame-duck Congressman, may have been offered the position of governor of Oregon Territory in 1849—he certainly could have had the secretary's post—but he refused to accept because of his wife's objections.) Not only was the territorial structure familiar, for many had lived under it elsewhere, but several political issues that confronted it were similar to those of the era of provisional government. Legislators, the territorial delegate, and appointed officials had to deal with land policy, military affairs, and race relations. The new issues that arose were concerned mainly with the quality and judgment of the officers appointed by the national government. In resolving the issues and in dealing with officeholders, Oregonians relied upon the theory of local self-government (often called popular sovereignty in the era), rooted in the American tradition, practiced by the settlers in the Middle West, and refined in the government of the wagon trains and in the provisional period. Popular sovereignty authorized white, adult, male citizens to determine their domestic policies—from education to slavery—with as little interference as possible from the national government.

The first issue resolved successfully in the territorial era was the security and availability of landed property. This agreement came in the Donation Land Act of 1850 as a reward to the pioneers for settling Oregon. Concerning race questions, the Organic Act itself had abolished slavery, and the territorial legislature continued the policy of its predecessor by voting, at its first session in 1849, to prohibit in the future the admission of free black persons to the territory. In Indian relations two concerns were paramount. One was to obtain payments from Congress for military expenditures authorized during the Cayuse, Rogue River, and Yakima wars. The other was to obtain support from the federal government to continue the wars against the Indians and to confine the Indians on reservations after the conclusion of military conflict. In both cases white Oregonians believed that the treasury or the military was too inclined to be suspicious of their requests and that Congress, also, was unsympathetic to their economic and military needs.

By the early 1850s Oregonians were showing their conservative tastes by importing another old political institution—the political party—to resolve their conflicts. The first party to be organized locally was an offshoot of the oldest in the United States. The founder of the Democratic party in Oregon was a twenty-eight-year-old Massachusetts journalist, Asahel Bush, whose newspaper, the *Oregon Statesman,* began calling for the formation of parties as early as 1851, buttressing its arguments, significantly, with quotations from eastern newspapers. In the following year the Democrats organized and became the most powerful party in Oregon until statehood. In short order the nucleus of the party, "the Salem Clique" to its enemies, had created a political machine comparable to those of eastern regions, like New York's Tammany Hall. The clique was interested almost exclusively in the pursuit of office and the distribution of plums such as the penitentiary and the insane asylum. Devoid of principle, the young men of the clique, including Bush, Matthew P. Deady, James W. Nesmith, and Orville C. Pratt, were able to maintain themselves in power by skillful exploitation of the realities of Oregon's political environment. Most migrants to Oregon were Democrats and the party's support of popular sovereignty—nationally and locally—kept them loyal in their new homes. Oregon Democrats admired enormously the charismatic Joseph Lane, a midwesterner like themselves, who had been a hero in the War with Mexico. President Polk had made Lane Oregon's first territorial governor, and, after he had been dismissed by a new administration in Washington, Oregonians elected him delegate (1851–1859) and then one of the state's first two senators (1859–1861). Lane's honesty, ability as a stump speaker, and skill in distributing patronage, plus his real accomplishments for the territory in Washington, redounded to the benefit of the entire party.

But the Democrats did not go unchallenged. In the northern counties of the state the Whig party was formed in 1853 to advance the interests of the commercial class and wealthier farmers of the territory. The local organization followed the national party in advocating strong federal intervention in the economy but was vague on local issues. Its principal spokesman, Thomas Dryer, editor of the *Portland Oregonian,* spent most of his time assailing the Democrats on the grounds of personality. In the next year emerged the Oregon subsidiary of another national party, the American or Know-Nothing, whose members feared the waves of immigrants to the United States, especially Catholics, and who built upon the superstructure of nativism and religious bigotry laid in the missionary era. Many Oregonians found appealing the Know-Nothing program opposed to short naturalization periods and alien voting and officeholding. Far more tolerant of human rights was the Free-Soil party, another national (or rather northern) party with an Oregonian following. The Free-Soilers, whose first northwestern branch was organized in Washington Territory in 1854, soon spread their platform into Oregon. The Free-Soilers were a radical, ideological party advocating free homestead legislation, abolition of slavery in the territories, and, in Oregon, prohibition of alcoholic beverages.

What galvanized Democrats, Whigs, Know-Nothings, and Free-Soilers into spirited conflict on the political stump and in their respective newspapers was the issue of slavery in the territories. In 1854 Congress passed the Kansas-Nebraska Act permitting the residents of the two territories named in it, and the rest of the West by implication, to decide by popular vote—the principle of popular sovereignty—whether or not to have slavery. Oregon Democrats supported the bill as an exercise in local self-government; Oregon Whigs opposed it, arguing that only Congress had the power to decide the issue of slavery in the territories. Most Oregonians favored the Democratic position, for it reflected their faith in local control of political matters and their hope that the principle could be expanded to include the election, instead of appointment, of territorial officials. By 1856, however, many citizens opposed to the Kansas-Nebraska law had coalesced to form a local organization of the new Republican party, a party determined to pass a congressional statute prohibiting the introduction of slavery in the territories regardless of the wishes of the inhabitants. In two years the party had acquired sufficient strength from ex-Whigs, former Free-Soilers, and dissident Democrats to become the second-largest party in the commonwealth.

As in the period of the provisional government, the most exciting political issue was the race question with its several ramifications. The legislature inadvertently repealed the black exclusion act in 1854 when it was mistakenly included on a list of laws to be repealed. Efforts to re-enact it failed, since few blacks were coming to Oregon, and most citizens feared the political turmoil that re-enactment would engender. The right to hold slaves was tested in court when Robin Holmes and his family, brought to Oregon as slaves of a pioneer named Nathaniel Ford, who settled near Salem, sued for their freedom in Judge George H. Williams's federal court. Williams, although not referring to the antislavery provision of the Organic Act, gave the slaves their freedom. Although there were not many black persons in Oregon, slave or free, their residence figured significantly in the crusade for statehood.

Ever since the first session of the territorial legislature in 1849, bills had been introduced to sample the sentiments of Oregonians concerning statehood. Three times a popular vote was taken on the question and three times it failed. Those who favored statehood stressed the power the people would obtain in the national capital with voting senators and representatives. Such authority would result in funding the war debts and in providing military protection against the Indians. A railroad to the Pacific would be only the most beneficial of federal gifts that statehood might provide. Democrats, being the majority party, favored statehood with the hope of capturing its host of elective offices. Whigs, for the same reason, opposed it. Opponents also argued that the expenses of state government, as opposed to federal funding of territorial expenses, would raise taxes prohibitively.

The catalyst for Oregonians' position on this issue, as on so many others throughout the decades, was a development on the eastern seaboard. Early in the spring of 1857 the Supreme Court of the United States handed down its opinion in the case of *Dred Scott* vs. *Sanford*. This momentous decision declared it illegal for either territorial legislature or Congress to prohibit slavery in any federal territory since only a sovereign state was constitutionally empowered to do so. To prevent even the possibility of slavery being legislated into Oregon, most citizens now swung over to support of statehood and voted by approximately a seven-to-one majority to call a constitutional convention.

Oregon's only constitution was drawn up at Salem in 1857 in a session lasting from August 17 to September 18. Sixty delegates were chosen; most were Democrats, and most were farmers or lawyers. Matthew Deady, a brilliant attorney and member of the Salem Clique, was elected presiding officer. In their deliberations the delegates over and over demonstrated the essential conservatism of the territory. This reliance upon the past emerged vividly at an early session of the convention when a historically minded delegate recommended that the convention employ a reporter, at the pay of $300, to make a complete transcript of the debates. In developing his point James K. Kelly reminded the delegates of the irreparable loss to posterity of a full record of the remarks of the members of the federal Constitutional Convention at Philadelphia. Immediately David Logan of Multnomah County was on his feet to challenge this expenditure: "The making of a constitution now," he declared,

> is not such an interesting proceeding as it may have been heretofore. What is said and done is not of that character, and the constitution that we may make, and every principle that we can engraft into it, has been discussed and decided time and again. It is no solution of new principles; it is no solution of new doctrines. We have a

number of models before us, and have only to select such as are applicable to the country at this time. Among the mass of principles which are already settled, we are only looking to the solution of those which are applicable to the present circumstances of Oregon.

Logan's view prevailed, and posterity's view of the constitution makers comes from the newspapers, not a verbatim official record.[11]

Nearly all the members of the convention were eager to incorporate the experiences of the past in the constitution. This made their task relatively easy, and as a result there was little time wasted on trivial matters, although a forty-minute time limitation on speeches was defeated ("Why, sir, I could not begin to have a good sweat on by that time"), and a motion to make the governor live at the seat of government was adopted ("Men coming from the extremes of the territory to see the governor wanted to know where to find him").[12] The models that Oregon's constitution makers followed most closely were those of the states of the Mississippi valley, the region which was a major source of migration to Oregon and was similar to it in its rural society. These constitutions were also written after the great depression of 1837 and reflected an agrarian people's distrust of the bankers and corporations who were blamed for that debacle.

With this heritage it is not surprising that the Oregon Constitution was hardly innovative in any respect. Nowhere was this conservatism more evident than in the provisions reflecting racial or ethnic prejudice. White foreigners were permitted to become citizens and the legislature was authorized "to restrain, and regulate" the immigration of nonwhites. Further, "No Negro, Chinaman, or Mulatto shall have the right of suffrage." Chinese migrating after the constitution was adopted were not permitted to work mining claims or to own mining claims or realty. Two other racial matters were considered too dangerous

11. Charles H. Carey, *The Oregon Constitution and Proceedings and Debates of the Constitutional Convention of 1857* (Salem, Ore.: State Printing Department, 1926), pp. 141–142.

12. Carey, *Oregon Constitution,* pp. 94, 227.

for the convention delegates to decide. These were the familiar issues of the residence of free blacks and the institution of slavery, issues that were left for the people, not the delegates, to decide. Accordingly, when the constitution was submitted to the voters in the fall of 1857, it was a document containing a traditional form of government. Legislative, executive, and judicial branches were established. Counties and municipalities were formed. The powers of these agencies were limited in a conscious attempt to cut costs, for there was little that an agricultural people desired by way of governmental activity and less by way of taxes. For as Deady said, "We have an agricultural community, and the domestic virtues incident to an agricultural people; and there is where you look for the true and solid wealth and happiness of a people." [13] The constitution accordingly prescribed rigid debt limitations upon the state and local governments. No government was permitted to become a stockholder or lend credit to a corporation. Indeed, only after a sharp and lengthy debate were limited liability corporations permitted at all. Salaries of governmental officers were meager.

In addition to the main body of the constitution the voters were asked to vote upon two separate provisions. They were asked if they wanted slavery in Oregon. Secondly, they were asked if they wished to permit the residence of free blacks. Between the adjournment of the convention and the vote upon the constitution, these racial issues were the ones most widely discussed. The debate was superficially extraneous, for there were few free blacks in Oregon and little possibility of slavery being introduced even if it were legitimatized. The subject received the attention that it did because of a pragmatic fundamental—the necessity that the constitution please not only Oregonians, but also Congress, which would vote upon admission.

Congress, and the nation, were torn by distressing news from another prospective state. Violent actions in Kansas Territory, deeds perpetrated by militants who wished to make the region slave or free, forced the slogan "Bleeding Kansas" upon the public consciousness. The doctrine of popular sovereignty

13. Carey, *Oregon Constitution,* p. 249.

proved unenforceable in Kansas as the citizens chose two governments, one proslavery, which formed a constitution at Lecompton, one antislavery, which drew up a constitution at Topeka, and President James Buchanan and his agents proved incompetent in resolving their controversy. Both nationally and in Oregon the Kansas conflicts and the failure of popular sovereignty to solve them split the Democratic party. In the Northwest the Salem Clique was unable to confine politics to the safe waters of local issues and local patronage. The party divided into a pro-Buchanan, pro-Lecompton wing led by Joseph Lane and a pro-Douglas, anti-Lecompton faction that included James Nesmith and Asahel Bush. This division gave the Republicans their opportunity to challenge seriously the majority party, and by the elections of 1859 they had become a formidable threat to the Democrats.

Earlier in the year, on Valentine's Day, the president signed a bill admitting Oregon to the Union. The long delay was caused, as Oregonians had feared, by northern and southern misgivings about the various racial provisions in the constitution, and by Republican fears of admitting a Democratic state. In the end a sufficient majority of Republican congressmen voted for statehood, against the wishes of their party leadership, to bring the state into the Union, and in time to cast its first presidential ballots in the momentous election of 1860. Voters in that campaign had a choice of four contenders. John C. Breckinridge of Kentucky represented the southern Democracy with a plank advocating a congressional slave code for the federal territories. Curiously, his running mate was Joseph Lane of Oregon, a man who had nothing to gain with his state's voters by his proslavery stand but one who adopted it out of conviction. Stephen A. Douglas's presidential race was based upon a defense of popular sovereignty. Abraham Lincoln's plank on slavery called for congressional prohibition of slavery in the territories. Both Douglas and Lincoln were pro-Union, adamantly opposing the Breckinridge-Lane stance that state sovereignty justified secession if the South's position on slavery in the territories did not prevail in Congress. A fourth nominee was John Bell of Tennes-

see, candidate of the Constitutional Union party, who equivo-
cated on the slavery issue.

Lincoln carried Oregon, although with a minority of the popular votes. His views on slavery, the Republican advocacy of
free homestead legislation and the construction of a railroad to
the Pacific, and the Democratic Congress's unwillingness to
discharge the debts of the Indian wars, secured his triumph in
the electoral college. If his votes and those of Douglas are combined, the pro-Union sentiment appears overwhelming. The
Lincoln-Douglas vote and the citizens' support of the Union
during the Civil War that followed is not surprising. The state
had always been nationalistic and conservative. The federal
government and its political institutions, and those of the states
as well, were satisfactory to the people of Oregon. To threaten
or to destroy the Union was a radical step that almost all
Oregonians found abhorrent to their self-interest and their principles.

III

Conservative as the settlers were in political affairs, they
were equally tenacious in matters of culture. In institutions and
ideals they were transplanters, not innovators, men and women
concerned with preserving a satisfying way of life in a new geographical and political environment. The basic organization of
life substantiates this generalization, for Oregonians belonged to
an extended farm family that was the fundamental social and
economic unit, although in the urban areas single males for a
time predominated. In contrast with the practice of Mormon po-
lygamy in Illinois and Utah or the almost exclusively male population of the California gold rush era, most Oregon settlers
were members of the monogamous families that were characteristic of rural America. Their economic occupations, both in
town and country, were familiar ones in the areas of largest
population, although new environmental challenges appeared in
the regions east of the Cascades.

The very buildings sheltering the people were built on eastern models. As the settlers put in their first crops, then found markets for them, they could in time afford more elaborate structures: a farm home developed in the pattern of log shanty, then log cabin, then frame house. Not that all houses looked alike, for Oregonians were both northern and southern in their heritage, and they recalled their native homes. What they did not draw upon for architectural inspiration was their new natural environment. Similarly, the pioneers' contempt for the Indian culture, although like their own in intimate dependence upon nature, precluded their learning from the earlier social environment for their housing. City residents, too, varying with their wealth and status, built their homes according to their memories of the dwellings of eastern people of similar position.

The most recent scholarship divides Oregon architecture in the formative period about the year 1860. Before this date the lumber houses built in Oregon were characterized by symmetry. The houses and the rooms within them were invariably rectangular. The chimneys and windows were in balance, and the roof was either flat or low-pitched. Houses built from these plans were constructed in one of three modes—hewn frame, balloon frame, or box construction, all of which had antecedents on the East Coast or in the Middle West. Exteriors of the most modish houses were classical revival or federal styles similarly transplanted from the East. The builders and owners, in making their architectural selections, were again choosing forms with which they were familiar from their own homes. In the Willamette Valley a traveller might encounter a house derived ultimately from the James River in Virginia or from Missouri or the French country of Illinois or even from the Dutch colony of New Netherland. After 1860 many of these modes continued to be employed, although there were new possibilities for the fashionably inclined as the Gothic revival, with its steep roofs, lancet windows, and multiple-volume floor plans became popular in Oregon.

Barns, like houses, were traditional. The norm was side opening barns, through which teams and wagons filled with wheat could be driven for unloading into lofts. This form was brought from sixteenth-century England to Jamestown and Plymouth and then transplanted the 3,000 miles to the Oregon Country. After 1860 barns became more technically complex in their design and construction but remained derivative. Mills, the only industrial enterprises of the era, warehouses, churches, and inns were also conservative. Even the radical communitarian settlement at Aurora, in its architecture, was a transplant from Missouri and Pennsylvania.

The Oregonians brought with them in vessel, wagon, or railroad car a respect, even love, for schools and churches. In these institutions, as in architecture, the hand of the eastern past shaped the Oregon present. The earliest primary and secondary schools, public or private, stressed the essentials of reading, writing, and arithmetic, in addition to the installation of moral values. The Catholic church had provided some religious instruction as early as 1844 among the French Canadians at French Prairie and later at Oregon City and Portland. In 1859 twelve sisters of the Holy Names who came around the Horn from Montreal to Portland established a school for six pupils, Saint Mary's Academy, still extant. The first Jewish school was begun by the Beth Israel Congregation in Portland in 1861 to provide instruction in both secular and religious subjects. Methodists had organized a school at Champoeg in 1834, originally for the purpose of educating the Indian converts, but it soon turned its attention to white children. In 1854 the Methodists founded Portland Academy and in 1861 Episcopalians established Spencer Hall Seminary in Milwaukie that, after a hiatus, was transplanted to Portland as Saint Helen's Hall in 1869. Eastern church members provided the bulk of the endowment for this institution, 300 dollars, for example, being given by students and faculty of Saint Mary's Hall of Burlington, New Jersey.

Public schools were more difficult to root than were private institutions. A territorial law of 1848 included two sections of public land in each township to be sold for schools, and in 1851 the first public school was begun in Oregon when the voters of Portland combined with those of Multnomah County to purchase a former private school building where a twenty-two-year-old Nova Scotian, John Outhouse, taught his first class of twenty pupils. The state's first public high school opened—in Portland—in 1869, although it was many years before this type of institution was regarded with general favor throughout the state.

Higher education also did not encompass many students. Several small academies, such as the Oregon Institute, which became Willamette University at Salem, grew up but their influence was small. Organized on eastern lines, they stressed a classical curriculum that was designed to prepare students for the professions. Indeed, in no respect was the educational system a product of the Oregon environment in terms of its structure or objectives. Teachers, administrators, and supporters of schools and colleges were educated in the East and convinced of the virtues of the eastern system. In their commitment to education Oregonians were not ungenerous, given the lack of material resources of an underdeveloped region. They wanted a literate citizenry for pragmatic reasons: to provide social cohesion, vocational opportunity, and an informed electorate, as Unitarian minister Thomas Lamb Eliot, grand old man of Portland "good causes," put it in an address in 1875 celebrating and justifying the public schools. They provided, he affirmed, "the supply of stable citizenship and conservative power—we must as a nation, pour in life blood from this system as a heart, if we would balance titanic material forces, and remain self-governed, without caste or chasm, free from the tyranny of man or mob." [14]

In the area of religion the Oregon frontier was similarly conservative. The transplanted institutions of the mission period were followed by the advent of other denominations until all of the major religious forms were represented. Yet not one single innovation emerged, either in polity or theology, unlike the Mormonism of antebellum western New York, or the Christian Science of late nineteenth-century urban America, or the proliferation of cults in twentieth-century California. Nor was there in Oregon a particularly large interest in traditional religion, and church membership, even among Methodists in the years before

---

14. Alfred Powers and Howard M. Corning, "History of Education in Portland," mimeographed (n. p., n. p., 1937), p. 78.

the Civil War, remained very low. A stable, self-satisfied, sufficiently prosperous people apparently felt little need for the support of religious institutions. This indifference, planted in the first decades, remains a distinguishing feature of the state's cultural life.

Beyond the basic institutions of home, family, school, and church, the people of early Oregon made some attempts at the "higher culture" of literature and the arts. What most interests the student of Oregon's history is the least conscious but refreshing writings, those of the diaries from the wagon trains, the correspondence of the missionaries, and the editorials of the frontier press. Although none of this material is great literature, taken as a whole it confirms the solidity of character, if somewhat unimaginative nature, of the early Oregonians and their practical aspirations, a characterization given further minor support by the total lack of folk songs contrived in Oregon wagon trains in contrast to the round dozen invented by those en route to the California mining camps. There are, of course, some notable exceptions to the stolid generalization: the humor of James Nesmith and the vivid sketches of Jesse Applegate from the Oregon Trail; the soul-searching of Narcissa Whitman; and the vindictive editorials of Asahel Bush and Thomas Dryer.

When one turns to fiction, drama, or poetry there is little that, by the standards of the day, was worthy of recognition beyond the borders of the region. A great deal of poetry was written for the local press, and a few novels and at least one play were published. In all these literary efforts the forms were traditional and the themes conventional. Most of the content dealt with the glories of Oregon nature, with romantic sentiments, or with personalities of the region. The two most interesting works, produced by two colorful although vastly different people, reflected these emphases.

Margaret Jewett Bailey was a member of the second Methodist reinforcement party of 1837. A contentious and pious young woman, she resented the overbearing manner of the Reverend David Leslie, who commanded this party, and her problems were magnified in Oregon when Leslie and Jason Lee refused to assign her the teaching position she had been promised before leaving the East. Angered by her continuing assignment to menial labor, by ongoing personality clashes with others at the mission station, and by the condemnation of her love affair with William H. Willson, a carpenter at the mission, Margaret Bailey published (under the pseudonym of Ruth Rover) a sensational exposé in 1854 entitled *The Grains, or Passages in the Life of Ruth Rover, with Occasional Pictures of Oregon, Natural and Moral.* In this work, whose characters had most transparent names when referred to derogatorily (Leslie was Leland; Shepard was S———), she laid bare the internal conflicts of the mission family, emphasizing how the secular activities of the missionaries hindered their ostensible purpose of laboring with the Indians. In the small circle of frontier Oregon the book became a piece not only for conversation, but also for angry debate, and all but two copies were destroyed by those who considered it immoral.

A similar work, at least in its notoriety, was *Treason, Stratagems and Spoils,* a play published in 1852 by William Adams in the pages of the *Oregonian* under the pseudonym of Breakspear. Adams, who had earlier sharpened his skills in the genre as a satirist in Kentucky, later became a leading antislavery editor. His play was a clever Whig attack upon the Salem Clique or ''Durhamites'' (so called because their early leader, Orville C. Pratt, had once sold a scrub bull as a pure-blood Durham), a play in which the clique leaders were mercilessly lampooned as self-seeking and incompetent spoilsmen. Tormented by the sharpness of the attack, the clique attempted to acquire, and destroy, all extant copies, but a few survived.

The touchstone of this cultural conservatism of Oregon was the relationship of the pioneers with the Indian peoples. The maritime traders, the explorers and scientists, and the early beaver trappers all had affected the Indian culture—as conservative as that of the Caucasian—in numerous ways, but their impact was relatively slight in comparison to the burdens placed upon the original residents by the white farmers and businessmen. It is surprising, indeed, that so many of the Indian ways of life survived at all. The pressures of white persons and institutions on the Indians took the form of disease, territorial encroachments, wars, and segregation on reservations. Certainly more lives were lost from the introduction of venereal disease, smallpox, measles, and influenza than from any of the declared or undeclared military conflicts of the era. For example, the members of the Kalapuya linguistic group who lived in the Willamette Valley declined in the century after 1780 from 3,000 to 351 persons, most of the loss the toll of malaria and influenza, while some coastal groups declined in population from 50 to 70 percent between 1850 and 1900.

White people brought these diseases in their role of occupants, not as sojourners. Although the missionaries certainly did not intend to destroy the Indians, they were the first to publicize widely the agricultural possibilities of the Willamette Valley. The advent of the pioneers led to a struggle for land between the old residents and the new, as farm making destroyed hunting and gathering terrain and as Indians in turn encroached on cropland. This type of conflict was evident as early as the 1840s in the Willamette region and then in the 1850s as the miners invaded Indian country all along the Rogue and southern coastal regions. Other miners in the 1860s were en route to the Idaho and Montana fields through the Klamath Lake area and in the Umatilla River region. Late in the decade and into the next, all other land desired by the white man fell from Indian control, as wheat farmers, cattlemen, and sheep growers occupied southeastern and central Oregon. These economic conflicts over incompatible land use patterns were irreconcilable and frequently led to war.

In the area of the original Oregon Country there were eight conflicts labelled wars between the Cayuse War of 1847 and the Bannock War of 1878. Not all were fought within the boundaries of the state of Oregon, but the Cayuse War, the Rogue River War, and the Yakima War were especially influential in the state's development and, indeed, had a national impact. The Cayuse War, carried on against the tribe whose members had killed the Whitmans, was instrumental in accelerating the demand of the pioneers for a territorial structure to replace the military impotence of the provisional government. In the Rogue River War, waged between 1851 and 1856, the territorial militia and United States forces defeated the Indians of southwestern Oregon. The Yakima War (1855–1858), against the Yakimas, Klickitats, Spokanes, and their allies, was fought on both sides of the Columbia but mainly in central Washington Territory, and together with the Rogue War forced a significant change in federal Indian policy.

Before the 1850s the national government had displaced the eastern Indians to the "Indian Country," a vast region of shifting boundaries west of the Mississippi River, where they were supposed to reside in perpetuity in conditions of relative freedom. The Oregon experience forced changes in the old policy and soon forged a new institution, the "small" Indian reservation. War and treaty-making produced the reservation. In 1855 at the Umatilla Reservation were gathered the Umatillas, Walla Wallas, and Cayuses. In the same year the Warm Springs Reservation was created for the Wascos, some of the Walla Wallas, and (after 1868) Paiutes. The next two years saw the establishment of the Grand Ronde and Siletz reservations on the coast for tribes of the Willamette Valley and the south, and in 1864 Congress commenced the Klamath Reservation which ultimately encompassed members of the Klamath, Modoc, and Paiute tribes.

The old policy of segregating the defeated Indians in areas separate from the victorious whites appeared as early as the regime of Joseph Lane, the first territorial governor, who also acted as Indian superintendent. The purpose was not only to prevent territorial conflict but also to avoid corrupting the Indians through contact with the dregs of white society. Lane argued for the separation of the races; Samuel Thurston, first territorial delegate, wished to move the western Indians east of the Cascades. Officials in Washington were willing to follow this time-honored policy, but Lane's successor as Indian agent, Anson Dart, realized that the Indians accustomed to the humid climate would be destroyed when they were moved to the semi-arid country to the east. Convinced that his position was sound, Dart in 1851 made treaties with the valley and coastal Indians. The treaties granted reservations in the west where there were no white residents, reservations which "consist for the most part of ground unfitted for cultivation, but suited to the peculiar habits of the Indians.'' [15] On these lands, presumably, the Indians were to carry on their historic fishing-hunting-gathering operations.

The theory of co-existence underlying these treaties was chimerical. Indeed the members of the United States Senate recognized this fact, for many settlers had complained to them; all of Dart's treaties were rejected; and he himself resigned in 1852. His successor was Joel Palmer, a pioneer of 1845, ''a plain, unpretensious [*sic*], practical and honest man, strong in the conviction that all people show their best traits when well treated.'' [16] Palmer further developed Dart's innovation of the small, specifically bounded reservation, but he abandoned both his predecessor's idea of reservations proximate to white settlement and the pioneers' wish for locating them east of the Cascades. Palmer drew treaties with the southern and western Oregon tribes that, coupled with executive orders of President Buchanan, established the Siletz Reservation and the Grand Ronde Reservation along the central section of the Oregon coast, an area he believed unsuitable for the white economy. By 1857 the Senate had approved these arrangements which, coupled with the treaties he and Isaac Stevens, governor of Washington, concluded with the Indians of the middle Columbia, cleared away the Indian ''title,'' at least as the whites understood this concept, to the land.

The reservation had two purposes. The first was to concentrate the Indians in areas undesirable to whites where any hostile actions could be easily detected. The second was to convert the Indian into a white farmer. To achieve the latter purpose the agents of the federal government included in the treaties provisions promising educational facilities and instruction in vocational arts and in agriculture. Sometimes directly, more often indirectly, the government encouraged the clergy to carry out their work among the Indian people. As in the Protestant missionary

15. Stanley Sheldon Spaid, ''Joel Palmer and Indian Affairs in Oregon'' (Ph.D. diss., University of Oregon, 1950), p. 79. Used with permission.

16. Spaid, ''Joel Palmer,'' p. 89. Used with permission.

era, the Caucasian culture was to displace that of the Indians, root and branch.

The discouragement and hatred of reservation life on the part of the Indians is not difficult to imagine. They were forced to farm, but the land was unsuitable for agriculture. Old tribal enemies were brought together on a single reservation. The entire culture was condemned as inferior or immoral. Family patterns were shattered, and the respect earned by the wisdom of the aged in solving the problems of the traditional culture disappeared with the advent of the challenges of the white civilization. The burden of assimilation fell principally upon the shoulders of the Indian agent and his staff and upon the younger Indian leaders. Their job, executed through cajolery, force, persuasion, example, or bribery, was enormous because the resistance of the Indian people was widespread.

What gave the advocates of assimilation hope, at least sporadically, was that the Indian resistance was selective. As anthropologist Theodore Stern has pointed out concerning the Klamath, there were certain aspects of the new culture that the Indians readily accepted. To work hard, to gain material possessions, to be practical were virtues of both worlds, and Indians needed no persuasion to assure agreement in these matters. Religion, clothing, even the names of individuals were matters of individual choice in the precontact era, and there was no objection from the tribe if an Indian assumed Christianity, the garb of white people, or a Caucasian name. What the Indian would accept only under duress was the economic system and the educational practices imposed by the national government.[17]

The precontact Indian throughout the Pacific Northwest was not a farmer. The practice of agriculture needed the tutelage of white teachers and the provision of seed, implements, and mills. None of these was provided systematically in either quantity or quality. During the transitional period, while awaiting the success of Indians in the new economy, the national government

17. Theodore Stern, *The Klamath Tribe: A People and Their Reservation* (Seattle: University of Washington Press, 1965), pp. 44–121. I have relied on this excellent work extensively throughout the book for my treatment of the Klamath reservation peoples.

had to supply food and clothing for the Indians. These goods were both inferior and in short supply. Other distractions appeared from time to time. On the Warm Springs Reservation the problems of early agriculture included raids by the northern Paiute Indians upon the reservation stock; the traditional attraction of the salmon fisheries, which took the men from the fields in the critical seasons of spring and fall; the absence of a mill, which made it impossible to provide poles for fencing; and the shortage of implements and harnesses, furnished by the agent, which created inconvenient delays at seedtime and harvest. On the Siletz Reservation troubles came with white encroachment for oystering, mining, and for the construction of a wagon road from Corvallis to Yaquina Bay. In time Congress responded to these pressures and whittled the reservation down in 1865 and 1875 to reduce further its potential as a means for the Indians to enter the mainstream of American economic life. The greatest frustration came to those Indians who had somehow survived the poor shelter, inadequate food, incompetent instruction, and insufficient equipment to become trained for the new economy. They found that not only did racial prejudice keep them out of the white world, but that the Indian economy lacked the base to provide employment for them in their new pursuits.

Another irony is that the Indian, ostensibly being prepared for Caucasian civilization, was required to live on reservations segregated from it. To assimilate off the reservation, as Dick Johnson and his family discovered, was undesirable. Near Yoncalla, Johnson and his family carved out a farm and made a success of it. They were Christians. They prized education. Indeed their desire for assimilation earned them the admiration of many of their white neighbors, including the respected pioneer, Jesse Applegate. Yet on November 28, 1858, Dick Johnson and his stepfather were murdered by a party of eight claim jumpers who coveted their farm. Although Applegate led a struggle to bring the murderers to justice and to guarantee the Johnson heirs their land, he and his friends failed. Law that prohibited the testimony of Indians in court, the lukewarmness of Indian Superintendent James Nesmith, and technicalities in the Umpqua treaty thwarted justice and equity.

Failure and frustration was also the harvest of Indian education. Designed to be both academic and vocational, to be offered in both day and boarding schools, the educational system was shaped to be comprehensive. Its main purpose was to make the Indian self-supporting, but the list of obstacles to the attainment of this goal was almost limitless. At the root, however, was racial prejudice on the part of the American public that precluded adequate congressional appropriations for suitable buildings and capable teachers. Without a more substantial recognition of the humanity of the Indians, their educational fate was to shiver in filthy and dilapidated buildings under the instruction of a succession of teachers, ill-equipped or incompetent, who attempted to prepare them for a world that would not accept them. By the 1880s Oregon Indians, for the white majority, were literally out of sight and out of mind, consigned to fringe regions, unworthy in their impotence even of hatred. They had become a sacrifice to the cultural conservatism of white Americans who transplanted racism in the wagon trains to the new land.

4

Intrusion of the Outside
World (1870–1920)

I

AFTER the close of the Civil War Oregon continued to furnish opportunities for new lives to thousands of migrants. From 1860 until 1920 the state's population grew at a far higher rate than did that of the nation, outstripping the federal rate of increase by an average of 37 percent every decade. Most of the newcomers came, as did those of the pioneer period, to better themselves economically, and although the great majority of the new Oregonians continued to be white, Anglo-Saxon Protestants, the state's population did become slightly more heterogeneous than in the antebellum era.

The American citizens who came to Oregon were easy for the pioneer generation to accept because both were people of a midwestern, agricultural background who aspired to settle in the Willamette Valley. Unlike the pioneers, however, many newcomers found the great valley settled, with the good land either already taken or priced prohibitively. Their solution was to cross the Cascades and to settle up farms and ranches in eastern and central Oregon or to reconcile themselves to an urban life along the Willamette or its tributaries. Indeed, urbanization in these years for the first time became an important feature of

Oregon life, and the city of Portland developed into the only metropolitan area in the state. Growth of population, the bridging of the Willamette, and the development of the electric streetcar all enabled the city to expand geographically and in many cases to annex adjacent small towns. The new markets of recent migrants permitted industrial expansion as the economy became more sophisticated, and an urban residence and job were the lot of most Americans who came to Oregon in these years. In spite of where they lived these American-born arrivals fit easily into the cohesive pattern of the state's culture and helped to forestall serious urban-rural divisions.

The majority of foreigners who came to Oregon after 1870 were equally adaptable and equally welcome. Germans were the most numerous throughout the whole period with Canadians, Irish, Swedes, English, and Scots following in a varying order, depending upon the particular census year. By and large these peoples, too, found a benign social environment since almost all of them were of the same color and Protestant religious preference as most older Oregonians. They came at a time of expanding opportunity and accordingly did not seem to threaten the standard of living of American citizens. They possessed the rudiments of education and probably had some experience, at least at the local level, with self-government. More importantly, their ideals were those of the native-born Americans. They came to Oregon to get ahead, because their ancestral lands in the old countries were too small to support a growing population, or because they dreaded the confined life of factory laborers in an industrializing European economy. They believed in hard work, in making a better life for their children, in the public school, in political democracy, and in a free press. Their contributions could be recognized and appreciated because, unlike the bulk of American immigrants of the day who were from central or eastern Europe, or from Asia, they were not handicapped by the ''wrong'' religion or color, or by inadequate educational and political preparation for life in the United States. Since the new migrants were so favorably equipped for life in America it is not surprising to find two German-born citizens elected mayor of Portland in 1869–1873, or Irish lodges given honored positions in the city's parade celebrating the completion of the Northern Pacific Railroad in 1883, or English-born Thomas H. Tongue chosen for the national House of Representatives from 1897 to 1903. The very lack of unfavorable notice of the northern European peoples in the public and private records of the state testifies to the overall smoothness with which they were assimilated into Oregon's culture. Furthermore, in the city of Portland, in contrast to most American metropolises, there were few foreign ethnic geographical enclaves, and the national organizations, such as the Sons of Norway, remained potent forces for a generation at most.

Oregon shared also, although to a very small degree, in the great migration of southern and central European peoples to the United States in the post-Civil War era. Those of northern European stock, aliens and citizens alike, found these newcomers to be useful in accepting positions of menial labor, but suspected them for their Catholicism and for their "exotic" ways. An expanding economy and their very fewness spared them, however, from the grosser forms of ethnic prejudice.

The building of the railroads in the Northwest brought Italians to the Pacific Northwest after 1880. Most came from southern Italy and from Sicily, driven from their farms by crop failures, soil erosion, and land monopoly. Their intention was to return home with a nest egg and hence most Italian migrants were single males ("birds of passage") willing to accept jobs with lower pay and more physical demands than would citizens. Italians worked in railroad building, in the mills and lumber camps, and in street and sewer construction. But in time at least half of the migrants decided to settle in Oregon, sent for their families, and began the arduous process of breaking away from manual labor to enter other occupations. Those who could afford the capital outlay took up the congenial occupation of truck farming around Portland, and some, or their children, secured a foothold in other businesses or professions.

By 1920 the Italian determination to stay and succeed was evident in the community's institutional structure. In the usual immigrant pattern the new residents founded benevolent societies, the first being the Columbia Lodge (1889), to cushion them against unemployment, sickness, and burial expenses, and churches to provide both divine and worldly consolation. The pioneer Italian Roman Catholic Church, Saint Michael's, was organized in Portland in 1901. In time political participation opened and the formation of the Italian-American Republican Club in 1916 signalled successful adjustment to this aspect of the American democratic process.

The Greek experience in Oregon, although beginning about twenty years later, resembled that of the Italians in many respects. The early newcomers, forced from their homeland by poor economic conditions, aspired to acquire sufficient savings to return to Greece. In America, they, like others from eastern and southern Europe, took construction work in the dry seasons and returned to Portland for the winter. In time many Greeks, too, decided their best interest lay in remaining in America and began the gruelling, often desperate, search for self-employment as bootblacks or retailers of candy, fruit, and cigars. Money laboriously saved was willingly spent in founding the Holy Trinity Greek Orthodox Church in 1907 and the Hellenic Social Club in 1912 as tokens of the intention to remain in the new world.

A small number of Russian and south Slavs also became Oregonians before the First World War destroyed the Czarist and Hapsburg empires. Most were "birds of passage" who worked as laborers or restaurateurs with the intention of returning home. Among the Russians of the Czarist migration not only Slavs were represented, but also Volga Germans and Jews. For Christians, the Holy Trinity Orthodox Chapel, built in East Portland in 1894, was their place of worship, and secular institutions included a Russian Club and a lodge of the Serbian National Federation.

In the 1880s eastern Europe also gave Oregon a renewed source of ancient culture. Jews from Germany had been a significant part of Oregon life since the days of the Rogue River gold rush in the 1850s when there were Jewish communities in Jacksonville and Glendale, and Aaron Rose, a tavern keeper, gave his name to Roseburg in 1851. In 1858 Oregon's first Jewish congregation was founded, Beth Israel in Portland, and German Jewish citizens became prominent in the business, professional, and political life of Portland. In that city Bernard Goldsmith (1869–1871) and Philip Wasserman (1871–1873) served successively as mayor. Jews of these years were akin to other German migrants in their educational and political background and in aspirations to participate fully in American life. In consequence they rarely fell afoul of anti-Semitism or other cultural discrimination.

The lot of the Jews coming after 1880 was rather different. Most were eastern Europeans from the Romanov or Hapsburg empires, poor people, of a strange and somewhat troubling background to Americans. Unlike the first Italians, Greeks, or Slavs, they were not "birds of passage." Unlike them, they did not go into construction work or the mills. Unlike the earlier German Jews, they were Orthodox rather than Reformist in their religious profession. The east European Jews made their way economically in Portland as tailors, as pawnbrokers, and in all varieties of retail and wholesale merchandise. They co-operated with German Jews in the founding of benevolent organizations like the local chapter of the National Council of Jewish Women, which established a social service organization, Neighborhood House, in 1904. They established several orthodox congregations such as Sharrie Torah and Kesser Israel.

By the early 1920s the diversification of Oregon through migration from southern and eastern Europe was over as disenchantment with the world, fear of a constricting economy, and disillusion with the world war led to the congressional imposition of minute quotas for migrants from these quarters of the world. Groups that had enriched the life of the state, particularly the city of Portland, with a heterogeneous cultural strain were now condemned as unworthy, not by Portlanders or Oregonians, but by the national legislature.

But older Oregonians themselves were not invariably pleased with representatives of other cultures. As before the Civil War, the burden of proof of their social acceptability was placed on the shoulders of nonwhite peoples. Many were never permitted equality of legal status with whites, contempt for their cultures was pervasive, and fear of physical violence was often their companion.

The newest of the nonwhite peoples to arrive in Oregon were the Japanese, whose numbers rose from two in 1880 to 2,501 in 1900 and to 4,151 in 1920. Although federal law throughout the years prohibited them from becoming American citizens, Japanese nationals migrated to Oregon before 1900 with the aspiration of making money so they could eventually return to the old country with enough funds to support their families in some comfort. The most influential of such early Japanese was Sinzaburo Ban, who became a contractor, lumber dealer, and shingle manufacturer in Oregon with branch offices in Tokyo, Wyoming, and Colorado. In the 1890s Ban began to supply Japanese labor on contract to the Oregon Short Line Railroad for construction work. Along the railway lines, in the logging camps and lumber mills of the Hood River region, and in Portland there developed a male-oriented, transitory Japanese community located in inexpensive restaurants, boardinghouses, and brothels.

Around the turn of the century the Oregon Japanese community took a new direction. Family groups replaced the male culture. Agriculture became the principal economic occupation as Japanese immigrants began farming in Hood River, Gresham, Salem, and, after 1910, in eastern Oregon around the small towns of John Day and Prineville. The life of these pioneers was arduous as they attempted to make the most of their labor by acquiring raw land on steep slopes, noncommercial woodlands, or poorly drained terrain; often the dream of a farm seemed chimerical as self-sacrifice brought them to the edge of hunger: "In those days a stray jackrabbit meant a feast and a cow killed by a passing train was a God-sent banquet." [1] But tenacity provided success, not only in material terms but in the development of a well-rooted and comprehensive set of cultural institutions like the Buddhist congregation founded in Portland

1. Quoted in Barbara Yasui, "The Nikkei in Oregon, 1834–1940," *Oregon Historical Quarterly* 74 (September 1975): 232.

in 1903 by a young priest, Shozui Wakabayashi. Japanese also began entering into American life and the children attended schools, learned the English language, and adopted American customs.

Although the Japanese exemplified the American ethic of hard work, material success, and desire for education, and were law-abiding and docile people, their reception among white Oregonians was not enthusiastic. In the twentieth century anti-Japanese feelings, beginning in California, spread northward along the Pacific Coast, although a minority, particularly among businessmen, hailed the industriousness of the Japanese. When Joseph Gaston, the railroad entrepreneur, published a history of Portland in 1911 he labelled a Japanese leader as a "typical representative of the progressive little nation which in the past half century has advanced to a greater degree than any other country in the same period," and W. E. Wheelwright, president of the Pacific Export Company, became in Oregon the principal white defender of the Japanese people.[2]

On the other hand, white small farmers and townspeople near Japanese communities either feared or resented the Asian immigrants. Many Caucasian citizens of Gresham and Hood River believed that Japanese were becoming "land monopolists," although they held only one-twentieth of 1 percent of the total acreage of the state in 1920. They were scorned as shiftless or slovenly, for the first generation of farmers spent the bulk of their capital upon land rather than upon sprucing their dwellings; they were regarded (in the face of contrary evidence) as inordinately prolific; and their community-mindedness was condemned as clannish or even politically sinister. Local prejudice developed concurrently with that of the nation, and when the United States and Japan agreed to limit Japanese emigration to the United States in 1907, coupled with the nineteenth-century ban against naturalizing Japanese aliens, an official seal seemed to stamp the Japanese as not only different but also culturally inferior to Caucasian Americans. In Oregon the development of

2. Joseph Gaston, *Portland, Oregon: Its History and Builders,* 3 vols. (Chicago: S. J. Clarke Publishing Co., 1911), 2:454.

anti-Japanese prejudice produced a bill in 1917, drawn by Sen. George R. Wilbur, an attorney, to prohibit land ownership by aliens ineligible for citizenship. Although defeated at this legislative session, it emerged again in the chauvinistic atmosphere after the First World War.

The social and economic position of another Asian group in Oregon, the Chinese, was the reverse of that of the Japanese: their conditions and respect, although not their legal status, improved with the passing years, while that of the Japanese simultaneously declined. Chinese had been among Oregon's earliest residents, having mined in the Rogue River Valley in the 1850s. In the following two decades the Chinese took up residence both around Portland and in eastern Oregon. They found their living in mining, railroad construction, and in the service trades, such as cooking or laundering, east of the Cascades. In the Portland area construction and services made up the bulk of the employment opportunities.

The Chinese migrants in the last decade of the nineteenth century resembled the early Japanese in that most of them were single men seeking economic opportunities in America with the intention of ultimately returning home. "I came to America," wrote an emigrant in 1897, "to labor, to suffer, floating from one place to another, persecuted by the whites, for more than twenty years. What is my goal for enduring this kind of pain and hardship? Nothing but trying to earn some money to relieve the poverty of my home. Do you know that both the old and the young at my home are awaiting me to deliver them out of starvation and cold?" [3]

In the late 1890s in China a spirit of change swept the country in the wake of the national defeat in the Sino-Japanese War. Many people left their homes after this debacle, including those who planned to make permanent residences abroad. Oregon was the beneficiary of many of these migrants, and by 1900 Portland

3. Chia-lin Chen, trans. and comp., "The Kam Wah Chung Company Papers, John Day, Oregon," typescript (Portland: Oregon Historical Society, 1974), p. 128. Used with permission from the Manuscript Collections of the Oregon Historical Society.

had a very large Chinese population, the second largest of any city in the United States.

The Chinese faced consistent prejudice until the turn of the century. Oregonians imported this prejudice from California, along with the Chinese, in the 1850s. After the Civil War Pacific Coast racists, led by demagogues from the Golden State, ensured that Chinese migrants were denied American citizenship, and in 1880 a treaty between the United States and China permitted Congress to legislate the regulation, limitation, or suspension of immigration of Chinese laborers. In 1882 Congress exercised this option by suspending Chinese immigration for ten years.

Although Oregonians did not create these federal measures, or the prejudice that undergirded them, they themselves were never tolerant of the Asian newcomers. Local mining districts often permitted the Chinese to work only the tailings of the mineral deposits. State law assessed a special tax on Chinese miners and merchants. Caucasians denigrated and ridiculed their customs and physically assaulted them sporadically. In the depression years of the mid-1880s and the mid-1890s the Chinese became the scapegoats for bad economic conditions and were unjustly blamed for the unemployment of American workingmen. In the last era the Populist-Democratic governor, Sylvester Pennoyer, ingratiated himself as the demagogic spokesman of anti-Chinese sentiment. The nurseryman Seth Lewelling had to shelter his Chinese foreman in his own home. Stores owned by Chinese and by those who employed them were burned in Portland in the early 1870s and Irish toughs cruelly abused the Chinese. In 1886 Chinese woodcutters were driven from Mount Tabor and forcibly deported from the woolen mills in Oregon City, and in the following year ten Chinese were murdered in Wallowa County.

Although conservative citizens condemned these outrages, the burden of the defense of the Chinese fell upon their own shoulders in almost all respects. "Chinatowns" were places both of residence and of refuge where Chinese could physically escape from the white world and could focus their cultural activities. Socially the Chinese depended for benevolent services, as well as for moral support, upon their clan organizations if they were members of large extended families. The less fortunate members of smaller families, denied the services of the clans, banded together into tongs to protect themselves both against the clans and against the Caucasian world.

After the turn of the century, as many Chinese left the city, as the remainder dispersed throughout Portland, as prosperity returned following the depression of the middle 1890s, and as the Japanese became the new targets of anti-Asian sentiment, Caucasians accepted the Chinese more easily. In the years until the close of the First World War the Chinese cultural life in Portland was centered in the Chinese Theater and in the Chinese Consolidated Benevolent Association of Portland, a federation of all societies that cushioned its members against the shocks of American society by providing advice and arbitration of disputes and also tried to abate the assimilationist temptations of the younger generation by founding a language school. By 1920 the last cause seemed to be almost hopeless. In eastern Oregon the store of Lung On in John Day was the center of not only the mercantile but the cultural life of the Chinese of that region. Temple, herbal doctor's office, gambling den as well as wholesale and retail mercantile institution, the store flourished until the death of its last proprietor in 1952.

Blacks, too, forged a cultural life in the teeth of white indifference. The constitutional amendments of the Civil War and Reconstruction eras freed the slaves, declared blacks to be citizens, and guaranteed the right to vote to the freedmen. Oregon's antiblack constitutional provisions were rendered invalid, but their nullification did not lead to a large migration of blacks in the late nineteenth or early twentieth centuries. Almost all Oregon blacks of these years lived in Portland, with a handful resident in La Grande and in other railroad division points. The occupation of the black populace was almost exclusively connected with transportation, and the newly arrived black people from the South filled jobs as Pullman porters, laborers in the railroad shops, cab drivers, and waiters. A few blacks became farmers, however, in Clackamas County. In Portland the black population was segregated in a ghetto area near the downtown business district until about 1890, when commercial expansion in the area forced the black community to move across the Willamette River into the independent city of Albina, a tough, brawling town that housed railroad shops and other industries.

Both in their old homes and in Albina, blacks maintained a cohesive and vibrant cultural life, one that partook of the worlds of both blacks and whites, since in the Oregon of this era there was no legal social segregation except for a ban on mixed marriages and a prohibition of integrated theaters from 1890 to 1900. Within the constraints of poverty and these legal barriers the blacks focussed their communal lives upon several thriving institutions. The roots of the First African Methodist Episcopal Zion Church (1895) were in the People's Church that had been founded in 1862. An African Methodist Episcopal church and several Baptist churches were founded before the First World War, and blacks were members of the prestigious Trinity Episcopal Church until shunted into Saint Philip's Episcopal mission in 1912.

Black women organized a variety of clubs and had a chapter of the Women's Christian Temperance Union. A Bad Rock Republican Club and later the New Portland Republican Club were founded for political cohesion, and debating and discussion societies like the Paul Laurence Dunbar Literary Society appealed to those concerned with more formal culture. The building which housed the Enterprise Investment Company was frequently used for parties after its opening in 1903. A more comprehensive organization was the Afro-American League that not only sponsored social gatherings, but also assisted blacks in obtaining employment. It also carefully watched the legal process to forestall illegal arrests or unfair trials. In a similar vein the Portland chapter of the National Association for the Advancement of Colored People was established in the early years of the twentieth century, first coming to public attention by its protest against the showing of D. W. Griffith's racist film, *Birth of a Nation*.

Black Oregonians also became active in the political realm in the last decades of the nineteenth century, although some had exercised the suffrage as early as 1872. One sphere of their activity was an attempt to repeal the racist legislation of the 1850s and 1860s. The constitution had discriminated against Negroes in a variety of ways. In 1862 a $5 poll tax was passed against Negro, Chinese, and Hawaiian residents. Interracial marriage was prohibited in 1866.

In the 1890s black leaders began the attempt to remove these measures. The pastor of the Portland AME (Zion) Church led a movement to have the mixed marriage law repealed in 1893, but it failed in the senate. The same session saw the Reverend T. Brown begin the effort to repeal the clauses of the state constitution prohibiting black residence and restricting the franchise to white persons. These two constitutional amendments came to the vote of the people in 1900 and again in 1916 but were defeated in both years, the first time because of a general anti-amendment sentiment and the second because of a misunderstanding about the terms of the measure.

Leaders of the black community, including Adolphus D. Griffin, a prominent real estate dealer and publisher of the *Portland New Age* (1899 to 1907), and McCants Stewart, Oregon's first black lawyer, were adherents of the Republican party, as were most of the state's black voters. In city politics also, the era was one of partisanship, and the blacks, although usually Republican, were not averse to switching parties. Charlie Green, a barber, was the first black elected to the city council, and black leaders attempted to deliver their race's votes in the traditional manner of ethnic urban political blocs. Bloc efforts were not unavailing, as instanced by the success of the New Portland Republican Club in getting a black, George Hardin, placed on the city police force in 1894. Whatever political pressure that could be exerted was a bonus, since the black community in Oregon was never far from the reality or memory of prejudice. Not only the ever-present symbols of racial prejudice, like the existence of the Coon Chicken Shack restaurant in Portland, but violent measures such as the deporting of a black from the town of Liberty in Marion County in 1893 and a lynching in Marshfield in 1902 were more vivid manifestations of the white Oregonians' heritage of racial bigotry.

The Indian, too, made slow progress toward recognition by Caucasians as equals, although the Oregon Indian's position in society altered somewhat in the years after 1880. In 1887 Congress adopted one of its most important statutes concerning the American Indian, the Dawes General Allotment Act. Convinced that communal ownership of property and tribal government were anachronisms that kept the Indian out of the mainstream of American life, white reformers, abetted by those who hungered for more Indian land, urged that the reservations be broken up and that Indians be given land in individual parcels in their own right. The principle underlying this allotment system was to force the Indians to become individual farmers with the aim of fully assimilating them into the white culture. Jesse Applegate, hearkening to Scripture, said the Indians, like Adam and Eve, should begin their new life in a garden. Contrary to the hopes of its advocates, however, the Dawes Act had its greatest impact simply in reducing the communal Indian land base. On the Siletz Reservation, for example, the 1,100,000 acres of 1856 were cut down to 3,000 acres by the middle of the 1890s. The Indians on the reservation held by then only 40,000 acres in allotment trusts, too small an amount for success as individual farmers. The theory of turning the Indian into a white farmer was also at the basis of education in the Indian schools, both day and boarding, in vocational and academic subjects alike; in 1901, for example, the *Course of Study for the Indian Schools of the United States* prescribed that in history classes, time should be devoted to the history of agriculture, a topic that "will assist the student much in his regular work in gardening, farming, etc., and tend to deepen his interest in those branches. The importance of this subject can not be overemphasized." Whatever the depth of commitment to this theory on the part of national policymakers, progress towards these objectives on the reservations of Oregon was painfully slow.

The most pitiable of all Indians were the Paiutes living in the Harney Valley near the town of Burns. These families were the remnant from the Malheur Reservation which had been discontinued by executive order in 1882. Transferred to the Yakima Reservation in Washington as punishment after the Bannock

War, they had slipped home again to live on the margin of subsistence, sustained in squalor by public benevolence. In 1898
they were granted 104 allotments of 160 acres, but this land was
unproductive, and charity alone continued to keep the Paiutes
alive.

The many tribes intermingled on the coast, in the Siletz and
Grand Ronde reservations, were scarcely better off. A special
census investigator reporting in 1890 detailed the plight of these
peoples. Declining population, rampant syphilis, squalid housing ("Those occupied by the old and infirm are nothing but
huts, giving but scant protection from the winter winds"), and
cultural loss ("No legends or traditions of these Indians are extant") characterized their lot. The Dawes Act was applied to the
Indians of Siletz (1892) and Grand Ronde (1901). Reservation
land remaining after the individual allotments had been made
was distributed and sold, far below its true monetary value, to
the United States Government. By the turn of the century the Indians of the former coast reservations had met, superficially, the
government's goal of assimilation, as they attempted farming,
listened to Christian missionaries, wore white man's clothing,
and lived in frame dwellings. Their children attended school
either locally or at Chemawa Indian School in Salem, but their
culture was largely gone and they had not succeeded in the economic world of the Caucasians.

Government agents also discussed allotments for the residents
of the Klamath Reservation in southern Oregon. Early recommendations from the Indian agents and other government observers opposed allotments, however, because the short growing
season of the high plateau of the reservation militated against
profitable farming. The economic hopes for the future, they asserted, lay in stock grazing or in lumbering. In spite of these
negative recommendations, the allotment process began in 1895
and was completed in 1906. The results, as predicted, were almost uniformly unsuccessful, for most Indian farmers lost title
to their unprofitable lands to white persons. Those obtaining
grazing allotments made a better living, but did so not by learning the business but by leasing their lands to Caucasians. But
the chief means by which the Klamath residents lived was by

apportioning the proceeds from the sale of reservation timber among the tribal members. These sales kept them well above the poverty line, but again accomplished nothing to integrate them into the economic mainstream.

Outside the economic sphere the Klamath Indians gained some political experience in dealing with their agent and with the Washington bureaucracy. Conflicts with the agent developed over a variety of issues, including the nature of the schools, appointments to the Indian police, and personality clashes. Indians who received the vote when they secured their land allotments also felt greater interest in making their case against the federal government. Here the principal controversies were the boundaries of the reservation and other claims against the United States. Indians learned to organize into political factions over both local and federal issues, and by the early days of the twentieth century they had developed the technique of sending tribal delegations to Washington to secure redress of grievances. One successful result of this pressure was the removal of Oliver C. Applegate (of the famous pioneer family) as Klamath agent because of Indian objections to his policies. In most cases, however, the political power of the Indians was minimal, although the experience gained had potential use if governmental policies authorized more autonomy in the future.

In social and cultural affairs Indians continued to display the veneer of white life as the old precontact society disintegrated. The solvent forces included the Christian church, which tended to replace the traditional religion or to fuse with it in a syncretistic pattern. Working patterns of some Indians took them into the Caucasian world either as employees of the white families of the agency or as workers in the cities off the reservation. The schools, too, attempted with mixed success to inculcate white values along with the curriculum.

The two large reservations of eastern Oregon similarly suffered from the painful pressures of existing between two cultures. At the Warm Springs Reservation economic discussions also revolved around allotments, although the desire for this procedure had come in part from the Indians because of frequent conflicts over the farming of the communal tribal lands. Under this system Indians who believed in individual operation of real property were often in dispute with their neighbors who continued to practice communal property ownership. Long before the Dawes Act, indeed in the original treaty of 1855, the principle of allotment was granted, but the practice itself was not begun until 1888. By 1900 almost all of the residents of the Warm Springs Reservation were self-supporting although in a status of poverty.

As in the case of the Klamath, the three tribes on the Warm Springs Reservation gained political experience in disputes with the federal government. Here, too, the boundary was an issue, with the Indians challenging the justice of the 1871 lines drawn by the federal surveyor. The Indians also argued that when they signed the treaty of 1865 the government interpreters had never read them the provisions in which they gave up their historic fishing rights on the Columbia River. Although objections on both of these issues were unsuccessful in this era they did bear fruit in future decades. Economic endeavors, political activity, and the efforts of clergy and schoolteachers were unavailing in stopping the discouragement and disillusionment of the Indians, a despair most poignantly reflected in the high rates of alcoholism among the residents of the reservation. Although its sale was prohibited on the reservation itself, liquor was readily available at The Dalles, and the agents and the members of the Women's Christian Temperance Union at Warm Springs were unable to stamp it out.

At the Umatilla Reservation the Indians were slower to adopt the trappings of Caucasian civilization. In 1890 the census taker reported that "a large number of the Indians of Umatilla can not be regarded as having adopted the habits of civilized life. They live in tepees or lodges, dress in blankets, leggings, and moccasins, wear long hair, paint their faces, and seldom converse in English." The Indians were reluctant to take up allotments that were authorized in a congressional statute of 1885, and even when the land was apportioned it was usually leased by the owners to white cattlemen or wheat farmers. At Umatilla, as elsewhere, the years 1870–1920 were transitional ones for the Indian people of Oregon. They were given a large dose of white civilization, but the taste was usually bitter. They had a harder struggle to retain their native culture if they were so minded. For the white citizens the Indians remained largely invisible, since they were distant from the centers of population and rendered almost powerless in terms of the state's economic and political structure.

II

The people of Oregon in the 1880s participated in one great transformation in their economic life, a change long sought and one with a great impact, although not always the one desired. The completion of railroads from the Mississippi and Missouri valleys to the mouth of the Columbia and to Puget Sound affected Oregonians engaged in the oldest pursuits of agriculture and fishing as well as the newer industries of lumbering and open-range ranching.

After 1880 Oregon agriculture continued as the principal economic occupation of the state. As in the pioneer era, the basic farming unit was the family-owned farm, with the state's proportion of owner-operated farms remaining far above the national average (in 1920, the respective percentages were 81.2 and 61.9). By 1880 almost all migrants had also admitted a less pleasant fact: the good land in the Willamette Valley was gone and the potential for new farms lay exclusively east of the Cascades.

In this region, especially in Umatilla, Gilliam, Morrow, Union, Wallowa, Wasco, and Crook counties, winter wheat became the dominant crop of the state. The soil was superb, the land was still abundant (the decade of the greatest use of the Homestead Act in Oregon was after 1910), and the railroad's expansion gave to vast areas an access to market. Farm families who arrived in the state by 1900 had the best opportunity to obtain the land that was adjacent to water and to timber, neither of which was abundant. Migrants coming after that date were often condemned to land without transportation facilities or were forced into futile competition with cultivators of better soils. Increasingly in the twentieth century, agriculturists required not only the assistance of nature, good fortune, and proximity to transportation routes, the successful farmer's immemorial allies, but they also needed capital and imagination as well. Capital was essential to acquire greater acreage for efficient operations and to buy costly machinery and stock to work it. Here again the long shadow of California fell across its northern neighbor, as most of the machinery of agricultural Oregon had been imported from the wheat ranches of the great central valley of California. But capital for land and for improved drills, harvesters, and combines, and for the horses and mules required to draw the largest machinery was not the only requirement for successful agriculture. Farmers had also to allocate time and energy for increasing political activity as counties proliferated and Grange and Populist organizations advocated solutions to rural problems. They had to set aside time for working with extension agents and agricultural college scientists in the quest for ever more bountiful strains of wheat or improved techniques of tillage, fallowing, and weed control that were the basis of prosperous dry farming.

For those migrants who wanted another chance to re-enact on a new frontier the American vision of the yeoman farmer and the country town, but who lacked the necessary luck or skill or money to realize it, for those who were shunted aside to the arid lands away from the railroad arteries and civilization, turn-of-the-century Oregon offered a progression seldom before encountered by white settlers: disillusionment, disappointment, despair. As the migrants' capital shrank with the failing crops, many of them, wrote novelist H. L. Davis in *Honey in the Horn,*

> were beginning to wonder, as most all or nothing gamblers
> sometimes will, whether they hadn't come a little too far, whether
> they shouldn't have gone somewhere else, whether they might not
> have been better off not coming anywhere. Mighty few prayers
> were ever addressed to the Throne of Grace as fervently as theirs
> were that old E. H. Harriman might be moved to build his railroad
> their way so the country would settle up and put civilization back
> around them again.[4]

4. H. L. Davis, *Honey in the Horn* (New York: Harper and Brothers, 1935), p. 299.

Frustration was also the lot of many in the fishing industry. By 1890 primacy in the salmon canning trade had been lost by the Columbia River packers to those of Alaska, and the relative importance of Oregon fishing continued to decline in the next three decades from overfishing, stream pollution, and irrigation ditches. As competition for the resource base sharpened, men turned, as in large-scale agriculture and lumbering, to increasing reliance upon mechanization. In the 1890s and at the turn of the century several inventions reduced labor costs. Axel Johnson developed a successful automatic canmaking machine and Edmund A. Smith's "Iron Chink," a device to cut, clean, and pack salmon automatically, did the work of fifty Chinese cannerymen. The cosmopolitan fishermen of the Columbia— Iberians, central Europeans, Greeks, and Scandinavians— cruelly exploited under a contract-labor system, fought many a bitter strike with management in the 1880s and 1890s, but thereafter the declining state of the industry and the departure of many of the packers to Alaska (packing began there in 1878) caused a decrease in militance.

The packers who remained on the river, like the contemporary farmers and lumbermen, were turning to large-scale organization to solve their production and labor problems. In 1887 nine cannerymen founded the Columbia River Packers Association to attempt to limit wages and maximize production, although a more constructive, but overrated, response for the industry was the interest private enterprise began taking in conservation of the resource. In 1877 the cannerymen started their own hatchery and by 1888 the United States Fish Commission, at the urgent behest of the industry, was fully committed to artificial propagation work on the Columbia. The state of Oregon, too, largely goaded by Robert D. Hume, salmon packer of the Rogue River, was convinced of the value of hatcheries by 1910.

In the forest products industry, always the most important manufacturing enterprise, the bases of operations remained the lower Columbia valley and the coastal area centering about Coos Bay. However, both of these regions continued to lag far behind the amount of timber that the state of Washington produced in these years, although there were some changes in the

Oregon industry. With the coming of the railroad the maritime trade was imperiled and began to decline by 1900. The railroad opened more extensive local markets and also the midwestern centers of Denver, Omaha, and Saint Louis. Business picked up in the urban areas of the state with population increase and continuing economic prosperity. A host of mechanical inventions ranging from the double-bitted axe to the steam donkey engine helped to meet these markets, although their cost required large capital investment.

With the depletion of the virgin white pine stands of the upper Middle West at the turn of the century, lumbermen moved to the Pacific Northwest. By 1914 the giant Weyerhaeuser Company had 400,000 acres of ponderosa pine and Douglas fir in Oregon which it was holding for future use. The advent of large corporations with vast holdings threatened the traditional pattern of Oregon timber ownership, the small "gyppo" mill, which was doomed by the heavy costs required for production efficiencies. The First World War saw an increase in production but Oregon still lagged behind Washington. Finally, the prewar years brought the rudiments of conservation with a state fire protection law in 1904 and the creation of a state forestry department five years later.

Oregon's cattle industry reflected the colonial condition of the state's economy although the classic days of the range cattle industry had disappeared by the middle 1880s. The four largest cattle ranches of eastern Oregon were all financed by Californians whose land base came from the acquisition of swamplands, or at least lands officially so designated. In 1870 the state took title to swamplands granted by the federal government at the time of statehood and began selling them at $1 or less per acre. Much of the land was not swampy but rather excellent grazing land. Many ranchers found even this cost exorbitant and freely helped themselves to the use of the public domain. For a time all prospered as new markets opened up with the advent of the railroad and the industrialization of the nation that created a demand for beef.

Cattlemen fed the growing cities of the Northwest in the 1880s. Until 1885 they continued the colorful long drives, begun in the 1870s, through the passes of the Rockies to the stocking ranges of the northern plains and Rockies. Some cattle were driven to Nevada and then sent by rail to San Francisco. In the cattle country from the Columbia to the Nevada line the names of Peter French, John Devine, Henry Miller, and James Hardin were merely the leading ones of a flourishing industry.

But the railroad which had been the catalyst for the range cattle industry also was the cause of its demise. The Northern Pacific, the Oregon Short Line, and the Union Pacific not only opened up new markets for Oregonians, they also brought new settlers east of the Cascades. These newcomers were farmers or sheepmen and were menacing to the cattle ranchers. The railroad made possible the raising of wheat in northeastern Oregon, and wheat farming was a more lucrative land use than cattle ranching. In the southeastern portion of the state the railroad made sheep raising profitable, and this enterprise drove the range cattle industry out of that region.

In the late 1880s and the 1890s the range cattle industry was in its death throes as competition for land led to bitterness and bloodshed among cattlemen, farmers, and sheep growers. Some cattlemen intimidated settlers and clubbed, shot, or poisoned sheep, but most reacted tamely by departing for Idaho, Montana, or Dakota. A lurid symbol of their defeat was the murder in 1897 of cattle baron Peter French by Ed Oliver, who in the face of the evidence was acquitted by a jury of his fellow settlers. Along with the farmers, the sheep raisers inherited the cattle country. After the middle 1880s thousands of wethers were driven east of the Rockies for finishing before slaughter. Other ranchers, especially the great trinity of central Oregon, Charles Cunningham, the Baldwin Sheep and Land Company, and the Dufur Brothers, went into wool production. The Baldwin firm was Oregon's largest, controlling 281 square miles by 1910, and for a time held the world record for annual wool clips. For a time, too, the railroad to central Oregon made the town of Shaniko one of the world's principal wool markets. These successes were products both of nature and of men. Sheep could go where topography prohibited cattle and farmers. Their wool was far more valuable to transport by rail than was beef. And, unlike the cattlemen, the sheep growers usually produced no rivalry for land with the farmers. By the early twentieth century the sheep industry was stabilized both by economics and government, and the new U.S. Forest Service began controlling land use through leasing grazing permits in the vast areas of the national forests. Also, by this date the remaining cattlemen had readjusted to the loss of the open range and were producing almost solely for local markets.

Although Oregonians resented the condition, they had to recognize their colonial economic status and to live within the context of dependence upon outside capital for development, the importation of a supply of labor, and the export of raw materials. In the 1880s their concern, especially that of Portlanders, was not to throw off colonialism but to assert themselves and secure its advantages by defeating the challenges of Seattle, Tacoma, Spokane, and other Washington cities for the position of metropolis of the Pacific Northwest. The principal weapon in this urban rivalry was the railroad. The Portland business community had to court the railroad magnates to acquire construction and service but had to avoid the trap of falling dependent upon a monopolistic line. At the center of both east-west and north-south transportation axes, the acknowledged metropolis of the Northwest, Portland in 1870 had the opportunity of obtaining competitive rail service if she developed her opportunities in all geographical directions.

The beginnings of this quest significantly involved foreign investors, German bondholders concerned about money sunk into Ben Holladay's railroad building south from Portland to California. Ultimately, one of their agents, the brilliant Henry Villard, in 1876 assumed the operation of the Holladay line and three years later began to invest his own capital in Oregon railroads. In 1881 Collis P. Huntington, the main force in the Southern Pacific, was threatening to buy the Oregon and California line and divert the traffic of the Willamette Valley to San Francisco, but Villard acquired control first and the railroad was finally completed in 1887.

More important was Portland's and Villard's quest to obtain a connection to the Mississippi valley superior to that of the Puget

Sound ports. To accomplish this link Villard established two holding companies to forestall the chief threat to Portland's hegemony, the Northern Pacific Railroad, which was being built from Saint Paul to Puget Sound, with a mere branch line to Portland. Portland's fear was that the Northern Pacific would construct a line from the confluence of the Snake and Columbia over the Cascade Mountains to Tacoma or Seattle and draw from Portland the wheat exports of those two great rivers, commodities that had hitherto flowed down the Columbia in the holds of the Oregon Steam Navigation Company vessels.

Villard's first holding company was the Oregon Railway and Navigation Company, formed in 1879. Through it he acquired the OSNC, which still held a monopoly of the Columbia River traffic; a line of steamships from Portland to San Francisco; and a railroad from the Walla Walla wheatfields to the Columbia River. The ORNC planned to build a railway along the south bank of the Columbia to prevent the Northern Pacific from using this route, which was superior to that on the north bank. In 1881 Villard formed his second holding company, the Oregon and Transcontinental, to control the Northern Pacific itself. His victory was complete, it seemed, for Portland and Oregon were secure from the Cascade–Puget Sound outlet.

The next decade proved this hope unwarranted. Railroad construction did move apace as the rails were laid from Spokane across the desert of Washington, down the south bank of the Columbia to Kalama, and thence north to Tacoma, the main terminus, and Seattle. But Portland was not to enjoy the benefits of this line exclusively, for the Northern Pacific freed itself of the grip of the Oregon and Transcontinental and completed its Cascade line in 1887. This tie to Seattle was a blow to Portland, for wheat increasingly was exported from Seattle, but the older city survived, in part by obtaining navigational improvements at the bar of the Columbia and in part by reaching toward the southeast.

Progress in this direction came from a link, called the Oregon Short Line, completed by the Union Pacific from Umatilla on the Columbia through Oregon and Idaho to the main line of the transcontinental at Granger, Wyoming, in 1884. This line not only opened up areas of eastern Oregon, but also provided a competitive shipping route to that of the Northern Pacific. Thus by the close of Oregon's railroad decade of the eighties, Portland had been able to salvage a fair share of the profits of regional development, although the construction of the Great Northern Railway to Seattle in 1893, the Alaska gold rush, and defense industries in the First World War enabled Seattle to attain regional primacy over Portland by 1920.

The railroad had other effects than those on the interurban rivalry. It made the basic exporting industries of wheat raising and lumbering competitive with California, Washington, and the South in the urban markets of the East and Middle West. The railroad not only functioned to continue the colonial role of furnishing raw materials, but it also supplied the imported manufactured goods that underdeveloped Oregon could not produce. The railroad as colonizer brought immigrants to Oregon in relative comfort compared to the overland trail or the Panamanian passage. Indeed, the railroad was more than a passive force in populating Oregon, for both Union Pacific and Northern Pacific maintained agents in Europe, in the East, and in Omaha to persuade migrants to settle on or along their lands in the West. The railroad advertising literature was reasonably accurate in describing the conditions in the Northwest, and railroad lands were quite inexpensive, since the roads' profits were to come from the freight traffic, not the sale of real estate. The railroad changed land use patterns by altering, as we have seen, the economy of eastern Oregon from cattle raising to one based on wheat or sheep. These changes—particularly the coming of agriculture—were welcomed by most "substantial" townspeople who preferred the familiar sedentary, civic-minded farmers (and their larger incomes) to untypical Oregonians such as cattle barons, cowboys, and sheepherders.

Yet in spite of their impact the railroads became less appreciated as the decades passed. Extravagantly hailed before their advent as the means to break down social isolation and promote economic growth, welcomed enthusiastically upon completion with golden spike ceremonies and municipal parades, the railroads soon became the target of disillusioned citizens. The railroads, critics now charged, demanded too-high rates; they discriminated between large and small shippers and among communities; they purchased favors from politicians (even the upright federal Judge Matthew P. Deady expected his annual passes from the ORNC and OSNC, and Sen. John H. Mitchell admittedly served the interests of the railroad magnates). The railroads brought too many drifters and too few farmers, and they laid their construction and financial plans in the interest of eastern capitalists, not sturdy Oregonians. Out of these charges, many of them true, came a counterattack against the railroads that lay at the base of the political protest movements of the post-Civil War years.

The workers and farmers whose skills underlay these economic changes were beginning to organize in these decades. Labor unions in Oregon were small in membership and quite ineffectual until the turn of the century. Probably there were only about 100 members of trade unions in Portland in 1880 and few elsewhere in the state, because the immature status of manufacturing limited the potential for labor organization. In the 1880s, though, with the development of manufacturing stimulated by the railroad, several groups arose. In 1880 was organized the Portland chapter of the Knights of Labor, a national organization that sought to unite all workers with hand or brain into a single organization that would humanize the industrial system. It had some periodic success locally, usually among the unemployed, until it perished in the depression of 1893.

Of far more importance was the organization of skilled workers into what became the American Federation of Labor. Samuel Gompers, the founder of this organization, was able in 1887, after a false start four years earlier, to organize fifteen skilled craft unions into a citywide trades assembly. Under the leadership of a great organizer, John L. O'Brien, the Oregon AFL unions grew in the years to 1900 and organized labor became more visible to the public. Portland brewery workers went on strike in 1888 and 1889, but their use of the boycott weapon lost them public sympathy and the strike in both years. In 1890, however, the city's building trades won a strike for the eight-hour day. Fishermen in Astoria organized the third group, the

Columbia River Fishermen's Protective Union, and conducted several unsuccessful strikes before 1900. In the railroad centers, such as La Grande and Roseburg, the shop unions and railroad brotherhoods were strong, and the Western Federation of Miners had a chapter in Baker.

In politics unions followed the AFL belief in nonpartisanship, although O'Brien lobbied in Salem in the eighties and nineties for an eight-hour day on public works projects, an improved mechanics lien law, and the secret ballot. Some labor unions were represented in the same decades in support of a farmer-labor alliance and Populist ideals, but organized labor lacked the numbers to be a powerful force in politics. Overall, the labor activity of the pre-twentieth century was conservative, following the lead of the national Knights of Labor and AFL in ideology, membership composition, organizing techniques, and goals, so that the historian of early Oregon labor concludes: "In fact, little that is unique can be found on the Oregon labor scene in that period." [5]

The next two decades produced prosperity; the Oregon System of initiative, referendum, recall, and direct primary; and the First World War. Oregon labor continued to be eclectic, but the ideas that it imported now tended to alarm the great bulk of the state's population, including many of its own members, whose conservatism remained staunch. In early 1902 the AFL unions founded the Oregon Federation of Labor at the initiative of George H. Harry, a sheet metal worker and recent migrant from California. Six years later the state federation embarked upon an extensive organizing campaign based upon the importation of the Seattle Plan (of 1903), which required that delegates to a city central labor council also represent their own trade section.

In spite of these institutional changes labor lost ground in the decade 1910 to 1920 as it became identified in the public mind with radicalism, lack of patriotism, and disregard of public convenience. Although most members of the AFL were not radical, the Portland Central Labor Council in 1907 did resolve to assist

5. Jack E. Triplett, "History of the Oregon Labor Movement Prior to the New Deal," (Master's thesis, University of California, Berkeley, 1961), p. 64. Used with permission.

the Industrial Workers of the World when that militant syndicalist group took over a Portland sawmill workers' strike. Also, after 1914, the AFL combatted municipal ordinances designed to silence the antiwar protests of the IWW. The AFL opposed military preparedness before American entry into the war (although not afterwards), for fear that a strengthened state militia would be used for strikebreaking purposes, and it objected to the Boy Scouts of America as dangerous to labor. The public disliked the boycott weapon.

The general public's most vivid impression of labor life before the close of the First World War was the rise of the IWW. This radical and colorful organization was created in 1905 by William D. Haywood, former president of the Western Federation of Miners, and other labor leaders disenchanted with the AFL. The IWW advocated a syndicalist state with economic and political power residing in the hands of the workers rather than in a system of capitalism and democracy. It opposed wars as conflicts between the exploiting classes. The techniques of the Wobblies, as they were derisively called, were almost as threatening to most citizens as were its goals, for they included inflammatory propaganda, speeches on street corners in defiance of municipal ordinances, the courting of mass arrests, and work slowdowns and sabotage. Ordinary Oregonians, accustomed either to a consensus society or one in which conflicts were resolved by the use of peaceful democratic machinery, were horrified by the starkness of the Wobblies' description of the social order, contained most famously in the preamble to their 1908 constitution:

> The working class and the employing class have nothing in common. There can be no peace so long as hunger and want are found among millions of working people and the few, who make up the employing class, have all the good things of life.
>
> Between these two classes a struggle must go on until the workers of the world organize as a class, take possession of the earth and the machinery of production, and abolish the wage system.[6]

6. Joyce L. Kornbluh, ed., *Rebel Voices: An I. W. W. Anthology* (Ann Arbor: University of Michigan Press, 1964), pp. 12–13.

The IWW had its greatest national success in organizing the lumber camps of the state of Washington. In the years of the First World War and in its immediate aftermath the Wobblies terrified the middle classes of the Evergreen State, and Wobblies and their conservative opponents clashed in bloody battles in Seattle, Everett, and Centralia. More than anything else the power of the Wobblies forced government intervention to maintain defense production in the lumber camps of the Northwest during the war by giving the employees the wages, hours, and working conditions for which the IWW was striking.

By contrast, IWW activity in Oregon was mild, although the first IWW strike in the Pacific Northwest was in Portland in 1907, ironically not for revolutionary goals, but for higher wages and shorter hours. In three weeks the strike was broken, and thereafter the organization became more ideological and less popular with each passing year. In 1912 the Wobblies tried to take over a strike of construction workers in Eugene and in the following year one of loggers at Coos Bay. Both strikes failed. In the great Northwest lumber strike of 1917 the Wobblies closed most of the mills in Astoria and Portland for about two weeks, but the relative insignificance of the lumber business in Oregon compared to that in Washington and the conservative nature of the state's population precluded much interest in Oregon woods or mills on the part of either the IWW or AFL organizers, and the strike in the state was ineffective.

The conservative social climate in fact defined the principal impact of the IWW in Oregon. Fear of the rhetoric of the Wobblies caused a variety of repressive responses by the citizens. In the summer of 1913 Mayor George Baker of Portland issued a proclamation prohibiting the use of the city's streets for IWW meetings, and veterans of the Spanish-American War helped enforce it by violence. In Klamath Falls a member of the IWW was arrested by a sheriff's posse and charged with arson after the destruction of a grain elevator, but he could not be convicted. And in 1919 the legislature adopted a criminal syndicalism law aimed at the IWW under which a few arrests but no convictions were obtained. The chief importance of the Wobblies in Oregon history was to demonstrate, by their militant and ideological contrast, the practicality of the traditional labor unions and the importance of organized labor retaining the confidence of the general public if it were to obtain its objectives.

III

In dictating a reminiscence for historian Hubert Howe Bancroft, the crusty and forthright Jesse Applegate summarized his views of the Oregon cultural record: "Oregon has no history. It has added no new fact to human knowledge—has produced no high illustration of any fact already known, has produced no statesman, warrior, or scholar in any branch of human knowledge, in fact not a *single* name that for any merit or act of its possessor *deserves* to live in the memory of mankind." [7] This judgment, rendered in 1878, however harsh it might seem, has a great deal of validity with respect to the higher culture for the next forty years as well. Writers of literature, poetry, and history were by and large parochial and second-class. In almost no sense did they touch upon the themes that were making the years to 1920 one of the most fruitful periods in American literature.

In fiction, authors emphasized nature and local history in such works as Frederick Homer Balch's *The Bridge of the Gods* (1890), Eva Emery Dye's *McLoughlin of Old Oregon* (1900), and Ella Higginson's *Mariella* (1904). Whereas the most compelling national literary movements were realism and naturalism, focussed upon universal themes in a contemporary setting in an "objective" and "realistic" mode, Oregon writers wrote of the pioneer generation in a romantic, personal, localized vein that stressed the heroic deeds of important men and women battling against the environment or the Indians. Indeed, except for Balch's *Bridge of the Gods,* writers ignored the Indians as authentic human beings. Balch conceived an improbable plot for his novel, the missionary endeavors and romance with an Indian

---

7. Jesse Applegate, "Views of Oregon History, etc. . ." [1878], Bancroft Library, University of California. Quoted by permission of the Bancroft Library.

princess of a seventeenth-century New England clergyman along the lower Columbia, but his reading and his interviews with Indians introduced their culture as worthy of serious literary treatment. Unfortunately he had no competent emulators in this respect for decades. Most of the abler novelists were women, and most novels were published outside the state, because the immature cultural life could not sustain an Oregon publisher. In poetry Oregon's most beloved author was the bibulous Sad Sam Simpson, who never realized his early promise, and its most notorious was "Joaquin" (born Cincinnatus Hiner) Miller, who deserted his wife Minnie Myrtle (born Minnie Dyer), the "Sweet Singer of the Coquille," and children before moving on to an evanescent reputation in California and the Old World. The themes of both poets were conventional romance and nature worship.

The writing of history, although also traditional in form, was more distinguished. The Oregon Historical Society, founded in 1898, opened an avenue for historical publication in its quarterly. At the University of Oregon Frederic G. Young and Joseph Schafer were professional historians of the new breed of the turn of the century: trained in graduate schools, assiduous in pursuit of sources, careful and clear in judgment, not particularly interested in literary style. Schafer's *History of the Pacific Northwest* (1905) was the first one-volume synthesis of regional development.

The best history was written by one of an earlier generation, however, Frances Fuller Victor, a migrant to the region from her native Ohio by way of California. In 1878 Hubert Howe Bancroft had employed her as one of the authors of his thirty-nine-volume series entitled *History of the Pacific Coast*. Ultimately she wrote four complete volumes in the series (the two volumes on Oregon; one on Washington, Idaho, and Montana; and one on Nevada, Colorado, and Wyoming) and probably parts of four others. Her Oregon volumes are still the beginning point for a study of the state's history: their detail, their ordering, and their judgments are all impressive. She also distinguished herself with a biography of the mountain man Joseph Meek entitled *The River of the West* (1870) and *History of the*

Indian Wars of Oregon (1894). Throughout her mature years Frances Victor also wrote poetry, newspaper and magazine articles, and a book of travel and description. Although income from her pen was modest, she was Oregon's best-known and most-respected resident author by the time of her death in 1902.

For two other authors Oregonians had less respect but equal concern. These men, "Oregon's Romantic Rebels," as Edwin Bingham styled them, were John Reed and C. E. S. Wood. Both were of wealthy Portland families, both successful in their fields, both critics of the established order, both, at least part of the time, shocking to the Portland citizenry. Wood, the older, stayed longer in his native city. Wood's critics found his personality to be bifurcated. A graduate of West Point who became a corporation lawyer and an important figure in the state Democratic party, Wood enjoyed the social amenities that were his birthright. A leader of the bar, he mingled easily with men of property and political establishment, but he was also a self-proclaimed anarchist, an attorney for advocates of unpopular causes like birth control, a defender of the Indian (one of his first published works was an article on Chief Joseph in the national magazine *Century*), and a worker for the initiative and referendum. Wood, too, was a talented painter and poet whose *Poet and the Desert* (1915) was the most lyrical evocation of the region east of the Cascades. Although his multiple talents and his radiant charm enabled him to retain the good will of Portland in spite of his radicalism, Wood in 1919 shook off the city's conventionality by fleeing to California with the poet Sara Bard Field.

One who departed earlier was John Reed, the only American to be buried in the Kremlin. Born to luxury in the Portland Heights area, Reed became a great war correspondent after a career at Harvard, gaining a national reputation in his coverage of John Pershing's campaign against Pancho Villa in Mexico that culminated in a personal interview with Villa. Reed became a prominent figure in the bohemian life of Greenwich Village; dramatized the IWW strike at Paterson, New Jersey, in 1912 through a pageant in Madison Square Garden; and for a time served as managing editor of the radical periodical, *Masses*. He also was a contributor to more conventional journals, writing domestic and foreign correspondence for *American, Century,* and the *New York World.*

On a visit to Portland in 1915 Reed fell in love with the poet Louise Bryant Trullinger, wife of a Portland dentist, who divorced Trullinger to marry Reed in the next year. Louise and Reed joined the Greenwich Village outpost at Provincetown, Massachusetts, where Louise for a time became the lover of Reed's friend, the then-obscure Eugene O'Neill. In time Reed was caught up in the Bolshevik Revolution and in 1919 published his masterpiece, *Ten Days that Shook the World.* This book breathed a spirit of romance and adventure, although the reporting was factual, celebrating the advent of Bolshevik power as the herald of the liberation of humanity. The book made him a hero of international communism—ironically for one of his independent and romantic views—and secured him a place in radical history that his early death in 1920 from typhus contracted in Finland and his Moscow burial helped to sanctify.

Whether shocked, titillated, or amused by Wood, Reed, and Bryant, Oregonians congratulated themselves that the romantic radicals were the exception to the conservatism that permeated their cultural life as thoroughly as in the era before the railroads. Education, for example, continued in the safe channels of the rudiments for all, vocational training for the many, and a liberal arts education for the few. The state passed compulsory attendance laws, required certification of teachers, and gave more generous financial support to education than in the previous era. The high school became normative and new institutions of higher education were founded. The Methodists established Portland University (its campus is now the site of the University of Portland), and Amanda Reed, widow of Simeon of the OSNC, left money that was used to found Reed Institute, later College, in 1911. On the other hand the state legislature abolished the meagerly supported three normal schools in 1909 and let the people select by initiative which they wished to retain. Only the college at Monmouth survived this test. The appropriations for the university at Eugene were always inadequate and in some cases referred to the people by the members of the legislature. Indeed, the state university had always been short of funds either from private or public sources. When Henry Villard of the Northern Pacific gave the university $50,000 in the railroad's bonds, the president of the regents, Matthew Deady, congratulated himself in the official report on the manner of his acknowledgment of this rare and generous gift: "I think I have done it in a way that will be acceptable to him . . . and at the same time point a moral in the right use of riches for the benefit of our local closefisted narrow visioned millionaires." [8]

Men and women of property had a somewhat better record in the patronage of the arts. Local people founded the Portland Art Association in 1892 with a small collection, and a building was acquired in 1905. Soon the museum added an art school that served a large number of students in its day and evening classes. After the turn of the century local artists gathered in the Art Association, the Little Club, and the Oregon Society of Artists under the leadership of Carl Walters, a landscape painter, lithographer, and ceramic artist; Anna Belle Crocker; and Harry F. Wentz. There were several amateur painters like Paul Trullinger, the first husband of Louise Bryant, but the two moving forces in art circles were Harry Wentz and Anna Belle Crocker. Wentz, a painter who loved the Oregon Coast at Neahkahnie, and who was the state's first landscape artist of repute, occupied himself almost exclusively with nature, depicting the remote mountains of the Northwest, the coastal areas, and detailed studies of floral life. The people in his paintings were also those in communion with nature: fishermen at Nehalem, hikers in the mountains, and ocean bathers. He also served as an inspiring teacher for thirty-one years at the Portland Art Museum Art School, to which he was appointed in 1910. Wentz, although committed to Oregon and its natural environment in his own paintings, was aware of the currents of international art and made visits to New York to visit the galleries and studios. His influence was immense.

Comparable in force was Anna Belle Crocker's curatorship of

8. Malcolm Clark, Jr., *Pharisee Among Philistines: The Diary of Judge Matthew P. Deady, 1871–1892*, 2 vols. (Portland: Oregon Historical Society, 1975), 2:420.

the Art Association from 1909 to 1936. She, too, was current with changing values in art, unafraid of modern art, and willing to test Portland's reception of it. She welcomed to the museum paintings that had been displayed at the Armory Show in New York in 1913, including Marcel Duchamp's "Nude Descending A Staircase" that confused or scandalized many in America who were introduced to "modern art" for the first time. Her leadership was consistently clear, forceful, and honest. In terms of theme, however much they might be impressed by modern art, most Oregon artists concentrated, as in former years, upon the world of nature.

The architectural life of Oregon in the late nineteenth and early twentieth centuries, in both town and country, remained for the most part derivative, although the cultural lag between the state and eastern centers closed, and the seminal figure of Albert E. Doyle began to influence regional architecture in new directions. The great American architects and landscape architects such as McKim, Mead, and White; H. H. Richardson; Richard Morris Hunt; and Frederick Law Olmsted had their Portland following both in clients and in architects. The Chicago World's Fair of 1893, officially titled the Columbian Exposition, had an influence in Portland in propagating the ideas of the "City Beautiful" movement that was sweeping the metropolitan centers, but the archetypical architectural monument of the early twentieth century was Portland's Lewis and Clark Exposition of 1905.

This fair was basically a promotional venture to advertise the economic assets of Portland and the lower Columbia valley, but its moving spirits had high aesthetic ideals. The director of architecture was Ion Lewis, who had moved to Portland in 1889 from his native Boston. The theme of the buildings was Spanish Renaissance, for no apparent reason, but it was carried out with grace and unity and in harmony with the landscaping. The fair made money, publicized the region, and gave Portland a beloved landmark, the Forestry Building (built of logs, not in Spanish Renaissance style) that survived until destroyed by fire in 1964. Yet the exposition was an eastern institution in almost all respects, as were the Portland city plan of 1912 designed by

Edward H. Bennett and the eclecticism of urban dwellings of the wealthy that drew from all cultures—and sometimes most effectively indeed—except that of the Oregon Country.

Although thoroughly trained in eastern modes and a devoted and brilliant practitioner of them, Alfred Doyle was also the first in Oregon architecture to reach for a native influence. Famous as the architect of the Georgian Portland Public Library, the terra cotta Meier and Frank building, and the French baroque Benson Hotel, Doyle was not confined by the eclectic tradition or the urban environment. At Neahkanie on the Oregon beach, a long popular resort, Doyle designed four cottages from 1912 to 1916 that were functional and freed from all prevailing European, English, or eastern United States styles. They cast a long shadow on the architecture of the next era.

The world of religious life was changing, too. Judge Deady, who was ubiquitous at religious services of every faith, attended morning worship on a summer Sunday in 1881: "Went to Methodist church in Salem. . . . The congregation was thin and looked lean. The glory has departed from Salem—particularly the Methodist part of it." [9] Although by no stretch of the imagination were pioneer Oregonians all Methodist or even church-affiliated persons, Deady was right in implying the rise in strength of other denominations after the Civil War. The coming of immigrants in large numbers from northern Europe, smaller groups from central and southern Europe, the more diverse origins of native migrants, and the rise in religious tolerance made for denominational cosmopolitanism. When a religious census was taken in the United States in 1906, the largest denominations in numbers were, in order, Roman Catholic, Methodist, and Baptist. These denominations held the same rank in Oregon. But in terms of total church membership Oregon continued, as in the pioneer era, to lag behind the national norm. Forty-three percent of Americans in 1906 had a denominational affiliation, but only 29 percent of Oregonians were church members. What did distinguish this era from the pioneer period was the greater concentration of the churches upon urban social

9. Clark, *Pharisee,* 340–341.

problems like prostitution and upon the establishment of cultural institutions for immigrants like Portland's Chinese Baptist Church.

Edwin V. O'Hara, a young Catholic priest, in 1912 assumed the presidency of the Oregon branch of the National Consumer's League to study the wage situation in the state. Using data compiled by Caroline Gleason, he became the moving force in persuading the state legislature to pass the first effective minimum wage law in American history in 1913. Rabbi Jacob Wise was a stalwart of the urban reform movement, and Thomas Lamb Eliot, longtime minister of Portland's Unitarian Church, was the conscience of the city in the establishment of the Oregon Humane Society, the [Orphan's] Home, and the Boys and Girls Aid Society of Oregon; he was also an advocate of enlightened aid to the criminals and the insane.

The most popular cultural institution in Portland was representative of the state's aspirations and level of concern. This was the Baker Stock Company, owned by George Baker, future mayor of Portland, who operated it from 1902 to 1915. Baker's resident stock company was, of its kind, among the best in the nation. It provided each year several weeks of theater by an able company whose members became temporary residents of the community—some indeed settled down permanently—and who were adopted by their admirers as old friends. The Baker Company gave performances of good plays that emphasized either comedy or action. Both the plays and the players were to emphasize proper moral themes and conduct (divorced actors and actresses concealed their previous marriages from the public). The appeal was to middle-class professional persons and white-collar workers: housewives attended the Wednesday matinees, family groups the weekend performances, and older couples the evening plays. Baker's customers were those whose taste ran between the vaudeville that appealed to the working classes and the touring productions from the East with the latest plays and stars, who often did not work very hard for the provincial audiences. The Baker Company was a model for urban Oregon in its emphasis upon tried and true plays staged in traditional modes for a middle-class audience.

When the excitement, the dislocations, and the disillusionment of the First World War began to clear away by 1920,
Oregonians who looked for support to their cultural past might
detect three basic characteristics of the years since the Civil
War. First of all, cultural life was overwhelmingly derivative
and conservative. The family remained nuclear although the rise
of cities gave wives and mothers more freedom of employment
and political action. In education there were no innovations at
any level in curriculum, teacher training, finance, or organization. Even the new schools, except for Reed College, which
prohibited Greek letter societies and intercollegiate athletics,
were modelled on eastern institutions. Architecture was basically eclectic, artists dealt with landscape in the traditional
modes, and theaters and musical groups neither performed original forms nor produced first-class local talent. In literature there
were some Oregonians of ability, but dissidents like Wood and
Reed left the state, and those who remained, like Frances Victor, did not break new ground in history and literature either in
philosophy or structure. Newspapers began to be homogenized
as the days of the personal journalist faded and those of the
mass advertiser emerged. The death in 1910 of Harvey W.
Scott, editor of the *Portland Oregonian,* marked the end of the
era that began with Asahel Bush and Thomas Dryer.

Cultural life was not only conservative, it was most admired
when it was most "practical," that is, most related to vocational opportunities. People endorsed public grade schools enthusiastically, but it took a sharp struggle to establish high
schools. Oregon Agricultural College at Corvallis was more
popular than the university at Eugene. Public support of art museums and of symphony orchestras was limited because most
citizens could not see their value in their own lives. Cultural life
was also parochial. Almost all painters, historians, poets, and
novelists emphasized local landscape and local themes. Few left
the state for extended periods of time or even explored other
regions or more sophisticated problems in the country of the
mind. In an era of enormous changes in the American intellect,
Oregon artists were far from the cutting edge of cultural progress.

5

Change for the Sake
of Continuity (1861–1920)

I

ETWEEN the firing on Fort Sumter and the close of
the First World War Oregon politics evolved from conservatism
to progressivism, at least in the machinery of government, but
the changes that occurred, although frequently misinterpreted
outside the state, did not drastically alter the political, economic, or social system. Reformers arose and reforms were
enacted by the legislature or the people through initiative or referendum so that "Oregon System" became household words in
America, but several basic political institutions of the antebellum era continued. The two-party system remained effective; the constitution of 1857 continued unamended in the nineteenth century; partisan journalism still flourished. By the end of
the period conservatives and reformers—after much strife and
excitement—had come to a rough agreement about the desirable
political responses to the new developments of post-Civil War
Oregon. They had grappled with the full-scale emergence of the
state's economy into world markets through its ever-increasing
reliance upon raw material exports. They had addressed themselves to the political and economic impact of the railroad, the
state's first modern corporation. They had taken into account the

forces of the city and the corporation: the boss, woman's desire for participation in political life, and urbanites' requirement of increased social services.

The most striking feature of state politics until the nineties was the alliance between business, especially the railroads, and government. The archetypical conservative political organization was the Mitchell-Dolph wing of the Republican party. Operating through the bosses of Portland's Republican machine, the law firm of John H. Mitchell and Joseph Dolph, plus two other partners, Joseph Simon and John M. Gearin, produced United States senatorships for all four members, men who supported the gold standard, the protective tariff, and federal aid to railroads. Mitchell and Dolph were retained by Ben Holladay and later by the Northern Pacific Railroad, and when Dolph won election to the United States Senate in 1882 he was attorney and vice-president of the Oregon Railway and Navigation Company. Although in time the Mitchell-Dolph wing was challenged by another faction within the party led by Joseph Simon and Henry W. Corbett, and Harvey Scott of the *Oregonian* waged a personal vendetta against Mitchell, the Republican internecine struggles until the mid-1890s evolved over office, not principle.

Mitchell was the most colorful politician in the history of the state, at least in his personal life. Courtly in manner, orotund of speech, patriarchal of beard, John H. Mitchell had the veneer of a statesman of rectitude. Yet his private life, which became increasingly an open book throughout his years of public service, belied his righteous exterior. Mitchell had deserted his wife in Pennsylvania and fled, with his three-year old daughter and his mistress, to California where he changed his name from Hipple to Mitchell. In turn he left his mistress behind in migrating to Oregon in 1861. The following year he married again, without benefit of divorce, and in a few years cast eyes upon his sister-in-law. His political enemies of course made much of his amours, ridiculing him for self-righteousness and hypocrisy (a favorite gibe was aimed at Mitchell's frequently delivered lecture on "Henry the Eighth and His Wives"). They were at times able to defeat him, but the legislature also elected him to the United States Senate four times, once in 1885 only a few days after the publication in the *Oregonian* of his captured love letters to Carrie Price, his wife's sister. These missives ("My thoughts have been of you, and you alone. . . . With you for my wife I would be the happiest man living. . . . *Read and burn.*") were sensational reading but little else. Judge Deady had rightly predicted the uselessness of this maneuver: [It] "must fix him with the decent part of the community, but with his particular henchmen I imagine that it will make no difference unless his pretensions to piety disgust them. He is alone in making fornication a means of salvation." [1]

An equally notorious representative of the casual morality of Oregon politicians in the postwar years was George H. Williams. A former free-soil Democrat, Williams had been elected to the United States Senate in 1865 as a Republican and had later been appointed attorney general of the United States by President Grant in 1872. In time it became rumored, then proved, that Williams and his spendthrift, socially ambitious wife had diverted Department of Justice funds to buy a small carriage, called a landaulet, and uniforms and wages of two servants for their personal use. Mrs. Williams had also extorted $30,000 from a New York firm in return for her efforts to halt a Justice Department suit against it. Even more seriously, Williams had misused government moneys to reward New York City spoilsmen for "political services." When disclosure loomed at the hands of an investigating committee of the House of Representatives, Mrs. Williams and a political retainer attempted to blackmail President Grant and members of his cabinet into forcing the committee members to abandon their inquiries.

In spite of his corruption and incompetence Williams escaped impeachment and was allowed to resign his seat in the cabinet. Indeed Grant nominated him, albeit as his fourth choice, for chief justice in 1875 but withdrew his name when it became obvious that he could not be confirmed. (One senator declared:

1. *Portland Morning Oregonian,* November 14, 1885, p. 2; Malcolm Clark, Jr., *Pharisee Among Philistines: The Diary of Judge Matthew P. Deady,* 2 vols. (Portland: Oregon Historical Society, 1975), 2:480.

"We have five hundred better lawyers in Massachusetts.") His reputation as a national figure shattered, stigmatized publicly as "Landaulet" Williams and privately as "George the Third" (his wife's first husband and her paramour had both also borne the name of George), Williams retreated to Portland where he resided until his death in 1910 as an honored citizen and sometime mayor.

Oregon also became an object of national political notoriety in the noisome presidential election of 1876. When the polls closed, it appeared that Samuel J. Tilden, the Democratic candidate, had won, but the electoral votes of South Carolina, Louisiana, and Florida, and one from Oregon, were contested. If all of these votes had been awarded to Rutherford B. Hayes, the Republican standard-bearer, he would have been elected by a single vote. The Oregon situation was extremely muddy. The three Republican electors had received the highest number of popular votes, but one of them, John W. Watts, was a postmaster on the day of election and hence ineligible under the United States Constitution, as a federal officeholder, to cast his vote for Hayes. Oregon law held that the office of a vacant elector would be filled by the remainder of the electoral college. When the electoral college met in December, however, confusion abounded.

The two Republicans re-elected Watts, who had previously resigned as elector. The secretary of state certified him as duly chosen. However, the Democratic elector who had received the most votes (fourth in the overall total), E. A. Cronin, himself unlawfully chose two other citizens as Democratic electors, neither of whom had been on the electoral ballot and one of whom had voted for Hayes. Gov. Lafayette Grover certified the three electoral votes of Oregon as Democratic. In the meantime Tilden's nephew, W. T. Pelton, was keeping in touch with Oregon events by coded telegrams. One of his agents, J. N. H. Patrick, endorsed by Sen. James K. Kelly, wired Pelton: "Must purchase a republican elector to recognize and act with democrats and secure the vote and prevent trouble. Deposit $10,000 to my credit with Kountze Brothers, Wall street." The sum of $8,000 was sent to Oregon, although there is no proof whatsoever that it was spent, let alone given to Cronin or Grover, who might well have been acting out of partisanship or ignorance of the law.[2]

To decide the matter of the disputed electoral votes from the four states Congress created an Electoral Commission, which decided that Hayes was entitled to them all and hence to the presidency. Grover, who had been elected to the United States Senate, was also scrutinized but was seated. In these two public investigations Oregon's politics became, for the first time since the statehood crisis, an object of national attention and some disgust.

II

While the two major parties were cementing an alliance between business and government, both state and local, and convincing the voters that their interests lay in assenting to this arrangement, there were occasional stirrings of protest. In the seventies and eighties the causes were economic as Oregon wheat became the chief staple export. The farmers of the Willamette Valley and eastern Oregon had little control over prices, and they blamed their inadequate income upon the transportation monopolies of the OSNC or of Ben Holladay or the Northern Pacific Railroad. Neither along the Willamette nor the Columbia they felt, was there effective competition and hence fair freight rates.

Beginning in 1872 local agriculturists met to form "farmers' clubs" that came into a state union in the following year. The thrust of these groups was to encourage farmers themselves to build steamboats and warehouses and to manufacture their own implements. A rival to the farmers clubs appeared simultaneously, the Grange, officially the Patrons of Husbandry, an offshoot of a national organization founded in 1867 in the East. The Oregon State Grange was born in 1873 and in the next year many of its members, although not the organization officially,

2. Philip W. Kennedy, "Oregon and the Disputed Election of 1876," *Pacific Northwest Quarterly* [hereafter cited *PNQ*] 60 (July 1969): 141.

joined with adherents of the farmers' clubs to organize a third party, the Independents, to run candidates for the legislature and for governor. In the elections of 1874 the Independents gained substantial strength in both the house and the senate although, for inexplicable reasons, they squandered their numerical strength when the legislature met and therefore translated none of their programs into law. The Independent party soon collapsed.

After this venture into political action farmers retreated from large-scale activism. What they did attempt was through the Grange, although its numbers were fewer in the eighties than in the previous decade. The Grange always demanded that the legislature adopt laws regulating passenger and freight rates and that Congress improve the navigable waterways of the region to provide an alternative to rail transportation. Grangers also organized some economic endeavors such as group marketing and purchasing ventures, but these efforts failed for lack of experience and capital. The organization did succeed in breaking down rural isolation through its social gatherings, and it advocated political rights for women in advance of other interest groups. But the chief importance of the Grange in Oregon history was to inaugurate and cherish the spirit of agrarian protest that became potent in the final fifteen years of the nineteenth century. In this crusade, as in the earlier Grange movement, Oregon imported its vehicles for reform.

By the late 1880s agricultural prices were still fluctuating wildly, although the usual drift was downward. Transportation companies remained unresponsive to the farmers' pleas for lower rates and improved service. Rates charged by grain elevators, often controlled by the railroads, were also believed to be unfair. In the cities, too, labor began to stir, and middle-class citizens of the professional and business classes became increasingly restive at the coalition of corporation with political boss and saloonkeeper. This combine delivered elections and government into the hands of machines dependent upon a "floating" vote of corrupt citizens who on election day moved from polling place to polling place voting repeatedly.

To take up arms against these conditions a Union party was

organized at Salem in 1889, about the same time as in other western states. The new party, composed of spokesmen of farmers, prohibitionists, and organized labor, pledged themselves to combat corporate monopolies and the liquor traffic. It provided the seedbed for the growth of the Oregon chapter of the Farmers Alliance and Industrial Union that had been organized in the South and Middle West in the late eighties. National and state alliance stood for the regulation of monopolies and a program of United States government loans to farmers at periods of low prices. In Oregon, although not nationally, the party supported prohibition. Although feared by many, the state alliance saw itself as restorative of older conditions, its platform preamble of 1891 declaring "that all monopolies are dangerous to the best interests of our country, tending to subvert and finally overthrow the great principles purchased by the fathers of American liberty." Pressures from the alliance and other reformers resulted in one important change in the machinery of government. Led by Edward W. Bingham, a Portland lawyer and sportsman (one of the first men to introduce largemouth bass to Oregon) who formed the Ballot Reform League, the state legislature passed a secret ballot law in 1891 that struck at the power of the boss and his "floating" voters.

In February 1892, the third national reform group began to develop its forces in Oregon. This was the People's party, better known as Populist, whose strength lay among the discontented farmers of the South and the Great Plains, and whose remedies for agricultural depression contained a thoroughgoing program of reform. The Populists advocated loans to farmers like the loans urged by the Alliance, nationalization of railroads and communications, a postal savings bank, the recapture by the government of federal lands granted to railroads, and inflationary monetary policies. As the nation plunged into depression in 1893 the Populist remedies gained attractiveness both nationally and in Oregon.

One convert to Populism was Sylvester Pennoyer, a Harvard graduate, who had served as mayor of Portland and gained both popularity and condemnation as a baiter of Chinese in the mid-1880s before being elected governor in 1889. Although a dema-

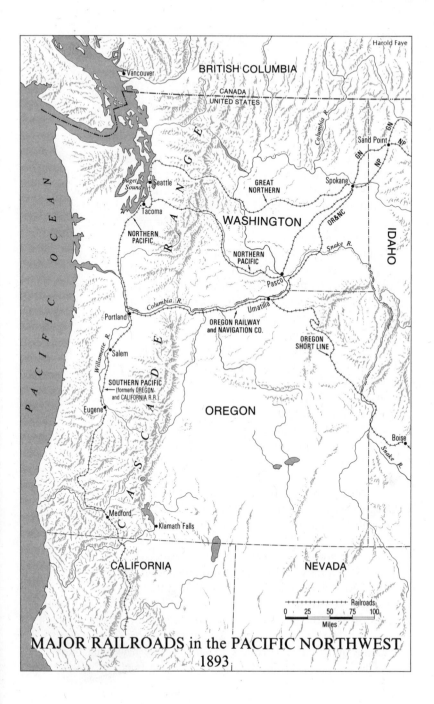

MAJOR RAILROADS in the PACIFIC NORTHWEST
1893

gogue, Pennoyer was also a man of acute mind (he had published three articles on economic questions in the prestigious *North American Review* between 1891 and 1893). His political astuteness was demonstrated by his switch to the Populist cause in time for re-election. As governor he became nationally famous for his disagreement with President Cleveland over monetary policies. Oregon's Populists supported the national program but also had a comprehensive reform program in Portland that included a free municipal boardinghouse for the unemployed. At the state level the Populists advocated free textbooks and a temperance law. They wanted Congress to finance government construction of a railroad along the north bank of the Columbia River to provide competition for the Northern Pacific.

The success of the Populists was mixed. Pennoyer gave active support to the cause by providing a pulpit for their views. The Populists elected some members to both houses of the legislature in 1892 and 1894. In the presidential contest of 1892 Oregon gave one of its electoral votes to James B. Weaver, the Populist candidate for president of the United States, making Oregon one of only six states where Weaver secured electoral votes. Populists were active in 1894 in the ranks of Jacob Coxey's "army" of the unemployed, which determined to march on Washington, D.C., to publicize its leader's demands for a public works program. The Oregon contingent of Coxey's force, which had a great deal of public sympathy, hijacked two eastbound freight trains but were stopped before leaving the state. Yet all of this activity was not translated into legislative achievement in Salem, and the Populists' principal legacy in Oregon was to keep the flame of reform alive, to publicize grievances, and to build a cadre of reformers that merged into the progressive movement that followed.

The failure of the Populists as an effective legislative force, even though they had some imaginative solutions for the gravest depression in national history to that time, was caused by the fact that they suffered splits in their own ranks, as did the Democrats, while the Republicans were temporarily able to paper over their controversies. The divisive issue for all three parties was the question of currency expansion and how best to obtain it. The Populists, in their early days in the East, favored cheap money created by federal coinage of large quantities of silver dollars—federal subsidies, in effect. Many Democrats and some Republicans also favored this particular Populist plank, although they could not accept the rest of the platform. Some Populists came to believe that they could turn this attitude to advantage and began to advocate "fusion" with members of other parties, that is, to advocate that Populists and Democrats (or even Republicans) nominate and support the same candidates for office on the silver plank. The fusion strategy had worked when both Populists and Democrats (the "Popocrats") had re-elected Governor Pennoyer in 1890, but fusion "stuck in the craw" of many Populists who feared that the abandonment of the balance of their platform was not worth the chance of gaining silver with Democratic aid. Many Democrats also feared that fusion would aid the Populists rather than their own party. In the Populist and Democratic ranks all over the nation this battle was fought and resolved in the electoral campaign of 1896.

At the national level the Populists and Democrats united in nominating for the presidency, on a silver plank without the other Populist measures, William Jennings Bryan, a former Democratic congressman from Nebraska. In the fall, however, in one of the closest and most exciting races in American history, William McKinley, the Republican candidate running on a single gold standard, was victorious. McKinley carried Oregon by only a few hundred votes, while Bryan won in the more progressive state of Washington and in silver-mining Idaho. In the two House races where the fusion strategy was employed, Republicans won the First District over a Democrat by 74 votes and the Second District against a Populist by 344 votes. The Populists also failed to capture control of the state legislature. Against the background of four years of severe depression and the worst harvest in forty-four years during the past summer, Oregon conservatism prevailed. Yet the cause of reform was not stilled, even with the return of prosperity in 1897.

III

The movement for reform in Oregon, born in Grangerism and developed in populism, reached fruition at the turn of the century in the progressive movement that produced the famous "Oregon System." Unlike earlier reformers, the progressives had an enormous faith that reason and morality could bring about changes in the political system. Progressives had a fervent hope that proper laws could remedy the baneful social and economic environment so that benign human energies could be released. In a newspaper interview the greatest of all Oregon's progressives, William S. U'Ren, proclaimed, "Things make men do bad things . . . conditions that can be changed." To free the citizens from corporation control the progressives believed that discovering the right set of political machinery would be the liberating force. The man who was certain he had come upon the correct instruments was William S. U'Ren.[3]

U'Ren was from Wisconsin, a blacksmith and lawyer who had migrated to Colorado and then to Hawaii in a vain search for improved health. When his health failed to improve in Honolulu he decided to return to the United States to die, arriving in Oregon in 1889, where he lived until his death in 1949. U'Ren was as tenacious of causes as he was of life (his niece reported that he looked "determined" even in his coffin) and sampled various crusades throughout his long career. A spiritualist, religious mystic, and disciple of the dietician Horace Fletcher ("never eat when you are sad or mad, only when you are glad"), U'Ren's intellectual searchings brought him to Henry George's *Progress and Poverty* in 1882. Written three years earlier, this influential work publicizing the single tax made U'Ren an instant convert: "I went just as crazy over the single tax as anyone else ever did. I knew I wanted the single tax, and that was about all I did know." The single tax was an economic panacea consisting of a confiscatory tax on unearned income or gain through speculation on land. George and his adherents contended that this measure alone would force speculators to disgorge their holdings and enable the landless American poor to acquire farms and homes in the traditional manner. Given a stake in society and freed from the serfdom imposed by indus-

3. Lincoln Steffens, *Upbuilders* (Seattle: University of Washington Press, 1968), p. 291.

trialism, the average citizen would recoup the freedom and dignity of an earlier era.[4]

U'Ren, soon after his arrival in Oregon, became a managing partner in the Lewelling nursery near Milwaukie, a position that, gave him entrée into the circle of high-minded reformers that gathered in the Lewelling home. Among the ideas discussed was another panacea, direct legislation, the plan to give the voters the constitutional authority to initiate laws and to have laws passed by the legislature referred to them. After a venture into Populist politics as a state representative, U'Ren decided to marry the single tax to direct legislation, for he became convinced that the corporation-controlled legislature would never adopt Henry George's reform without popular pressure. All his considerable political talents were put into the fight for the initiative and referendum.

By the late 1890s the elements for progressive reform in Oregon had coalesced. Earlier critics had challenged the old order. A great depression had just ended. The electorate had for years heard rumors of corrupt politics. A remedy and a leader were at hand. And the catalyst was a break in the ranks of the old guard. The Republican party in Oregon was sagging badly from years of internecine struggle when, in the spring of 1897, the time came to choose a United States senator. The Simon-Corbett wing of the party, as always, was at loggerheads with the Mitchell faction, but Mitchell's group itself was divided. Mitchell had been a silver Republican until the presidential campaign of 1896, when he had reluctantly endorsed McKinley on the gold standard platform. This decision alienated his most formidable ally, Jonathan Bourne. Now Mitchell's chances for re-election were compromised by Bourne's defection. Bourne himself had his eye on the speakership of the Oregon House of Representatives but lacked the necessary votes to secure the post.

U'Ren fished skillfully in these waters. Although theoretically committed to democracy and to rational persuasion, he "now

4. Esther G. Weinstein, "William Simon U'Ren: A Study of Persistence in Political Reform" (D. S. Sc. diss., Syracuse University, 1967), p. 5. Used with permission.

decided to get the reforms by using our enemies' own methods.'' The enemy of the machine now determined to use
ruthless methods to champion democracy. As a leader of the
Populists in the legislature U'Ren worked out a plan with
Bourne. Bourne would agree to support the initiative and referendum and to finance the room, board, and entertainment of
legislators who agreed to oppose Mitchell, since they would
draw no pay until the legislature organized (U'Ren himself got
$80). U'Ren for his part agreed to persuade enough senators and
representatives to absent themselves so that the legislature could
not be organized for lack of a quorum. Bourne rented quarters
in two hotels, he and the Mitchell force spent wildly, the local
banks ran out of hard money, and gold and silver had to be imported from Portland. Without organization of the legislature
Mitchell could not be elected senator. Of course, no one else
could be elected, and no laws could be passed, but in U'Ren's
mind these inconveniences were a small price to pay for the aid
of Bourne in the struggle for direct legislation. The strategy
worked and the legislative session of 1897 was never held.
U'Ren had deprived the people of one senator and a year's
laws, and he and his supporters had received money from the
wealthy Bourne, who was the attorney for the Southern Pacific
Railway. Reminders of these actions were hurled in U'Ren's
face thereafter, but he brazened it out. Other Oregon progressives also, for all their talk of the popular will, were not always
respectful of the citizenry. C. E. S. Wood, for one, had little
regard for the average voter: '' 'The mass of men will not study
a law which is of abstract interest, or of great length and legal
technicality . . . and therefore it seems to me the people will
not vote intelligently on any but clearcut, briefly stated questions.' '' [5] For the progressives the popular will had to be
guided.

In 1898 U'Ren formed a new organization to obtain the direct
legislation that would allow the people's will to emerge clearly
and decisively. This was the Direct Legislation League, and

5. Weinstein, "U'Ren," p. 23; James D. Barnett, *The Operation of the Initiative,*
Referendum, and Recall in Oregon (New York: Macmillan Co., 1915), p. 37.

through it, in a few years, U'Ren's political genius was able to achieve the constitutional amendments that gave the initiative and referendum. His task, although aided by the reform tradition, was formidable, for amendments to the basic law had to be adopted by two successive legislatures, and the legislature met only every other year. Amendments also had to be approved by the vote of the people. The constitution, indeed, had never been amended since its adoption in 1857.

U'Ren and his direct legislation advocates moved skillfully to overcome these barriers. They recognized the failures of the narrowly based reform movements of Grangers and Populists, which were largely agrarian in their composition, by adding to the farm coalition. City people wanted greater freedom from the control of the legislature. Suffragettes desired the vote and antiliquor interests, prohibition. Businessmen wanted better services from railroads, especially shippers who confronted a chronic shortage of boxcars. A speaker at a business convention in Eugene in 1906 denounced the president of the Union Pacific, which also controlled the Southern Pacific: "Mr. Harriman has money enough to buy up other railroads—then let him buy enough cars for Oregon shippers." Another speaker at the same meeting urged his fellow businessmen "to construct a financial club with which to batter the wizard of Wall Street." Believers in representative democracy advocated freedom from the old-line political conventions in which a small group of delegates ruled by controlling the proxy votes of absent members. The direct legislation cause thus added a potent urban constituency, including some very conservative men who supported it because they wanted to take money out of politics, to prevent more radical measures, to make legislation more difficult to enact, or simply because they thought it right or inevitable. Even Harvey Scott and John H. Mitchell, conservatives and implacable personal foes, supported U'Ren's amendments, as did the president of the state bar association, Stephen Cornell, and the bankers, William and Charles E. Ladd. U'Ren's tactics also fit into the cohesive, conservative spirit of the state. He was a persuader, not an arm twister, a reasoner, not a shouter, a man described by Lincoln Steffens as "slight of figure, silent in motion, he speaks softly, evenly, as he walks; and they call him therefore, the 'pussy cat.' '' [6]

U'Ren was also extraordinarily determined in pursuit of his objectives. Unlike many reformers he did not insist that all his remedies be enacted at once. He put nothing in the way of the cause, neither personal political ambition nor desire for fame, and he was not a partisan, although after the demise of the Populists he labelled himself a Republican. Nor did he refuse to work with people who had once opposed him or who continued to oppose him on other issues. He bore no grudges. As he himself once declared: "I'll do nothing selfish, dishonest, or dishonorable, but I'll trade off parties, offices, bills—anything for [the initiative and referendum.]" The Direct Legislation League sent out literature, provided speakers, and lobbied in Salem during legislative sessions. The fruits of the new constituency, of U'Ren's personal qualities, and of his tactics of persuasion were harvested initially in the 1899 legislative session when the initiative and referendum amendments passed in the house by a vote of 43 to 9 (with 8 absences) and in the senate 20 to 8 (with 2 absences). The next year came word that Utah and South Dakota had obtained direct legislation, and in 1901 the two amendments passed the legislature for the second and final time, unanimously in the house and 28 to 1 (with 1 absent) in the senate. The last hurdle was cleared in 1902 when the voters adopted the amendments by an overwhelming vote, 62,024 in favor and 5,668 opposed. [7]

Progressivism was spurred forward after the enactment of the Oregon System by sensational revelations concerning the misuse of federal land laws in Oregon. In 1900 a three-man Portland syndicate was formed to take advantage fraudulently of an enlightened measure of the national government, the Forest Reserve Act of 1897, designed to create timber reservations on the national domain. Under this law, when the reserves were created, previous owners of land within them could take other fed-

6. O. K. Burrell, "Shortages of Freight Cars an Old Problem in Oregon," *Oregon Business Review* 14 (September 1955): 4–5; Steffens, *Upbuilders,* p. 288.

7. Steffens, *Upbuilders,* p. 316.

eral lands as a substitute. The three Portlanders, Franklin P. Mays, Steven A. D. Puter, and Horace G. McKinley, in collusion with the Eugene branch of the United States Land Office, had prepared a series of fraudulent entries in remote portions of the state within the bounds of the potential Cascade Forest Reserve, lands which they anticipated exchanging for excellent timber stands after the reserve was proclaimed. The entries were approved by the General Land Office in Washington.

When their plan was exposed to special investigators of the Department of the Interior it had numerous unpleasant ramifications for Oregonians. President Roosevelt appointed a special prosecutor, the crusading San Francisco attorney Francis J. Heney, to handle the case. In time several cases were prepared and prosecuted (one before a jury "that would crucify Christ"), and by the time the affair ended in 1910 several cases concerning misuse of the public domain in Oregon had been brought to trial. As a result Senator Mitchell was convicted of accepting bribes to expedite fraudulent claims before the General Land Office by influencing the commissioner, Binger T. Hermann, an Oregonian and a Mitchellite. U. S. Rep. John N. Williamson and a Prineville employee of the General Land Office were both convicted of conspiracy to defraud the government. Three former state senators suffered the same fate, as did U. S. Attorney John Hall. Binger Hermann, by the vote of a single juror, escaped conviction.

The Oregon land fraud trials publicized policies toward natural resources and the conflict between America's old and new attitudes. One historian contends that the trials not only ended the grossest abuse of public land laws, but more positively helped form in the minds of the general public and federal officials such as President Roosevelt the conviction that conservation should be pushed aggressively. In a sense, then, nationwide publicity about Oregon politicians, both corrupt and honest, the Mitchells and Williamsons as well as the U'Rens and the Lewellings, fostered the American progressive movement.

Oregon's transformation from a corrupt state, unable to combat the power of corporations or other modern forces, to a commonwealth that so speedily adopted innovations in the machinery of its government, has called forth a multitude of explanations. The Swiss experience with direct legislation that was carried by immigrants to U'Ren's Oregon home of Milwaukie; the lack of an urban-rural cleavage in the state; the high level of literacy of the population; the provision for county use of the referendum in the original constitution are all sound explanations. One might also note that the nature of direct legislation was, as U'Ren often said, that of tools. The tools could be used to build or to destroy, or to build different legislative structures. Two conclusions follow from this fact. One is that the neutral nature of the tools appealed to both conservatives and reformers. The other is that the tools would be used by a cohesive people who, even in reform moods, were not radical. Neither their rhetoric nor their use of direct legislation was destructive of the existing order. Frederick G. Young, a political scientist at the University of Oregon, exemplified in his speeches and articles this progressive modernization of the old order. Young's faith in reason and the ability to learn from history led him to believe that the contemporary Oregonian, having inherited from his ancestors who crossed the overland trail the pioneer notions of liberty, equality, and democracy, could adapt their values to form a modern society characterized by a socially conscious rather than an excessively individualistic citizen. Young's faith in his contemporaries was such that he believed the modern Oregonian, like his pioneer ancestor, would play the role of "the most representative American of his time." [8] U'Ren, too, in his advocacy of direct legislation was employing new devices, although even they were imports from other states, for an old purpose, the restoration of the family farm and the small business via the single tax.

Once equipped with direct legislation the voters of Oregon used it repeatedly in the fifteen years after 1902 to attempt to restrain the powers of corporations and to improve the lot of working people. The various constituencies of progressivism had something to show in this legislative harvest. Farmers and

8. Quoted in George A. Frykman, "Frederic G. Young, Regionalist and Historian," *PNQ* 48 (April 1957): 36.

small businessmen obtained a railroad commission, road legislation, and laws regulating banks; organized labor secured a child
labor law, a minimum wage law, a statute regulating the hours
and conditions of female labor, and a workmen's compensation
act; small businessmen approved the banking and railroad legislation and a statute scrutinizing securities issues; middle-class
urbanities got home rule for cities; people of integrity of all
groupings gained a responsive government. Yet the people were
not—either through direct legislation or their elected representatives—prone to measures requiring expensive appropriations
or those destructive of the existing system. Their changes were
remedial, not radical.

Indeed, Oregonians continued to be as fascinated with further
changing the machinery of government after 1902 as they were
with adopting social and economic legislation. To further this
aspect of reform the Direct Legislation League, reshaped into
the People's Power League in 1905, pushed for the direct primary and for the popular election of United States senators.
U'Ren drafted the direct primary law, but he drew upon the experiences of Minnesota, Maryland, and Wisconsin in preparing
it. Supported by all groups it passed with ease. More controversial was the attempt to acquire for the voters the right to elect
directly their United States senators. Under the American Constitution the election of senators lay in the hands of the state
legislatures, which meant that in effect powerful and well-
organized interests assumed this sovereign power. Reformers
around the nation were interested in giving the people the right
to elect directly their senators either by amending the federal
Constitution or by some mode of circumventing it, and in
Oregon the People's Power League adopted the second alternative in devising what became known as "Statement Number
One." The league persuaded the legislature to draw up a law
that included the names of candidates for the United States
Senate so that voters could express their preference for the office. At the same election the state legislative candidates were
asked whether they promised, if elected, to vote for the winner
of the preferential primary ("Statement Number One") or if
they would use their own personal preference ("Statement

Number Two"). The first test of the new law came in 1906 when U'Ren managed Jonathan Bourne's campaign for the United States Senate. Bourne's wealth made possible the use of a direct mail campaign, an innovation that, along with other expenditures, cost $50,000. Victorious in the primary and general election campaigns, Bourne awaited the vote of the legislature in the spring of 1907. The legislature, without cavilling, chose him to become the first United States senator elected in conformity to the popular majority. This triumph was the highwater mark of U'Ren's influence, for the people would not follow him into more fundamental reforms. In 1909 U'Ren drew up a constitutional amendment that drastically reshaped the governmental structure of the state, but the people were not ready for six-year terms for governor and members of the state legislature; for annual legislative sessions; and for awarding the governor the power to appoint all state officials, including sheriffs and district attorneys. They defeated U'Ren's amendment for a more centralized government by a substantial margin.

The great irony of U'Ren's career, however, was his failure to persuade the people of Oregon to adopt the single tax. He began serious work for this project in 1909 when he met with board members of the Joseph Fels Fund Commission. This group was a project of the wealthy Philadelphia soap (Fels-Naptha) manufacturer, Joseph Fels, like U'Ren a devotée of Henry George. The Fels commissioners and U'Ren agreed that Oregon would be a likely place to enact the single tax, and from 1910 to 1914 the fund poured thousands of dollars into Oregon to secure the adoption of this measure. Success came only in 1910 when an amendment permitting the single tax at the county level was adopted. The Fels money helped publicize this innovation, but the fundamental reason that it passed was that it was stated in a duplicitous manner so that the voter had no idea for what he was voting. The first words of the amendment read: "No poll or head tax shall be levied or collected in Oregon." The poll tax had several years earlier been repealed anyway, but few remembered that and few read on to the other sections of the amendment. When charged with mendacity, U'Ren responded: "I never went hunting deer with a brass band." When the measure was exposed in 1912 it was repealed, and the single tax failed of re-enactment in 1914, 1916, 1920, and 1922, when the long struggle was abandoned.[9]

In 1912 U'Ren and the People's Power League not only lost the single tax but they sustained two other defeats. One was the campaign to re-elect Senator Bourne. Bourne had strong opposition in the Republican primary from Benjamin Selling of Portland, a contender who elicited an unusual response from men ostensibly dedicated to clean government. Bourne paid U'Ren the sum of $500 to hire a firm of private detectives to gather evidence charging Selling with failure to report campaign contributions. The results were not conclusive, but U'Ren was undaunted: "Although no formal charge was made, it was hoped that the publicity would cost Selling votes." U'Ren's troubles were compounded when he and Bourne, the great advocates of rule by the citizens, refused to accept Selling's primary victory and decided to mount an independent campaign in the fall general election, a stratagem for which they were denounced by some within the People's Power League, including C. E. S. Wood. Neither Bourne nor Selling, but the Democratic candidate, Harry Lane, won the election. The final blow for U'Ren in his disastrous year of 1912 was the defeat of another of his proposals to reorganize drastically the state government. Two years later he ran for governor and finished third.[10]

Another influence of the progressive movement on state politics lay in the realm of parties and party government. The elected leaders of the Oregon reform movement were George Chamberlain, Oswald West, and Harry Lane. All were Democrats in a Republican state, but their elections indicated that the voters were now prepared to support the candidate rather than the ticket. Chamberlain was governor (1903–1909) and United States senator (1909–1921). West was governor from 1909 to 1915, and Lane was mayor of Portland (1909–1913) and United States senator (1913–1917). The nonpartisan tradition of Oregon politics that continues to the present began in this era when the voters realized that in a cohesive state the need for powerful

---

9. Robert C. Woodward, "William Simon U'Ren: In An Age of Protest" (Master's thesis, University of Oregon, 1956), p. 114.

10. Woodward, "U'Ren," p. 146.

parties to represent specific interests was far less strong than the requirement to adjust politics to the social needs of the industrial era.

The years of the rise and fall of the People's Power League were also years of progressive reform in municipal government. In Portland the city had been long bossed by Walter F. "Jack" Matthews, who organized the business interests in support of friendly politicians for the mutual benefit of each. "All politics," he said, "are selfish; therefore politics is mere selfishness." A shy and secretive man who never permitted interviews and who became enraged at being photographed, Matthews did not even list his name in the city directory or the telephone book. An easy master, Matthews ruled by persuasion, resembling U'Ren in that sense, and by providing politicians the wherewithal and strategy for victory. The facade for Matthews and for the Portland machine was the venerable George H. Williams, his venality and misjudgment on the national scene forgotten. Behind Williams's distinguished appearance the city lay in the grip of business interests, gamblers, and thugs, all of whom obtained their special requirements from a complacent city hall vigilant only to extract its payment in money and votes. Williams was first elected mayor in 1902 at the age of seventy-nine, the oldest mayor in the country. Although there were some achievements during his administration, such as the creation of a full-time fire department and the improvement of streets and sewers, Williams and his cronies became notorious as sponsors of gambling dens and houses of prostitution (one of the last, painted a flamboyant scarlet, was anchored in the Willamette River), whose proprietors were levied upon by the city periodically as a valued source of revenue. Although supported by the vice business, the old guard Republicans, and the *Oregonian,* Williams also had a legion of enemies who included the clergy, church members, and progressive businessmen who fought him on the grounds of religious morality or municipal efficiency.[11]

---

11. Scrapbook 261, Oregon Historical Society, Portland, Oregon, p. 142. Used with permission.

For a time the champions of reform in the city found a leader in the unlikely person of Harry Lane, who defeated Williams for mayor in 1905 and was re-elected in 1907. The grandson of Joseph Lane, the new mayor was a physician, mushroom hunter, bird watcher, and a man of courage and humor. Although he was caricatured by his opponents in his first campaign as one who would "make a mushroom bed out of the city park and build little houses up in the trees for people to live in," he had substantial support from middle-class business and professional people. Their progressive creed was articulated in the pages of the new *Oregon Daily Journal,* founded in 1902 and published by the crusading journalist, Charles S. "Sam" Jackson, who had launched earlier the *Pendleton East Oregonian.*

Once elected, Lane and his police force had considerable success in enforcing city ordinances against prostitution and gambling. As ex-officio chairman of the city water board he was able to persuade its members to reduce the municipal water rates, although the city council defeated his plan to establish a sinking fund to redeem the city's debt. Lane reformed the police department and refused to create needless jobs for patronage plums. Although less vigorous and successful leaders, two later mayors, Allen G. Rushlight (1912) and Harry R. Albee (1913–1917), also carried forward the fight for honest government. Albee was the first mayor to serve under the commission form of government, a typical progressive device that replaced the old councilmanic ward system when reformers instituted a new city charter in 1912. Lane himself was elected to the United States Senate in 1913 on the basis of his municipal achievements.

The progressive movement in Oregon was not confined to altering the machinery of government or cleaning up state and local politics. Perhaps its most important contribution, arising from its basic philosophy of faith in human reason and the innate morality of persons, was the expansion of the state's constituency by the adoption of woman suffrage. Although woman suffrage was a progressive crusade in the sense that it was achieved in the era bearing that label, women's participation in civic life in Oregon had a long history.

In the famous Oregon Donation Land Act of 1850 Congress granted wives as much land as husbands. At various times the legislature had expanded the political rights of women. In 1866 married women obtained the right to own personal or real property in their own name and six years later acquired the right to sue and be sued. Women twenty-one years or older who were taxpayers gained the franchise in school elections in 1878 (in 1889 all women with school-age children were included) and women were admitted to the practice of law in 1885. The powerful farm lobby, the Oregon State Grange, had often taken positions favorable to the increasing participation of women in public life. In 1881 the Grange passed a general resolution declaring that women must have equality "where their interests are concerned." In 1882 it favored equal treatment for women in the settlement of estates and the guardianships of minors, and in the same year it declared for suffrage for women taxpayers and their right to serve on school boards. In 1889 it asked that the governor appoint women to the board of Oregon Agricultural College, now Oregon State University.

The moving figure in the long struggle to obtain woman suffrage in Oregon was a pioneer of the overland migration of 1852, Abigail Scott, who had crossed in a wagon train at the age of seventeen. In Oregon she married a farmer, Benjamin Duniway, whose life was dogged by financial misjudgments and by accident and ill-health. Much of the burden of family support accordingly fell upon Abigail's competent shoulders (her mother had died on the Oregon Trail) and she established herself as a milliner and as a newspaper publisher in Oregon. Publishing was not just a vocation for Abigail Duniway but a means for political reform. Her first interest in public affairs had been the temperance cause but, like U'Ren, she had turned to a means, woman suffrage in her case, to reach her original objective. In time she abandoned her first goal because it was interfering with the realization of the second.

In 1871, after the family's move to Portland from Albany, Abigail Duniway began to publish the *New Northwest*. Although the paper contained news of general interest, its focus was on the cause of woman suffrage, and the Duniways, for husband and six children also worked on the paper, made it the most influential organ of the cause in the Pacific Northwest. The year 1871 also brought a second significant political experience to Abigail Duniway when she accompanied the famed reformer Susan B. Anthony on a three-month speaking tour of the Northwest. The tour was indeed more valuable for Duniway than Anthony, who had small audiences and mixed reviews. For her part Duniway gained from the tour not only the reputation as the foremost suffragette in the region but also a plethora of new ideas, some money for the cause, and additional subscriptions for the *New Northwest*. The interest base provided by the newspaper enabled Duniway to institutionalize her cause in the formation of the Multnomah County Woman Suffrage Association in 1873 and the Oregon State Woman Suffrage Association founded two years later. Yet her preparations were of greatest impact in Washington Territory and Idaho rather than in her home state.

On their tour in 1871 Anthony and Duniway had organized a Woman Suffrage Association in Washington Territory, and Duniway had pushed for woman suffrage bills in Olympia in 1873 and 1875 and at the state constitutional convention in 1878 but without immediate success. In 1883 Washington adopted woman suffrage only to repeal it four years later when men became convinced that it was being used for the cause of prohibition. This reaction was an important influence in Duniway's subsequent political strategy for it marked the end of her personal advocacy of prohibition. In 1872 she had declared: "Women must have a chance to vote, and legislate whiskey hells out of existence," but now her political pragmatism forced her to repudiate the prohibitionists as liabilities.[12]

In Idaho Duniway became almost an institution in the suffrage campaign. She paid her first visit to the state in 1876 and

---

12. The quotations on woman suffrage are from Abigail Scott Duniway, *Path Breaking: An Autobiographical History of the Equal Suffrage Movement in Pacific Coast States* (New York: Source Book Press, 1975), pp. 192, 157, 236, 114, 162, 238; T. A. Larson, "Home Rule on the Range," in *Western American History in the Seventies,* ed. Daniel Tyler (Fort Collins, Colo.: Robinson Press, Inc., 1973), p. 81; and Larson, "The Woman Suffrage Movement in Washington," *PNQ* 67 (April 1976): 54, 56, 59.

returned frequently to speak. She also contributed periodically to the Idaho campaign through her suggestions in the pages of the *New Northwest*. The climax of her Idaho career came in 1887 when she addressed the constitutional convention, but she continued to work in the state until 1895, although she founded no suffrage organization there as she did in Washington and Oregon. In the nineteen years of her Idaho itinerancy Duniway gave 140 public lectures and travelled 12,000 miles in addition to distributing 500,000 copies of the *New Northwest*.

In Oregon the woman suffrage cause had moved slowly until the 1890s. It had been linked with the Women's Christian Temperance Union since 1883, but by 1890 the two causes were split since Duniway broke with the temperance forces. Not only was she impressed with the loss of woman suffrage in Washington because of the fear that it would lead to temperance, but she herself was afraid that the temperance people would form a third party if women gained the right to vote. This was particularly abhorrent, for Duniway was an ardent supporter of the Republican party and feared that a third party would cut into its support. Finally she became less and less certain of her Christian faith with the passing years and less confident of the moral underpinnings of a Christian organization. In time she turned her considerable sarcasm against the prohibitionists, assailing them as women who "had never lifted voice or finger to secure their right to vote, but had often sat in the sanctuary singing 'Where Is My Wandering Boy Tonight,' when the little hoodlum was kicking up a rumpus at my suffrage meetings."

Out of the wreckage of the old alliance Duniway organized the Oregon State Equal Suffrage Association in 1894. The association in Oregon immediately went to work using methods of quiet persuasion, what Duniway called a "still hunt," among the legislators. The woman suffrage amendment passed the legislature in 1895 and 1898 but the electorate defeated it by some 2,000 votes in 1900. After the initiative became law the Equal Suffrage Association took advantage of this process to put the suffrage question on the ballot in 1906, 1908, 1910, and in 1912, when victory was finally attained.

The campaign for woman suffrage, in both its arguments and

tactics, is a model of Oregon progressivism. The cause was couched in typical terms for Oregon reform, and the appeal of Abigail Duniway and the OESA seemed certain to gain ultimate, if slow success, for it avoided "fanatical" arguments while it echoed traditional appeals. Duniway took care that the cause could not be branded as advocacy of prohibition. She frequently admitted publicly the harm prohibitionists had done to the suffrage cause in nearby Washington and took care to disassociate her Oregon work from the WCTU. She also repeatedly insisted that woman suffrage would not bring about a revolution between the sexes and place men in leading strings to "man-hating," revengeful women ("Show me a woman who doesn't like men, and I will show you a sour-souled, vinegar-visaged specimen of unfortunate femininity, who owes the world an apology for living in it at all"). Her own happy family life, her success as wife and mother, also gave credibility to her insistence that the ballot would not cause women to forsake the home and compete economically with men. Indeed, she seemed to accept in part the argument of many conservative opponents of woman suffrage, that there were innate psychological differences between men and women, when she declared: "The home instinct is inherent in woman, and cannot be created or destroyed by laws of men's or women's making." After her earlier flirtation with prohibition, Duniway and her forces shied away from the advocacy of woman suffrage as the means to any forms of sumptuary legislation. In other words, the Oregon suffragists did not hold out the hope that votes for women would purify politics or regenerate society, as was the cry in other areas.

What Duniway and the OESA did advocate was the right to vote as one of the traditional American ideals. In the 1899 campaign, for example, Oregon suffragettes sent an appeal to each legislator, "basing it wholly upon the fundamental right of self-government, that inheres in the individual, which the Declaration of Independence and the Constitution of the United States had taught us to revere." In Oregon the woman suffrage appeal was mainly to principle: one student has shrewdly noted that the eastern suffragette advanced her cause by arguing that women's votes could be used to protect Anglo-Saxon institutions against the immigrant hordes now coming to America from central and eastern Europe. Given Oregon's cohesive population such an appeal would have been meaningless.

Not only did the woman suffrage movement appeal to the past but also to the conservative experience of other states. "Women," Duniway declared, "under normal conditions, are evolutionists, and not revolutionists, as is shown by their conduct, as voters, in Wyoming, Colorado, Utah, and Idaho." Yet at the same time Duniway avoided the dangerous waters of overreliance upon assistance from outside the state. Her lesson had been learned in the campaign for the initiative in 1906 when the OESA allowed the cause to be directed by officers of the National American Woman Suffrage Association, which conducted a campaign marked by ballyhoo and noise and resulted in a convincing defeat. Even earlier, in her Idaho work, Duniway had been wary of eastern suffragettes, calling them "invaders" and "leeches," a suspicion that caused them to regard her as a prima donna who was, in Susan B. Anthony's words, "amply sufficient not only unto herself, but unto the whole state of Oregon as well." Carrie Chapman Catt was blunter: "Mrs. Duniway is a jealous minded and dangerous woman." By 1906 Duniway was assailing the new president of NAWSA, Anna Howard Shaw (whose name she invariably spelled "Pshaw"), as a "liar" and threatening her with court action if she came to Oregon. In the end it seems that Duniway got the better of the argument, for her undoubted fame in American woman suffrage came from her quiet and effective methods in Idaho, Washington, and Oregon.

Oregon obtained woman suffrage two years later than Washington and Idaho. The state was conservative in taking its time to adopt the reform, but when it did occur, as in the case of the Oregon System, it came with the support of all elements of the citizens. Men and women, rural and urban, rich, middling, and poor, supported the cause in 1912. They found it to be based on principle, threatening to no group, and presented with quiet conservative techniques under the leadership of an independent but not radical woman, a successful wife and mother, who was a veteran of the Oregon Trail. As Solomon Hirsch, stalwart Mitchellite and political spoilsman, declared in 1908: "I am naturally conservative, but I advocate woman suffrage because it is right."

The movements for the Oregon System and for woman suffrage are characteristic of the progressive period in Oregon. Both reforms were instrumental, not substantial. They were based upon broad principles rather than small single-interest groups. They were threatening to no large group but were potentially useful to all groups. They passed with a relative lack of passion and ill will because they were guided by men and women who understood the cohesive nature of Oregon society and its tradition of quiet change. Once in force, the instruments were used to adjust tradition to contemporary forces so long as the changes made were adjustments, not radical alterations. When radical change was pushed, it either failed or lasted only for a short time. Prohibition, nationalization of railroads, and drastic restructuring of the form of state government were too advanced for Oregon progressives, and U'Ren went to his grave advocating the single tax in vain.

A failure to understand the nature of Oregon progressivism characterized Americans at the time and to some extent subsequently. Certainly direct legislation and the work of Abigail Duniway were nationally known through the work of journalists and politicians who made pilgrimages to Oregon. The adoption of direct legislation became nationally known as "the Oregon System" (somewhat inaccurately, since South Dakota had the initiative and referendum in 1897 and Utah in 1900) and the state's governmental experiments were its principal political influence upon the United States. Oregon received an enormous amount of publicity in books, pamphlets, and, above all, in the crusading, "muckraking" as they were called, journals of the day where the state was labelled as one "Where the People Rule"; "the Home of Direct Legislation"; "the Most Complete Democracy in the World"; and a "Political Experiment Station." Perhaps the most laudatory of all appraisals was by the greatest of the "muckrakers," Lincoln Steffens. In *American Magazine,* in March 1908, appeared an article, "U'Ren, The

Law Giver,'' that Steffens later republished in a book on American reformers entitled *Upbuilders*. Steffens wrote effusively in delineating U'Ren's moral character and his political astuteness, but he also asserted that the Oregonian had an influence far beyond his state. ''They call this man,'' said Steffens, ''the Father of the Initiative and Referendum in Oregon, but that title isn't big enough. U'Ren has fathered other Oregon laws, and his own state isn't the limit of his influence.''

In another, more concrete, sense Oregon came to national attention via the federal court system when the constitutionality of one of its social laws was challenged. This statute was one passed in 1903 that limited the hours of women in factories and laundries to ten hours per day. On a September day in 1905 Mrs. Edward Gotcher was required by her employer, the Grand Laundry of Portland, to work more than the legal maximum. The owner of the laundry, Curt Muller, was convicted under the statute and his conviction was upheld by the Oregon Supreme Court. He appealed to the United States Supreme Court, contending that the law restricted the liberty of women to make contracts, constituted class legislation, and was an unlawful use of the police powers of the state.

At the time Muller appealed the case it became an object of concern to a national organization, the National Consumers League, which was dedicated to social welfare causes, especially protective labor legislation for women and children. The leaders of this group, the renowned Florence Kelley and Josephine Goldmark, sought a distinguished counsel to defend the Oregon law and determined to persuade Goldmark's brother-in-law, Louis D. Brandeis, to take the case. Brandeis was one of the nation's most distinguished reformers, a Boston attorney who had a great reputation as an opponent of industrial and transportation monopolies. Brandeis agreed to accept the case on two conditions: that he represent the state and not the league and that the league staff gather data for him on the effect of long working hours on women employees. With both conditions met, Brandeis then drew up a remarkable brief in arguing the ten-hour law in the Supreme Court.

His task was to show the court that it was reasonable for the state to limit the hours of working women even though such regulation restricted their freedom to work as many hours as they chose. The task was difficult because in the Lochner case (1905) the court had ruled unconstitutional a New York ten-hour law for men and women employees. Brandeis had to gather data that proved women's health, but not necessarily that of men, suffered by long hours of labor. With the aid of the Consumers League, Brandeis presented a unique brief, so seminal a document that it thereafter was known simply as the "Brandeis brief." His argument devoted only two pages to matters of constitutional law and judicial precedents, but more than 100 pages dealt with legislation, foreign and domestic, and with more than ninety reports of various agencies from all over the world, the bulk of which concluded that woman's physical constitution made her uniquely susceptible to dangers from long hours of employment.

The Supreme Court accepted the Brandeis arguments in unanimously upholding the constitutionality of the Oregon law. The Brandeis brief, in its use of economic and sociological data, was the first occasion where overwhelming emphasis was placed upon other than constitutional arguments before the Supreme Court. It became an enormously important precedent for courts in assisting them to adjust the law to changing economic and social realities. Although the immediate effect of the Brandeis brief in American constitutional law should not be exaggerated, for it took some time for Brandeis's educational work to be fully accepted by jurists, the Muller case did call national attention to Oregon's progressive spirit.

Yet it must be remembered that the forces of conservatism, even reaction, were still powerful in these years. In Portland, for example, the progressive mayoralty of Harry Lane was followed by the long regime of George L. Baker. Baker built upon his connections and enormous popularity as a theater impresario to become leader of the Fourth Ward, the largest in the city, where he operated in the conventional and time-honored manner of the political boss. Ubiquitous, handsome, and gregarious ("Fraternal affiliations are the finest things a man can make. I attribute all my success to the contacts made in these"), Baker distributed patronage jobs and other favors to the poor. He also ingratiated himself with the middle class by his showmanship—he led the annual Rose Parade—and by his public displays of puritanical virtue (he once protested at a meeting a speaker's use of the word *virginity:* ''Mr. Chairman, I object to the use of this insidious word in the presence of women''). In 1915 the Fourth Ward elected him to the city council, where he became commissioner of public affairs; his sole platform in the campaign was a promise to reinstate the city hall janitor, a drunken incompetent, but a Civil War veteran who had been dismissed by the previous reform administration. Baker made good on his promise and then embarked on a program of public entertainment, spending on municipal band concerts, bathing beaches, rifle ranges, and golf courses. In 1917 his endeavors paid off with his election to the position of mayor, which he held until 1933.

The chief issue in the mayoralty campaign of 1917 typified the decline of progressivism and its faith in reason and human nature. Baker and his opponent, William H. Daly, clashed over an ordinance on the ballot aimed at unions and at the Industrial Workers of the World. The measure would have made it almost impossible to boycott, picket, or display a banner in any labor dispute without running the danger of a conspiracy conviction. Daly, the candidate of organized labor, seemed to be the favorite to win the race as an opponent of the anticonspiracy ordinance, but several days before the election his house was ransacked; then the *Oregonian* published on the eve of the election Daly's application to join the Socialist party, an application made out in 1910. In the wartime years any identification with socialism was fatal, for the party opposed the war effort. Baker won the race by a little more than one thousand votes and was triumphantly re-elected thereafter, his alliance with business, the *Oregonian,* and the Republican machine solidified.

At the state level, also, progressivism failed to survive the 1910s. When the Republican party failed to nominate Theodore Roosevelt for president in 1912, he and his supporters walked out of the Chicago convention and formed the Progressive or ''Bull Moose'' party with Roosevelt as the candidate. The party stood for increased governmental regulation of industry and greater structural changes in the national government (e.g., the recall of judicial decisions) than advocated by Woodrow Wilson, the Democrat, or by the incumbent Republican, William Howard Taft. In Oregon, under the leadership of disgruntled Republicans, the Progressives marched under the same banner of reason, integrity, and individual and public morality that had characterized the campaigns for direct legislation, woman suffrage, and social and economic legislation.

But the limits of progressive accomplishment had been reached in the state by 1912. The two-party tradition remained adequate for the mass of the voters. Indeed the Oregon Progressive party never adopted a state platform and instead concentrated upon its efforts to elect Roosevelt. In so doing its members were handicapped by the fact that they had seemingly deserted the Oregon System by not supporting the winning candidates in the Republican primary. Tarred as hypocrites, their campaign did not stir the voters' interest, and Wilson carried the state. Two years later the party candidates for governor and United States senator were beaten, and in 1916 the state Progressives, like those nationally, returned to the ranks of the two older parties. Indeed, many wondered why they had ever left, for most progressive Oregonians were satisfied to provide the balance of power within and between the Democratic and Republican parties, to endorse such men as Oswald West, George Chamberlain, and Harry Lane, rather than to support a more radical third party. To win the voters' support progressives, with or without the capital *P*, had to be bipartisan, reasonable, and, paradoxically, relatively conservative. By the time of American entry into the world war in 1917 Oregon progressives, for the most part, were satisfied with their work.

When war broke out Oregonians supported it overwhelmingly. By every measurable index, from the purchase of war bonds to the rate of voluntary enlistment, the state's contribution to the war effort was in the first rank. Qualitatively, too, Oregonians supported the cause wholeheartedly, as the emotionalism and violence of war ended, at least temporarily, the progressive dream of a world of reason and morality. Those who did not endorse the war, or even the specific programs of the Wilson administration, were pilloried. Anything smacking of the German cause, indeed even of Germany, became anathema: the streets of Portland with German names such as Rhine or Bismarck were altered to those of American or Allied military leaders. A Portland clergyman proclaimed: "There is no place on the top side of American soil for a Pacifist. . . . There is no room in this country for a Pacifist. If you have one, shoot him." Mayor Baker and the press demanded the dismissal of M. Louise Hunt, a young employee of the Multnomah County Library in Portland, for her refusal to buy war bonds on account of her pacifist convictions. Although the members of the library board, principally composed of conservative professional and business men, refused to do so ("the right to one's own conscientious opinion is the very foundation of human freedom"), Hunt resigned and left the state. Criminal syndicalism laws were passed to combat the antiwar activities of the IWW and the Socialist party, and several prosecutions were instituted under them, although few convictions were secured. So far had the spirit of harmony and the hope of progress disintegrated since the bright morning of the Oregon System.[13]

13. Annette H. Bartholomae, "A Conscientious Objector: Oregon, 1918," *Oregon Historical Quarterly* 71 (September 1970): 220, 227.

6

People and Politics (1920–1970)

N the last half-century the people of Oregon have modified but not discarded their major political, economic,
and social characteristics derived from earlier historical
eras. That Oregonians have survived international wars, a global
depression, and enormous cultural changes without drastic modi-
fications of their traditional patterns is a tribute to the tenacity
with which they are devoted to moderate conservatism. They
continue to accommodate themselves to change but not to welcome it.

I

Oregon's ethnic composition has remained fundamentally homogeneous, and the state's historic social prejudice has not
prevented nonwhites from gaining greater material advantages,
legal rights, and cultural respect, especially in the years after the
Second World War. The majority Caucasian group that had
grown enormously in the late nineteenth century and at the turn
of the century was reinforced by the defense workers of the First
World War whose motive for migrating, economic advancement, and whose geographical background, southern and western, were the same as those who had preceded them and those
who would come in the 1920s. In the Great Depression, how-

ever, the white immigrant participated in an experience that was unique.

By the middle of the 1930s thousands of farmers and urbanites, mainly from the northern Great Plains region, were driven by depressed economic conditions, which in the case of agriculture reached back into the twenties, to seek homes in the Pacific Northwest. Although far less publicized than those who departed from Missouri, Arkansas, and Oklahoma, perhaps because they had no John Steinbeck to write about them, their numbers were larger and their fate, in some respects, was similar to those of the "Arkies" and the "Okies" of *The Grapes of Wrath*.

Like their predecessors, the depression migrants were seeking economic opportunity in Oregon, preferably in the agricultural life that was familiar to them. They were not seekers of adventure, rootless drifters, or individuals drawn by an aesthetic appreciation of the Northwest's natural environment. They were white, literate, family members who accepted the American social and economic system. But they were different too. Most came within a very short span, 1935–1937; they had little luck in finding a prosperous farm and had to take urban jobs, if any; and, above all, their reception, in its chilling unwelcome, was unlike the fate of their Caucasian predecessors who had been almost invariably regarded as economic and cultural assets to a developing region. Now the migrants seemed to threaten the old residents who perceived the newcomers as competitors for scarce jobs, as sources of increased taxation for relief, and as socially dangerous malcontents. Although Oregonians never emulated Californians in using violence against the migrants or in passing laws forbidding the entry of indigents, there was a great deal of grumbling that dissipated only with the absorption of the unemployed into the armed services or defense plants after Pearl Harbor.

The Second World War brought thousands of Caucasian migrants to Portland. In the twelve months after American entry into the war 160,000 new workers, mainly white, came to the Portland area, most for shipyard employment. The major defense firm, the Kaiser Corporation, desperate to recruit labor, had advertised throughout the country for war workers. The response came from throughout the nation and special trains, called "Kaiser Specials," brought many of the shipyard employees. Perhaps the most remarkable contribution, at least in numbers, was made by the John H. Braukmiller family from Iowa, whose twenty-five members included fifteen who worked on the graveyard shift at Kaiser's Swan Island yard.

After the war the population of Oregon continued to rise at a higher percentage than the national rate, mainly stimulated by migration of Caucasians. These migrants tended to resemble the bulk of previous white residents, although their income and educational levels were somewhat higher. Many of the new Oregonians of this era were employees of the so-called "footloose" industries, those not located because of the proximity of raw materials or cheap transportation and therefore free to select their sites, subject to the availability of skilled labor. Although most of these most recent immigrants came for economic gain, and were thus traditional, the social and economic amenities of the state were also powerful pulling factors in their decision to migrate.

In their reasons for leaving their old homes the post–Second World War Oregonians also differed from their predecessors. No longer simply economic misfortune, but social problems such as urban crime, pollution, and educational decay drove them from their former places of residence. And, ironically, their very migration to "unspoiled" Oregon has put greater pressure not only upon natural resources, but also upon social services, as the affluent and well-educated newcomers demand power boats, vacation homes, air conditioning, and additional schools. Their demands and their increasing numbers cause the old guard to turn against them in a manner reminiscent of the antimigrant hostility of the Great Depression, so that neither skin color, economic competence, educational level, nor affluence can secure the newest immigrants against the derision, scorn, and fear of the older citizens.

If the fortune of the new Caucasians has changed markedly for the worse in the last thirty-five years, that of the Japanese and Japanese Americans has undergone the opposite transformation. During and after the First World War anti-Japanese sentiment began to intensify in Oregon in various portions of the state and to take the form of pressure upon the legislature. The Caucasian citizens of Klamath Falls became panic-stricken at the rumor that thirty or forty Japanese planned to acquire farms in the area. Near Redmond in Deschutes County a plan by local people and George Shima, "the potato king," to raise seed for Shima's California farms led to the "potato affair." Although the work on Shima's Oregon enterprise was to be done by Caucasians, the Deschutes County Farm Bureau passed resolutions against the rumored introduction of "several thousand Japanese tenants." The project was dropped.

The town of Hood River was the site of the most virulent prejudice and was the source of both state and national legislation reflecting it. In 1917, it will be remembered, a local attorney and legislator, George Wilbur, introduced a bill prohibiting aliens ineligible for citizenship from owning land in Oregon. Pressure from the American State Department, which feared the consequence of this assault upon Japan's national honor, forced Wilbur to withdraw it. California influence was present, for not only had that state passed an alien land law in 1913, but after the war it had begged Oregon to adopt a similar statute so that California bigotry would not stand alone in the nation's eyes. In 1919 Hood River citizens organized the Anti-alien League to obtain both the land law and a federal law barring further immigration of Japanese aliens. In 1923 the Oregon legislature passed the alien land law. The Hood River post of the newly formed American Legion persuaded the national convention of the veterans' organization to pass a resolution calling for Japanese exclusion. Aided by similar pressure from California and Washington, Japanese exclusion was adopted in the immigration law of 1924.

In the aftermath of this brief era of prejudice the Japanese of Oregon moved ahead economically in the 1920s and suffered with the rest of the population in the depression years. Children of immigrants now were not only Americans, since they were born in the United States, but increasingly Americanized. They learned the English language, worked into the economic system, and rebelled against their parents' ways. Prejudice against them became less overt than in the wartime era.

This typical progression of an immigrant group was interrupted, first by war alarms and then war itself. Shortly after Pearl Harbor, the army, with the concurrence of President Roosevelt and Congress, as a war measure, established a military zone along the Pacific Coast in which residents of Japanese ancestry were first placed under curfew, and then deported to interior concentration camps. Although this drastic measure did not originate in Oregon, neither was it opposed by most of the state's white population, whose outrage against the bombing of Pearl Harbor coupled with the traditional economic and cultural fear of the Japanese justified the harshness of removal in their eyes. (One Portlander, answering the doorbell in the city's first blackout, found a second-generation Japanese-American soldier, and yelled in terror: "The invasion is here!") Oregon's principal cultural group, the Japanese American Citizens League, went along with the evacuation order under protest and the people in the affected area met at Portland in May 1942 to be sent to their camps.

One man at least protested the order more forcefully. Minoru Yasui, born in Oregon, a graduate of the state university, and an officer in the army reserve, intentionally violated the curfew order to test the constitutionality of the program, claiming that it could not be applied to American citizens. Sentenced to a $5000 fine and a year in a prison road camp, he appealed his case to the United States Supreme Court, which upheld the constitutionality of the curfew order.

In January 1945 came a twofold turning point in the hostility toward the Japanese. Both events occurred in Hood River. The local American Legion post removed the names of sixteen Japanese-American servicemen from its roll of honor. A national outcry led by President Harry Truman forced their replacement. In the same month three hundred residents of Hood River signed a petition urging that the Japanese returning from concentration camps be given a cordial welcome. This sentiment reflected that of the future, for although other Hood River citizens published a statement of hostility to the returning

Japanese, and there were public meetings in Gresham and other localities urging the strict enforcement of the alien land law and harassment (economic and otherwise) in various points, leaders of public opinion such as banker E. B. MacNaughton and Gov. Charles Sprague helped deflect this sentiment. Unlike California and Washington, Oregon saw no violence over this question.

In contrast to wartime, the Japanese of Oregon found the postwar years far more fulfilling than any previous era. Economic progress continued, informal prejudice declined, and discriminatory legal actions disappeared. In 1949 the Oregon Supreme Court declared the alien land law unconstitutional. In 1965 Congress effectually eliminated the principle of Japanese exclusion by banning race as a barrier to immigration and naturalization. Six years later Congress repealed the emergency detention clause of the Internal Security Act of 1950, a section that might have been used to legitimatize another group detention comparable to that suffered by the Japanese in the Second World War. Less satisfying was the disposition of claims for loss of property during the war. Congress permitted litigation to recover these losses, but when the final payment of Oregon claims was made in 1961 the Japanese residents of the state were awarded only 25 percent of their claimed losses, and many who lacked the means to litigate or had lost faith in American justice did not file claims.

The war had also first brought large numbers of Spanish-speaking people to Oregon until today they constitute the largest minority group in the state. As early as the nineteenth century, members of this ethnic group had come to the Northwest as miners, muleskinners, sheep raisers, and cattlemen, and in the 1920s the first migrant agricultural workers began to arrive. The last group, mainly from Texas, was like the first in that it was almost entirely composed of single males who came for economic purposes. When war broke out, demands of the military and defense industries created a grave shortage of labor in the fields of the Pacific states. To meet the requirements for harvesting, Congress established the *bracero* program with Mexico to ensure a labor supply of Mexican nationals who came to the United States, followed the crops, and then returned home after the last harvests. This program was extended until Congress, at the urging of organized labor, terminated it in 1964. Long before its demise, Spanish-speaking American citizens had become indispensable ingredients in Oregon's harvest fields, until by the end of the 1950s only 13 percent of Oregon's forty thousand migrant workers were Mexican nationals and a mere 2 percent were year-round residents of the state. Because of their forced rootlessness and the indifference of white Oregonians to dark-skinned groups, the pitiful lot of both American- and Spanish-speaking workers long went unpublicized. Not until an investigation by the Oregon Council of Churches in 1956 were the low pay, poor sanitation, inadequate housing, and lack of education for children made public knowledge. People who cared now discovered that the migrant worker was a family member, not a single person, with all the problems inherent in establishing a normal pattern of domestic living in the dislocated world of the migrants dominated by labor contractors and the growers.

The investigation by the council of churches produced further scrutiny of migrant labor conditions by an interim committee of the Oregon legislature whose chairman was Rep. Donald S. Willner. In turn this led to the creation by the governor of an interagency committee from the executive branch to assist the interim committee. Out of these investigations and the attendant publicity came several acts in 1959 designed to aid the migrant worker by protecting his health and by licensing labor contractors. The laws lacked teeth, however, and were not effectively enforced.

In the decade of the 1960s the Spanish-speaking ethnic group changed substantially. Increasingly its members became permanent residents and the state's most urbanized minority, rather than men and women who spent the winters in California or the Southwest. Mechanization, government regulations, and federal programs shrank drastically the ranks of migrant farm laborers. This residence gave them a base from which to operate politically and culturally, and organizations controlled by Spanish-speaking people have developed in the recent past, ranging from cultural centers in Woodburn and Cornelius to Colegio Caesar

Chavez, the former Mount Angel College. The first cultural center was founded in 1969 near Woodburn on a sixty-three-acre plot purchased by an arm of the Roman Catholic church, and its initial activities included a bilingual library, a monthly newspaper, and radio programs. Although federal government programs were of some importance in the migrant labor phase of the Chicano experience—the Education Act of 1965 established special programs for the children of migrant workers, and the Office of Economic Opportunity funded a Valley Migrant League in 1964—with permanent residence the Chicanos have gained control of their newer organizations and the Spanish-speaking society is itself reaffirming its heritage.

The Indians of Oregon have had diverse experiences in the years since 1920, and the very different fate of two groups of them have had a substantial influence on American Indian policy. The failure of the Dawes Act and the attempt to make the Indian a participant in the mainstream of American economic life became more evident with each passing year, not only to Oregon but throughout Indian America, until the fact became widely recognized in the 1920s. By that time the Indians had not only been apportioned their lands but, by one means or another, had lost at least the more productive lands to whites. Critics of the Dawes Act had become convinced that salvation for the Indians could come only in the repudiation of the principles of that law and its replacement by a policy that recognized communitarianism rather than economic individualism as the basis of Indian culture.

This philosophy was the basis of the Wheeler-Howard Act of 1934 that permitted, not forced, Indians to regroup into federally chartered tribes with limited powers of self-government and with eligibility for programs of federal economic assistance. In Oregon the three tribes in the Warm Springs Reservation organized under this new statute in 1938 but were not able to take advantage of it fully until 1960. In that year the tribal council spent $2 million of a settlement from the United States Government for the loss of its Celilo Falls fishing grounds on the Columbia River (for the construction of a dam) to purchase a resort on the reservation called Kah-nee-ta. This tribal enterprise became the foundation for other economic developments, such as a forest products factory and an electronics assembly plant, that have made the Warm Springs Indians among the most successful in the United States and have belatedly vindicated the principles of the Wheeler-Howard law.

Indians living on the Klamath Reservation suffered a far different fate when, in the 1950s, they encountered another of the changing Indian policies of the federal government. The Klamath peoples had not organized under the Wheeler-Howard law, nor had those on the Umatilla Reservation, and they continued to live, as they had before the First World War, from the proceeds of the timber sales from their reservation and from casual labor. In 1953 Congress adopted the new termination policy, a throwback to the philosophy of the Dawes Act. Under termination, reservations whose residents were presumed capable of making their way in the economic mainstream were to be broken up if their members preferred to take their individual per capita share of the tribal assets. Special government programs to assist Indians were to be terminated for them. Unlike the Dawes Act, however, the principle of voting was incorporated into the termination policy, although the government reserved to itself the decision whether to submit the question of termination to any given tribal group. In 1954 Congress passed a law requiring that the Klamath tribes vote on the termination question. In the ensuing election that took place in 1958, 77 percent voted to take their per capita shares and to withdraw from the tribe; 5 percent voted that their property shares remain under the trusteeship of a private organization, ultimately the United States Bank of Oregon; and 18 percent cast blank ballots (they were then assumed to have voted for trusteeship). Those who took the large per capita settlements, and the children who acquired them when they reached maturity, rather soon regretted their choice, since most of their money was dissipated. In 1969 the trustee Indians voted to abandon their bank trust and to accept their per capita share of it, a result ultimately accomplished when the United States Government bought their remaining land for a part of a national forest. The failure of termination on the Klamath Reservation, coupled with the similar outcome in Wisconsin on the Menominee Reservation, although too late to save the economic fortunes of the Indians, forced the abandonment of the policy.

This belated responsiveness to the desires of Oregon Indians and their allies elsewhere is also reflected politically in the settlement of the Warm Springs Reservation boundary, the prospective legislation for the restoration of tribal status to the Siletz tribes whose reservation had been terminated in the 1950s, and the decision of a federal judge in Portland guaranteeing the Indians a proportionate share of the Columbia River fisheries as they had been promised in the original treaties. Oregon Indians, who now make up 1½ percent of the state's population and are increasingly urbanized, have also moved in directions that are not exclusively political, such as the Chicano-Indian Study Organization at Camp Adair and a museum and study center at Coos Bay. In both areas the Indian, like the other ethnic minorities, is more and more a creator of his own destiny, rather than a reactor to the Caucasian culture.

The Oregon black community in the 1920s and 1930s grew in traditional patterns based upon employment in the railroad industry. Cultural life continued to be centered in black rather than integrated organizations as the Williams Avenue YMCA, founded in 1921, and the weekly newspaper, the *Advocate,* published by Beatrice Canoder, joined the churches as cultural centers. The major accomplishment politically was the repeal of the racist provisions of the state constitution. In 1926 a committee of the Portland League of Women Voters that included Lenore Freeman, a black woman, and the *Advocate* led a successful campaign to abolish the residence clause. In the following year the voters repealed the antiblack and anti-Chinese suffrage clause as well. Extralegal discrimination continued, however. In the 1920s blacks were excluded from the Catholic schools of Portland and also segregated in the schools of Vernonia. Hotels, restaurants, and unions also practiced discrimination; Portland real estate agents refused to sell to blacks except in the Albina ghetto; automobile insurance rates were higher for blacks.

Just as the Second World War greatly affected Oregon Japanese and Chicanos, so did it greatly affect Oregon blacks. On the eve of American entry into the war the 1940 census reported Oregon's black population to be 1,800, the majority of whom were supported in the traditional transportation and hotel industries. The Kaiser shipyards brought a large increase in the black population throughout the war until a peak of approximately 20,000 was reached in early 1945. Most of the newcomers resided in federally financed housing projects operated by the Housing Authority of Portland. The largest of these was Vanport, an entirely new community built in north Portland by the Kaiser firm but operated by the local housing authority. In Vanport the Portland white community had its first experience with large numbers of black residents and many southern blacks had their first exposure to a partially desegregated life.

Government fair employment regulations opened up the unions to blacks and guaranteed equal pay and employment opportunities. Off-the-job life was segregated to the extent that all black war workers were assigned to residences in the Vanport or Guild's Lake housing projects, and the Vanport blacks lived in blocks of housing separate from other residents. Responsibility for segregated housing was denied by the housing authority, but it is evident that it did create this policy either on its own initiative, as a reflection of prewar segregation patterns in Portland, or in response to the prejudices of the white residents of the housing projects. The other institutional aspects of life in Vanport, schools, shopping centers, recreation halls, and church facilities, were open to all on a nonsegregated basis.

Although morale of Vanport residents of any race was not high, a far larger proportion of blacks remained there after the war than did whites. This fact was not so much the result of preference but rather the lack of job opportunities elsewhere; whites could move out, blacks could not. Thus when the city of Vanport was washed away in the floods of Memorial Day, 1948, many blacks left the Portland area, for they could not get housing elsewhere in the region. Yet the war migration did not totally evaporate, and the black population of Portland in 1950 numbered 9,495 compared to 1,931 in 1940.

For many black persons the wartime period in Portland had provided steady and high income. It had strengthened older community organizations like the NAACP and had stimulated new ones like the Urban League. Blacks were the most active in the Vanport churches of any group and led the way in other community activities. On the base of the war years the now-expanded black population could build a greater cohesiveness, one that flourished in the civil rights movement of the postwar era.

For the Oregon white community the migration of black ship-yard workers was also important. The newcomers gave the Caucasians an opportunity to deal with blacks other than as members of a tiny minority and gradually to erode Oregon's racist heritage. A Committee on Interracial Principles and Practices was established, and white organizations such as the Portland Housing and Planning Association and the League of Women Voters finally forced the local housing authority to terminate its segregated Vanport housing policy early in 1948. The *Oregonian* refuted rumors of a disproportionate amount of black crime in Vanport and pointed out that black migration into white residential areas did not destroy property values. And there were very few, if any, interracial conflicts in Vanport.

After the war Oregon blacks participated in the burgeoning civil rights movement. The first major result of this was a state fair employment practices law adopted in 1949, followed by measures abolishing the ban on interracial marriage, opening the National Guard to all ethnic groups, and desegregating public accommodations. Economic opportunities became more diversified because of these government pressures, and prosperity and the greater freedoms opened to blacks the opportunity to participate more widely in both older activist organizations, such as the NAACP and the Urban League, as well as in groups that had become prominent more recently, such as the Congress of Racial Equality and the Black Muslims. Yet a recent student concludes that there is a "special conservatism of Oregon Negroes, which make them, similar to most other Oregonians, highly selective in their acceptance of exogenous novelties." [1]

1. Thomas C. Hogg, "Negroes and Their Institutions in Oregon," *Phylon* 30 (Fall 1969): 285.

II

In the last half-century Oregon's political life has been characterized by more or less successful attempts to adjust the principles and institutions of the Progressive Era to industrialization, urbanization, and resource depletion. The period opened, however, with a savage reaction against the spirit of progressivism that made Oregon nationally notorious. This development was the rise of the Ku Klux Klan in the urban areas of the state, coupled with an attempt to close the parochial and private schools by initiative petition. The openness of Oregon's politics and the tools of direct legislation that U'Ren believed were to be used for progress now became the instruments for reaction. The postwar Ku Klux Klan was an organization, strong in both North and South, dedicated to restoring private and public morality by attacking those it judged failures to meet its moral standards; blacks, Jews, and Catholics automatically qualified as deviants. There were few members of these groups in Oregon in the early 1920s, but the state acquired a large and influential Klan membership nonetheless.

In 1921 the Klan came to Oregon, moving north from Medford with its message of racial hatred until it developed its greatest numerical strength in Portland. Originally derided and opposed by established politicians such as Gov. Ben W. Olcott, the Klan plunged into politics in 1922 and almost defeated him in the Republican gubernatorial primary of that spring. In the general election that followed, the Klan endorsed Olcott's opponent, Democrat Walter Pierce, and the school initiative measure. This proposal would have required parents to send their children of ages eight to sixteen to public schools (only 7 percent of Oregon pupils attended private schools) and would have virtually destroyed private education in the state. When the votes were tabulated in November both Pierce and the school bill won overwhelmingly.

Their victories may be attributed to Oregon's traditional social cohesiveness, racism, and reluctance to face change and to the newer progressivism. Pierce not only supported the school bill; he was an avowed foe of Japanese land ownership and an advocate of the old progressive crusade of higher taxation on utilities combined with a lowering of individual tax rates. The school bill not only conformed to nativism but it also appealed to the egalitarian sentiments of a people largely middle class, a people whose ethnic homogeneity spread throughout the state. The twin appeals of the compulsory school measure were caught superbly in a work of propaganda entitled *The Old Cedar School,* by George Estes. Mainly written in a rural vernacular, the pamphlet attacked the subversiveness of Catholic education ("the Academy of St. Gregory's Holy Toe Nail") and the snobbishness of "Piscopalyun Oxford Hall" ("there's a hull lot of big bishops an' fellars that wear their collars and vests buttoned in the back . . . an' eat good grub an' draw big salaries an' you have to pay an awful price for the learning").[2]

The compulsory school bill was sponsored and supported by others than the Klan, including the Scottish Rite Masons, the Federation of Patriotic Societies, the Knights of Luther, and the Loyal Orange Institution. Its enemies numbered George Putnam's *Salem Capital Journal* and the *Portland Telegram,* although most of the state's newspapers approved it or were neutral. Pierce supported the bill, although he neither endorsed nor repudiated the Klan. Governor Olcott opposed both Klan and bill in the strongest terms.

In 1923 the legislature quickly adopted the bill under the leadership of the Speaker of the House Kaspar K. Kubli, a Portland stationer and the son of a pioneer, but all parties agreed that it would not be enforced until tested in court. The fate of the law was finally settled in 1925 in the case of *Pierce* vs. *Society of Sisters* when the United States Supreme Court unanimously declared it unconstitutional as a violation of the parents' right to educate their children in schools of their own choice and of the property rights of the proprietors of parochial and private schools. But long before this decision was rendered the Klan

2. Quoted in Robin Huffman, "An Analysis of the Interrelationship between the Oregon School Law of 1922, the Press of Oregon, the Election of Walter Pierce and the Ku Klux Klan" (Master's thesis, Portland State University, 1974), p. 32. Used with permission.

had disappeared, a political phenomenon of three or four years, shocking but evanescent. Internal wrangling, rumors of corruption, and the second thought of the public destroyed it, although its influence lingered throughout the decade.

Most of the period between the world wars was not marked by the bigoted reaction of the early 1920s but rather by conservative or moderate political life. Even in the depression the Oregonians voted for Franklin Roosevelt but did not heartily embrace his New Deal policies, especially those that required the spending of money. Both political parties remained divided and weak, a product of personal rivalry as well as the reforms of the Oregon System and the lack of powerful antagonistic interest groups. Republican conservatives were ascendant during the twenties, although the progressive wing of the party, led by Charles Linza McNary and Charles Sprague, gained in the following decade.

Senator McNary was the state's only national figure in these years, and his legislative impact was in the most crucial area of domestic politics for Oregonians, that of natural resources. McNary was of an old pioneer family, an urbane and sophisticated progressive of amazing equanimity, who recovered quickly from a one-vote loss in the Republican primary for state supreme court justice in 1914. McNary was the major force in pushing the Clarke-McNary Act through Congress in 1924, an innovative measure that strengthened the triple alliance of federal Forest Service, state government, and private timbermen in fire protection. The statute also provided seedlings to states, and in various other ways was the motivating force in making Oregon state forestry effective. McNary also received a great deal of publicity for his sponsorship of the McNary-Haugen bill for the relief of agricultural prices that were declining throughout the 1920s. The measure called for a government corporation to sell farm surpluses abroad; farmers would be paid by government the difference between the lower world price they received and the higher domestic price of farm products; once prices were raised they would remain high behind a protective tariff barrier. Although passed twice by Congress, the bill never survived vetoes by President Coolidge, yet its advocacy of large-scale government intervention in the farmers' interest was an important precedent for New Deal farm legislation.

When Republican party strength in the 1930s was reduced to a handful in the United States Senate, McNary was chosen as minority leader, where he served effectively to keep the party alive, chiefly by condemning a policy of diehard opposition to the New Deal that would stamp the party as hopelessly reactionary. Although McNary did not support Roosevelt in 1932, he prevented the party caucus in the Senate from expelling progressive Republicans who did so. Three years later he denounced Republican negativism ("We ought to accept and acknowledge the good that is to be found in the Administration program") and in 1936 he sat out the presidential campaign rather than oppose Roosevelt.[3]

The personal friendship and political compatibility of minority leader and president worked to Oregon's advantage in the Bonneville Dam project. After Roosevelt successfully urged Congress to adopt the Grand Coulee project in the state of Washington, primarily as a work-relief measure, McNary provided the impetus for the second of the great Columbia River multiple-purpose projects at Bonneville. This dam, when placed into operation in 1938, provided low-cost electrical power for farmers, public utility districts, and farm co-operatives, all of which received preferential rates, and for industry. It also was instrumental in bringing aluminum and other defense industries to Oregon during the Second World War. McNary rounded out his career in national politics as Wendell Willkie's vice-presidential candidate on the Republican ticket in 1940, a tribute to his progressivism, as the GOP tried to shed its reactionary image. In this role McNary was the second, and to date the last, Oregonian after Joseph Lane in 1860 to reach this height in national politics.

In the interwar years the Democrats, too, were divided. Oswald West, his progressivism cooling, was the leader of the

3. Arthur M. Schlesinger, Jr., *The Politics of Upheaval* (Boston: Houghton Mifflin Co.), p. 525.

conservative forces, as the spokesmen of the state Grange and organized labor took the field for progressivism. This internal clash caused the party to muff a golden opportunity in the depression decade to replace the Republicans as the majority party, for although some Democrats won office—Charles Martin as congressman and later governor and Nan Wood Honeyman and Walter Pierce as congressmen—wrangles over patronage, public power policy, and personalities kept the party split. The coup de grâce of lost opportunity came in the late thirties when progressive Democrats joined with a few Republicans and Socialists to form the Oregon Commonwealth Federation, which called for public ownership of natural resources, utilities, banks, and monopolies. The OCF did defeat conservative Governor Martin in the spring primary of 1938, but the radicalism of the OCF was too much for the voters, who chose progressive Republican Charles Sprague as governor in the fall. Sprague's victory was symbolic of the state's measured response to the depression, for the unparalleled economic crisis produced in Oregon very little support for drastic radical measures in comparison with those proposed in Washington ("the soviet of Washington" as it was described by James Farley) or with Upton Sinclair's socialistic End Poverty in California movement, or Dr. Francis E. Townsend's plan for government payments of $200 per month to the aged. Oregonians were grateful for New Deal measures such as agricultural payments and resource projects, but they were little inclined to reward local Democrats for these plans, let alone push for more radical measures.

After the Second World War Oregon continued its moderately progressive course. Institutionally the state firmly established a two-party system as hard organizational work, attractive candidates, and an influx of Democrats among the war workers enabled the Democrats to attain first major- and then majority-party status by the 1970s. So far as issues were concerned, environmental resources continued to dominate political affairs, although with a shift to equal emphasis upon amenity as well as economic conservation. The legislature enacted a scenic rivers bill, regulated field burning, provided for a Willamette Valley "Greenway," and created a land conservation and development commission, among other resource laws.

The major national political figure of these years was Wayne Lyman Morse, whose career exemplified, indeed in doubly distilled form, Oregon's use of the progressive tradition to alleviate both state and national political problems. Morse came to Oregon from Wisconsin in 1929 as assistant professor in the Law School of the University of Oregon, and in 1931 he was chosen its dean. There he quickly developed a reputation as an effective teacher, inspiring administrator, and a nationally known arbitrator. In 1944 he was elected to the United States Senate as a Republican. On the larger Washington stage Morse became known as a man of brilliance, articulateness, and integrity. His independence was manifest not only in his defiance of special interest groups but more spectacularly in his abandoning the Republican party in 1952, then serving as an Independent, and finally joining the Democrats in 1955. He was an advocate of civil rights and of organized labor and an early and unremitting foe of American military intervention in Southeast Asia. Throughout his public career, which ended with his death while campaigning for the Senate in 1974, Morse drew deeply upon the progressive tradition of both his native Wisconsin and his adopted state, a tradition rooted in the years of political ferment at the turn of the century.

Morse exalted the use of educated reason. One of his two principle legislative accomplishments, in his own judgment, was his sponsorship of federal aid to education statutes, including the Morse-Green Act of 1963 and the Higher Education Act of 1965, which together provided grants for university building construction, scholarships, and loans to students, among other provisions, and established the precedents for billion-dollar federal outlays in this sector. He also argued that his own decisions as senator were based upon his impartial study of the facts and the answer to the question, "What do these facts show the public interest to be?" The freedom that impartial scrutiny of public issues demanded led to his determination that all public policies be examined carefully, regardless of the power or prestige of those advocating them, and to his equal determination that dissenters, regardless of the depth of their convictions, utilize only weapons of peaceful persuasion rather than violence in their opposition. Morse himself refused to employ pathos or sentimentality in his public addresses.[4]

Morse was progressive not only in his professional obligations, but also in his insistence upon the rule of law. In this respect his greatest contribution came in the advocacy of collective security under the aegis of the United Nations, and he was a strong supporter of United States intervention in Korea under the UN banner and of Israel's access to the Gulf of Aqaba in 1966–1967 under the protection of a UN resolution. What gave Morse his international reputation was his opposition to American involvement in Southeast Asia, a position that went back to his refusal to endorse the congressional Formosa Resolution of 1955, which regarded an attack on the small offshore islands of Quemoy and Matsu as an attack upon Formosa.

Morse opposed the Vietnam War from the beginning of American entry, not because he opposed the use of economic aid or military force to American allies (he objected to rapid disarmament after the Second World War and endorsed the Marshall Plan, Truman Doctrine, and NATO), but because the war was illegal: "In Vietnam," he declared, "we have totally flouted the rule of law, and we have flouted the United Nations Charter. This lipservice given by the United States to the United Nations and its international law provisions and procedures has done our country great injury among many international lawyers around the world." When in 1964 the administration succeeded in persuading Congress to adopt a resolution condemning the North Vietnamese attack upon two American destroyers in the Gulf of Tonkin, Morse was one of two senators who opposed it. He had been informed by sources within the Navy Department that actually the United States had been the aggressor, and he chose correctly to believe his source rather than the secretary of defense. In time, of course, the Morse position in opposition to

4. This quotation and those following are drawn from Morse speeches as recorded in the *Congressional Record* on various occasions from 1945 to 1969.

the war became the national view, although it cost him his place in the Senate in the election of 1968.

Although Morse became famous nationally for his position on the Vietnam War, as well as earlier opposition to the Eisenhower resource policies, he also was popular within Oregon because he caught and responded to the spirit of what its citizens wanted done within their state. Morse's conviction that there was a public interest apart from the desires of pressure groups, a classic progressive faith, led to his refusal to be partisan and to the voters' insistence that he be rewarded, not punished, for his change of parties. He opposed gun controls, advocated nuclear power to solve energy needs, and objected to a bill to create an Oregon Dunes Seashore Park because it contained a provision for government condemnation of private land (''They've got public property running out their ears down here''). Morse's defense of free enterprise (''The threat of world communism is a threat of economic totalitarianism, out of which political totalitarianism is bound to be a certainty'') and his opposition to the demands of pressure groups (''I have never made a commitment to a labor organization, to an employer organization, or to any political pressure group in this country . . . and I do not intend to start with the CIO in the State of Oregon'') also helped earn him election to the Senate four times, where he became one of the most intelligent, conscientious, and forthright members of that body in the twentieth century.

On public issues beyond Vietnam, Oregon's impact upon the national consciousness was most marked concerning the natural resources policies of the Eisenhower administration. These involved men and measures crucial both to Oregon's political and economic life. As a part of his ideological conviction that the federal government played too large a role in the development of natural resources as opposed to the states and private enterprise, Eisenhower shortly after his inauguration in 1953 unveiled what he called the ''power partnership policy.'' Under the direction of Douglas McKay, secretary of the interior and former governor of Oregon, this program called for the government and private utilities to divide the costs of future power projects.

On the Hells Canyon of the Snake River the Idaho Power Company, supported by the Eisenhower administration, proposed a series of three low dams suitable for the production of power, but inadequate for purposes of flood control, navigation, and recreational facilities. Advocates of these additional purposes, including most Oregonians of both parties, favored a single high dam at Hells Canyon and carried their case to the Federal Power Commission, to Congress, and to the electorate. The Hells Canyon project was the reason for Morse's switch to the Democratic party in 1955, and the issue became even more dramatic when McKay, at Eisenhower's urging, and against his own wishes and those of the leaders of the state Republican party, resigned from the cabinet to oppose Morse for the Senate seat in 1956. In an exciting race Morse focussed on the Eisenhower-McKay resource policies (McKay was rhythmically pilloried as "Giveaway Doug McKay"), and McKay unwisely tried to make Morse's personality and party-switching the central issue of the campaign. Morse won handily and in the national perspective the defeat of McKay forced Eisenhower to abandon his ideological conviction that westerners wanted less rather than more federal participation in developing the resources of the region. Oregonians had helped persuade the president that their support of him—he carried the state handily in both 1952 and 1956—was a vote for less federal government; this may have been the rhetoric of the Oregonian, but in practice he continued to desire federal assistance.

At the local level postwar Oregon politics turned slightly toward a more progressive cast as both Republicans and Democrats moved to limit the influence of conservatives within their ranks. In 1948 the state had been clearly Republican. It was the only western state to vote for Dewey against Truman, and the Republican party had a majority of registered voters. The party also elected all but one of its statewide candidates to office and recaptured control of seventy of the ninety seats in the state legislature. By the middle 1950s, however, the picture had changed. Younger Democrats fresh from the world war took advantage of the presence of the large number of Democrats who came to the state as war workers to mobilize them behind the issues of fair employment practices, the Brannan plan for agriculture, and federal aid for education, so that the party's strength developed election by election. The party leaders also were wise enough to abandon causes like the Columbia Valley Authority, a program modelled on the Tennessee Valley Authority, when it became apparent that the scheme rubbed against the grain of most Oregonians, who regarded it as a bureaucratic nightmare divorced from familiar controls on river development maintained by Congress and old-time federal agencies such as the Corps of Engineers and the Department of the Interior. Richard Neuberger, a nationally known journalist-turned-politician, was elected as a Democrat to the United States Senate in 1954, a tribute not only to his personality and grasp of the issues, but also to a drop in the economy and the effective organization of his labor and party supporters. Senator Morse joined the Democrats the following year and in 1956 led the party to its greatest victory. Not only did he defeat Douglas McKay, but the first Democratic governor since 1934 was chosen, and the party gained control of the legislature. Oregon had become a two-party state.

Quickly taking a cue from their rivals, the Republicans fought back by limiting the power of their conservative wing. Almost from the time of the great Democratic victories of the 1950s the Republicans adopted a policy of seeking out attractive candidates, muting ideology, and moving toward the center. By the 1960s they were re-established as solid rivals of the Democrats.

In state government Oregonians secured measures that were mostly progressive but inexpensive. As always, the voters were almost parsimonious, and it became routine for them to insist that tax increases be referred to them. In 1963 an income tax measure was beaten, and in 1969 a sales tax suffered the same fate, as it had in 1933, 1934, 1936, 1944, and 1947, although a cigarette tax was adopted in 1965. A civil rights law was enacted in 1949 and laws protecting migratory labor a decade later. The legislature reapportioned itself before this reform was mandated by the United States Supreme Court. The nonpartisan, privately financed Citizens Conference on State Legislatures appraised the Oregon legislature in 1971 as twenty-seventh among the fifty states in its overall efficiency, twenty-eighth in functional ranking, but—in a significant tribute to the legislature's traditional responsiveness to the voters' wishes—fourteenth in accountability. In other words Oregonians have secured what they wanted in postwar politics: a two-party system composed of weak parties, a responsive state government, and laws and legislators, state and national, that are moderately progressive, avoiding ideological rhetoric and radical or reactionary programs.

Although the politics of Oregon have not had the national impact that they contributed in the antebellum era or at the time of the Oregon System, the state has from time to time had a political influence. Oregon's flirtation with the Klan produced nationwide revulsion. Battles against the power partnership policy helped shape natural resources policy, and the opposition of Senators Morse and Mark O. Hatfield to the Vietnam War gained national attention. In its presidential primaries Oregon also had something of an influence in nominating politics when in 1948, in the last primary before the Republican convention, Oregon Republicans chose Thomas Dewey and thus destroyed the presidential ambitions, for that year, of Harold Stassen. Similarly in 1964 the Oregon primary revived the campaign of Nelson Rockefeller, at least temporarily, when Rockefeller defeated Henry Cabot Lodge to eliminate him from the presidential race. Finally, in its attempt to pass legislation to protect the natural environment, the state has created interest around the nation, both at the state and federal level, in measures that might become models in other political jurisdictions. In contrast to the Progressive Era, Oregon is becoming known for the substance rather than the structure of its politics.

7

The Struggle against Modern Life

I

N the interwar years Oregon's economic life followed its customary patterns of dependence upon lumber and agriculture, but during the Second World War and after, some alterations began to appear in this traditional structure. In the 1920s and 1930s the Oregon economy grew at a rate slower than that of the nation, except when federal expenditures began to take hold during the Great Depression. Exports from farm and forest enabled the state to balance its imports, although by no stretch of the imagination did the state's continuing colonial status place it in the ranks of the most affluent of American commonwealths.

In the Second World War the federal presence that became manifest in the programs of the New Deal expanded enormously in shipbuilding and aluminum, and Oregon, although its base was far lower, led California and Washington in the percentage increase of value added by manufacturing during the years 1939 to 1947. After the war the boom continued into 1951, fell off briefly, and then was further stimulated by defense contracts in lumber, plywood, and food during the last two years of the Korean War.

But for the 1950s as a whole Oregon did not keep pace with

the average rate of growth of the rest of the United States because her exports of manufactured goods, with the exception of pulp and paper, lagged. In the decade of the fifties national real income rose 21 percent, but Oregon's income appreciated only 4 percent. The causes of this lag included a decline in the labor force, the declining value of farm income, the slower rise in wages, and the fact that the rest of the nation was industrializing at a faster rate. The hopes of the thirties and forties that cheap power or some other panacea would convert the state into another California or Texas in economic development proved to be chimerical.

Since the 1950s the economic scene has turned more prosperous and more diverse. The lumber business has intensified a conversion that began in the mid 1940s to the diversified forest products industry, in which a variety of by-products has saved the old lumber enterprise from stagnation. As the population of the area has increased, new manufacturing has been required to meet the needs of an ever-more-affluent society. Cheap power, although getting more expensive, continues to be a factor, and "footloose" (amenity-attracted) enterprises like electronics have contributed to Oregon's wealth.

Throughout the years since 1920 the lumber industry has continued to be a staple of the Oregon economy. In the last year of the prosperous twenties lumber production was at an alltime high, accounting for about one-half the value of goods exported from the region. Four years later, however, the industry was at its nadir, a victim not only of depression, but also of the trends developing since the close of the First World War. Indeed, in the years 1919 to 1933 lumber industry production averaged less than 40 percent of the value of other manufacturing industries in the country. New technology was one cause for the doldrums of the industry, as rubber, plastics, and light metals, for reasons of expense or convenience, began to replace lumber in the construction industry. Architectural changes also hindered lumbermen: newer homes were designed with fewer rooms and lower ceilings than in the prewar period. To meet their competition for markets lumbermen became frantic to cut more and more trees as prices dropped, a remedy that led only to a disastrous condition of overproduction. The underconsumption of the Great Depression was only the final blow.

Between the wars Oregon lumbering also changed. The state at last passed Washington, in 1938, as the leading lumber producer in the nation, since most of the readily accessible virgin timber in the Puget Sound area was milled. Symbolic of this fact, the headquarters of the West Coast Lumbermen's Association was moved to Portland from Seattle in 1945. Within Oregon there were geographic changes as well, as corporations began to cut heavily in the regions of the southern Willamette Valley and in the southwest to replace the stagnant production of the Columbia River and northern Willamette valleys.

Although the postwar years were far more profitable than the thirties, the lumber industry never recovered its position as the dynamic factor in the state's economic development that it held in the forty years before 1920. Even in the era of unparalleled affluence after 1945 the lumberman has been on the defensive. Although the industry has taken seriously a variety of conservation methods, ranging from fire protection to tree farming, it has had trouble in bringing its resources to bear upon matters of research and marketing. As a far less concentrated enterprise than any other major American industry, it has had some difficulty—in the face of threats from foreign lumbermen and domestic producers of rival building materials—in bringing its many companies to co-operate with each other to meet these challenges.

Oregon's other historic industry, agriculture, has remained an important, although shrinking, portion of the state's economic sector. Wheat is still the most valuable crop east of the Cascades, where it has been dominant for a century, but products of irrigated agriculture like apples have risen in importance along with the production of specialty crops like filberts. Indeed, from 1935 to 1959, while the nation's farm acreage declined 20 percent, Oregon's farmland actually increased in extent, chiefly because of the spread of irrigation in eastern Oregon. In the decade of the 1960s, however, Oregon farms conformed to the national agricultural standard as productivity increased, the number of farm acres fell, and the farm population declined. The exodus from agriculture was a result not only of the increase in productivity caused by the use of chemical fertilizers, improved seeds, and sophisticated machinery, but also of the wide gap between farm and nonfarm income that has lured hundreds of farm children to urban centers.

In recent years the old cattle and sheep industries have taken on new life. Now the cattle feeding business is a major enterprise. Centered in the Tule Lake–Klamath Basin area, it produces beef for the regional urban centers. This industry arose during the Second World War based on the state's large acreage of grazing land, the nutritious feed produced on its farmland, the well-developed transportation network, and the expanding regional market outlets. Sheep raising has come full circle, for since the close of the Second World War the largest number of sheep in Oregon are again west of the Cascades where the enterprise began in the 1840s. During the war high prices for wool and mutton revitalized the sheep business, but the shortage of skilled labor after the end of the war, caused by higher wages in other forms of employment, coupled with the loneliness of the sheepherder's lot, made the life of the eastern Oregon sheepherder unappealing. In the postwar era the majority of the state's sheep are grown in the southern part of the Willamette Valley, mostly in Douglas County, as an adjunct of farming operations. Ironically, cattle that the railroad replaced with sheep in the eighties and nineties have now, in turn with the rise in beef prices, supplemented sheep in the eastern regions. Mining and commercial fishing, the other nineteenth-century staples, have almost disappeared as important ingredients in the economic life of the state.

In the Oregon economy the stable or declining industries have been replaced or augmented since the Second World War by promising new ventures. Chief among these is the broadening of the old lumber industry into a diversified forest products industry. One technological key to the salvation of the Oregon woodsman was the invention of the whole-log barker, which opened the way to use an entire log for lumber, for fibre for pulpwoods, and for chips. The lumber and paper pulp industries, historically rivals, now became complementary. This integrated use of logs meant an integrated corporate structure, since firms now could produce the full range of forest products rather than confine themselves to single lines such as lumber, pulp, or plywood. Integration requires capital for the high-priced machinery of barkers, chippers, and conveyors, and many smaller lumber firms, unable to raise this capital to diversify, have perished. Another technological advance has been the invention of the Kraft process for producing pulp from the residues of nonwhite trees like the ponderosa pine that is the dominant forest type east of the Cascades.

The pulp and paper industry of Oregon is a product of the years since 1946. Technology, the enormous growth in national wealth, and the depletion of large logs cut from the virgin forests have made it possible for surviving lumbermen to diversify to stay solvent. The modern pulp and paper enterprise is large and fully integrated; it uses small trees and is expanding to the Pacific shore where these smaller trees are growing.

The plywood and hardboard enterprises have also developed as important components of the Oregon economy since the Second World War. Although there had been a plywood firm in Portland as early as 1904, most companies were located in the state of Washington, where timber was more accessible, sounder, and younger than in Oregon. After the wartime interlude when production slowed, plywood in Oregon grew mightily because of the availability of timber and of the desirability of harvesting old-growth trees before their quality declined. Douglas fir was particularly adapted to plywood production because it had large logs that the original mechanical peelers could easily handle, and its uniform texture made for an attractive finish. By the 1960s, however, Oregon plywood was facing vigorous competition from the South as old growth timber declined, and the invention of sheathing plywood, used for concealed structural strength, made surface appearance unimportant.

Hardboard, production of which began in Corvallis, is also an invention of the late forties. This wood aggregate takes up the slack when lumber and plywood are no longer available or suitable. Hardboard flourished when high-grade raw log supplies for lumber and plywood decreased and when cost efficiencies demanded a ruthless crusade against waste of any wood product. Postwar housing booms, with their insatiable demand for any type of suitable building material and more tolerant architectural trends, have also opened the way for the hardboard industry.

For years Pacific northwesterners had dreamed and hoped for federal production of hydroelectric power to make possible a more diversified economic base in the region than reliance upon the extractive industries. With the advent of the Bonneville Dam in the late 1930s this hope became firmer and was realized after Pearl Harbor. During the war the aluminum industry came to Oregon because of the availability of cheap power and because it was close to the aircraft producers of Washington and California. In Oregon the Aluminum Company of America built and operated a plant at Troutdale in the war years for the United States Government, a plant that was sold in 1949 to the Reynolds Metal Corporation, and in the 1950s the Harvey Aluminum Company opened a plant at The Dalles.

In the 1950s aluminum production as a herald of state prosperity began to disappoint its supporters. It became clearer that the cost of power was becoming the least important factor in the total cost of aluminum production. Other regions closer to major aluminum customers became a growing threat, but in the sixties production picked up with a decline in regional freight rates and an increase in large contracts for aircraft production.

Food processing was another industry spurred by the Second World War with its high prices for products and the absence of rationing of fruit and vegetable products. Canneries boomed because of the demands of the armed forces for food supplies in compact and concentrated form. After the war frozen and dehydrated foods became important ingredients of an industry based upon a rich truck gardening area that was close to urban markets and that was blessed with an outstanding transportation network.

A final new category was "footloose" industries. These enterprises, such as electronics and others, are not dependent upon local raw materials and nearby markets for their locations because of low transportation costs. They may be sited almost anywhere that a skilled work force can be gathered, which meant that Oregon's natural and social environment, attractive and uncrowded, and with well-educated residents, was magnetic for them, although even they cannot escape from the impact of federal government policies and the demands of extraregional markets.

The tourist industry was rooted in such developments as the founding of Crater Lake National Park in 1902 and the visits of occasional wealthy tourists of the nineteenth century (Rudyard Kipling, after fishing for steelhead on the Clackamas River in 1889, proclaimed "I have lived!") and of landscape artists of the same era (Albert Bierstadt painted in the state in the 1850s and 1860s).[1] Yet tourism was really a product of the automobile age. Gov. Oswald West persuaded the legislature to declare the state's ocean beaches as public highways in 1913, thus protecting them against private land ownership. The mass-produced automobile led to the good roads movement in Oregon and to the construction of the first part of the scenic Columbia River Highway in 1915. Oregon enacted the nation's first tax on gasoline in 1919. In 1921 another incentive to tourism was added when the legislature created a state parks system under the authority of the highway commission. Later in the decade Commissioner Robert W. Sawyer pushed for the acquisition of more state parks, arguing that they would attract tourists to use the highways and thus to support them through gasoline tax revenues. Sawyer also arranged the appointment of Samuel H. Boardman as first superintendent of the state parks, a man who in his twenty-one-year tenure acquired thousands of acres for the system. Yet the rise in tourism, presaged in the twenties, was largely unfulfilled during the depression era and the Second World War.

In the last year of the war the first systematic attempt to orga-

---

1. E. H. Eby, ed., " 'American Salmon,' by Rudyard Kipling: A Sketch from American Notes," *Pacific Northwest Quarterly* [hereafter cited *PNQ*] 60 (October 1969): 177.

nize the tourist business began when Gov. Earl Snell called a conference that established a committee to set up a program to publicize Oregon's tourist attractions. A dozen years later an officer of the United States National Bank was still extolling the tourist as a desirable source of revenue: "The people who come to see the mountains, the ocean, the forests, and the rivers are not like locusts that consume every living thing. . . . They leave the beauty of the scene for ours, and theirs, and other eyes. They are profitable business." [2] Certainly the tourists were profitable for Oregon as national affluence, transportation improvements, and the westward movement of population to the states of the Pacific Coast produced a large pool of potential tourists with the means to visit Oregon. These "birds of passage" were regarded favorably by most citizens until the last few years when they became objects of suspicion as competitors for recreational sites and as potential residents.

Whether old or new industries, based on natural resources or "footloose," Oregon's enterprises have been increasingly affected by the federal government. The most obvious and most important economically are the multiple-purpose projects along the Columbia River that began, in Oregon, with Bonneville, a measure advocated by Senator McNary and largely managed through Congress by him. Although these dams were supported by most citizens, their legislative proponents had to overcome some opposition. When the NcNary Dam was proposed in the middle forties, for example, it was assailed by commercial fishermen, who feared for the salmon runs; the National Association of Electric Companies, who objected to federal power protection as a threat to free enterprise; John L. Lewis and the United Mine Workers, who were apprehensive about hydroelectricity as a threat to coal; and various eastern interests alarmed by industrial competition and the employment of their tax dollars for western enterprises—the typical "mother country" objection to the colonies. Although all the industrial hopes for cheap power were never realized, the federal projects were of

2. Marshall N. Dana, "New Mood Found in Pacific Northwest Forest Industries," *Oregon Business Review*, 16 (May 1957): 4.

enormous value, not only to manufacturing, but also to rural people in electrifying the farms and irrigating the semiarid regions.

The national government also fostered the excellent transportation network in Oregon. In 1944 federal road aid was extended to urban areas, a decade later the highway act raised the federal contribution to highway construction from 50 to 60 percent of costs, and in 1956 the interstate highway system authorized by Congress increased the federal contribution to 90 percent of the construction costs.

The policies of the national government concerning the housing industry were decisive for Oregon's lumber and forest products manufacturers. In the early thirties, Congress established, as antidepression weapons, a Federal Home Loan Bank, a Home Owners Loan Corporation, and the first federal housing act. In 1935 came direct federal funding of public housing construction. From the New Deal forward federal regulation of interest rates and the supply of money have had much to do with the rate of national housing starts and hence with the health of the Oregon economy; e.g., three times in the 1950s tight money policies contributed to a recession in the state's economy.

Farm legislation, environmental regulations such as the ban on DDT in the national forests, and transportation and freight rates are further obvious manifestations of the federal presence. One sector in which the nation has been of minimal effect in Oregon since the Korean War is in military expenditures, a matter of great significance in California and almost of economic life and death in the state of Washington. At the height of the Vietnam War, in the period July to December 1969, Oregon's prime defense contracts numbered but 0.3 percent of the national total, and there have never been large military installations in the state. Although often cited as proof of the impotence of Oregon's senators and representatives in contrast to the influence of those of other states, the paucity of military spending has contributed to the evenness of economic development.

Since the era of the "Red Scare" of the First World War and early twenties, when most citizens automatically identified organized labor with radicalism, the men and women of

Oregon's labor force have progressed impressively until the urban areas of the state have become among the most highly unionized in the United States. Most of this gain in membership has been accomplished in unspectacular fashion, although there have been many strikes, some marked by violence. The passage of the Wagner Act in 1935, another example of the federal impact, guaranteed the right to organize and bargain collectively. This statute unleashed a wave of organizational efforts and produced, in the process, the Congress of Industrial Organizations, dedicated to organizing the unskilled industrial workers in the face of the older American Federation of Labor concern for the skilled crafts. This rivalry produced temporary confusion in the minds of workers, management, and politicians (the AFL, which had helped elect Nan Wood Honeyman to Congress in 1936, repudiated her in her losing campaign two years later, after she supported the CIO).

A portion of Oregon labor, although certainly not the largest, participated in the spectacular waterfront struggles of the 1930s. The International Longshoreman's Association had been organized in the 1890s and conducted unsuccessful strikes in 1901, 1916, and 1919–1921. Conditions along the waterfront had always been bad: labor contractors, hiring favoritism, company spies, dangerous working conditions, ethnic rivalry, and loan sharking were omnipresent. Out of these conditions, magnified by the depression, came the maritime strike of 1934. This great strike began on May 9, 1934, in all the major ports of the Pacific Coast. The strikers demanded union recognition and the closed shop, control of the hiring halls, and a reduced work day. The employers resisted adamantly and tried to break the strike by importing nonunion labor and by using special police to guard the strikebreakers. On July 5, 1934, "Bloody Thursday" in longshoreman's annals, the employers attempted to open the coast ports and to destroy the union. Police officers battled against the union pickets in all cities, a brief general strike broke out in San Francisco, and several men were killed, although there were no deaths in Portland. In the end the longshoremen won a complete victory. Three years after the strike, in 1937, the Pacific Coast longshoremen broke away from the

ILA, because of dislike for its local and national leadership, to form the International Longshoremen's and Warehousemen's Union, an affiliate of the CIO.

After the Second World War there was a major West Coast dock strike in 1948, the expulsion of the ILWU from the CIO in 1950 on account of the left-wing policies of its leader, Harry Bridges, and then a period free from major strikes until 1971. These more amicable relations surmounted such problems as control of hiring halls, relinquished by the union for a large monetary settlement in 1960, and the threat to employment brought on by the handling of bulk freight through containerization. Aside from the waterfront, woods workers and millmen also went through a time of troubles in the 1930s. The forest products corporations recognized the unions in 1935, but labor unrest caused by depression and CIO opposition to the old AFL unions continued throughout the decade. Union membership rose enormously but temporarily during the war with ship construction; there was a bitter strike against the *Oregonian* and *Journal* newspapers in Portland beginning in 1959; and there were other labor disputes scattered throughout the state. But with the exception of the longshoremen, Oregon's modern labor relations have not differed from the national developments.

The last fifty years have also seen the amplification of the hesitant conservation measures of the Progressive Era. The fisheries have received assiduous attention from state and nation in legislation for closed seasons, size of nets, prohibition of certain equipment, requirement of fish ladders at dams, and artificial propagation expenditures. Yet the effort has been, if not wasted, at least from the vantage point of the seventies, not successful. The commercial fishing industry has almost entirely disappeared and the sportsmen are now the most vigorous, because most numerous, in the conservation struggle. Whether their efforts can prevail against the desire of industry, agriculture, and transportation for use of the waters of the Columbia Basin remains conjectural.

In the forests of the Northwest, conservation has become more successful as the old triple alliance of state-federal-private forestry has expanded. After the Clarke-McNary Act was adopted the national government matched state and private expenditures for fire protection and reforestation. In 1928 Congress adopted the McSweeney-McNary Act to finance forest research and experimentation along the lines of earlier agricultural experiment research. In 1937 the theory of sustained yield was applied to the Oregon and California land grant forests in Oregon by the Department of the Interior, which managed this timber. Sustained yield was a principle whereby forests would be cut and replenished and lumber marketed at a rate sufficient to maintain profits, employment, and trees indefinitely. In 1944, again under the leadership of Senator McNary, Congress passed a law extending the triple alliance co-operation to the practice of sustained yield. In Oregon state forestry began in the 1930s when the people adopted a bond issue to acquire abandoned forest land. The first state efforts were in the area of the Tillamook Burn in western Oregon, where 311,000 acres had burned in 1933. Private corporations also pushed conservation measures. The first tree farm was established in Washington in 1941, and the idea took hold in Oregon after the war. Lumbermen began publicizing the "Keep Oregon Green" slogan in the early forties and expending large sums for research and development for both forestry and forest products enterprises.

Beginning in the 1950s the economic conservation endeavor became intermixed with the desires of hunters, fishermen, campers, and preservationists to protect the American environment. Congress responded to these newly powerful interests, which gathered strength because of urbanites' disenchantment with city pressures and their sufficient influence to do something about it. Several important measures were passed that, in part at least, dedicated public forests to interests other than commercial forestry and grazing. What the outcome of this legislation will be, in harmonizing both those who look to nature for economic sustenance and those who desire nonmaterial rewards, is in doubt. What is clear is that contemporary Oregonians no longer take the existence of Eden for granted.

II

Jesse Applegate's assessment of one hundred years ago that there was not one Oregonian worthy of memory for any endeavor has long since been disproved. The cultural life of the state, especially in the last half-century, has been marked by the achievements of several men and women who have done notable work. Yet when their accomplishments are assessed, one must still conclude that the familiar patterns of conservatism and eclecticism continue to predominate.

In institutional religion Oregon has the second-lowest percentage of church membership of any state. The most likely influence to account for this condition, which is a longstanding one, is the homogeneous population. A people without sharp ethnic or class divisions, a people of a conservative collective personality, and one whose natural environment is generous, need not depend upon religion for social control, since the great mass of the population is self-disciplined. Why there is no greater need felt for church membership for individual salvation is less clear; the facetious explanation is that when one already lives in Eden there is no need for salvation, but it is evident that Oregon has produced no new religion, no new church polity, and that no religious leader of national impact has long resided in the state.

In education the modern era continues the eclecticism of the past. In primary and secondary education, public, private, and parochial, the trends of modern educational philosophy have washed over the state from the East or California, but no noteworthy local innovation has emerged. The taxpayers have been willing to expend the money to provide a literate population, but as elsewhere have not been overly generous with tax dollars. Hemmed in by the state's constitutional requirement that no taxing unit (including a school district) may raise its tax base more than 6 percent over that levied in any one of the preceding three years without approval of the voters, school administrators and parent groups are required to spend much time and effort in cajoling the electorate for funds.

At the level of higher education, five four-year institutions have emerged since the close of the First World War. The citizens finally consented to expand the number of teacher-training institutions, and Southern Oregon College and Eastern Oregon College were founded in 1926 and 1929, respectively. The Sisters of the Holy Names of Jesus and Mary established Marylhurst College for women in 1930, and the Church of God started Warner Pacific College in 1937. After the Second World War, under the leadership of Stephen E. Epler, came the genesis of Portland State University, established as a two-year extension school for military veterans in 1946, a four-year degree-granting college in 1955, and a university in 1969.

Other important developments in the realm of higher education include the progress of Reed College, which by the quantitative measures of percentage of graduates attaining doctorates, Woodrow Wilson Fellowships, and Rhodes Scholarships is in the forefront of American private liberal arts colleges. After a power struggle among the alumni, faculty, and local legislators of Oregon Agricultural College and the University of Oregon in the late twenties and early thirties, the legislature established the Oregon State System of Higher Education to oversee all the state institutions of higher education. In addition to the rise of Portland State to university status, the post-Second World War years have seen the development of a thriving group of two-year community colleges in the old Oregon tradition of appreciation for vocational education. The largest of these, Portland Community College, founded in 1962, flourishing under its philosophy of an "educational shopping center," has grown to an enrollment of more than 15,000 persons in the middle 1970s. Although the public has taken some pride in these advances, the state's overall commitment to education has not been deep in appreciation or expenditures.

In literature and scholarship the story is much the same. There are certainly far more able men and women writing in the state of Oregon than at the time of Frederick Balch and Frances Fuller Victor. Yet in first-rate national figures the list is sparse. The first to attain this status was H. L. Davis, born in Yoncalla in 1896, and a practitioner of various trades from cowboy to typesetter in central Oregon, until he emerged from a year at Stanford and another in the army to win the prestigious Levinson Prize of Harriet Monroe's *Poetry Magazine* in 1922 (other winners of the early twenties included Wallace Stevens, Robert Frost, E. A. Robinson, and Amy Lowell). Davis next emerged as polemicist, not poet, in the biting diatribe, *Status Rerum*, written with James Stevens in 1927, which labelled the creative writers of the state as either mediocre or mercenary: "Is there something about the climate, or the soil, which inspires people to write tripe? Is there some occult influence, which catches them young, and shapes them to be instruments out of which tripe, and nothing but tripe, may issue?" Challenged to do better than those he scorned, Davis responded with a long novel, *Honey in the Horn* (1935), that was awarded the Pulitzer Prize in 1936.[3]

In this work, the first excellent novel to be written about the state, Davis dealt with the rural people of Oregon in 1906–1908. He realistically described, with deft characterizations of the average settlers and with sensitive attention to their natural environment, the ambitions, frustrations, and failures of the later pioneers who were too late to re-enact their parents' and grandparents' success in finding agrarian fulfillment in the Oregon Country. Lack of humid land, and the prohibitive cost of irrigation, farm machinery, and fencing, prevailed against their courage and left them only hopeless and embittered. *Honey in the Horn* is the account, perhaps too harsh to be fully accurate, not of the disintegration of the older values, but of the impossibility of their attainment in the new century.

Not until the 1960s did two other Oregon novels of first rank appear. In 1960 Don Berry published *Trask,* an excellent historical novel based upon a journey of the pioneer Elbridge Trask and two Indian companions along the Oregon Coast south from Clatsop Plains to open up the land on the shores of Tillamook Bay to white settlement. Using the raw materials of pioneer sources, Berry's imagination developed a plot that brilliantly enlightens the modern reader about the indigenous values of white settler and Indian occupant and their redefinition when the two cultures intersect. The evolution of Trask into a searcher for the Indian culture, the tragedy of the young Wakila without a place in either race, the integrity of Kilchis, chief of the Tilla-

3. Warren L. Clare, ed., " 'Poseurs, Parasites, and Pismires,' *Status Rerum,* by James Stevens and H. L. Davis," *PNQ* 61 (January 1970): 27.

mooks, and the insight of Charley Kehwha, Trask's Indian mentor throughout his quest, express this theme in vivid characterization. Berry followed his first success with *Moontrap* (1962), the trials of an ex-mountain man and his Indian wife in attempting to adjust to a life of farming and to the bigotry of their Oregon City neighbors in the 1850s, and with *To Build a Ship* (1963), which deals with the efforts of Tillamook Bay settlers to construct a homemade vessel to transport their goods to outside markets.

Four years after the publication of *Trask,* Ken Kesey's *Sometimes a Great Notion* appeared. Although dealing with universal themes and written in a vein that made it a favorite of the "counterculture" of the sixties, the novel superbly catches the meanness of smalltown life on the Oregon Coast, the pride of the logger in his conquest of the forest, and, above all, the varieties and impact of nature upon the hero, Hank Stamper, proprietor of a "gyppo" logging operation. The Wakonda Auga River, flowing by the Stamper home, sets the tone of the novel's grim action, and Kesey also illuminates the changing seasons in their various moods. Kesey's Stamper family is a testimony, although often a sordid one, to the enduring independence of Oregon's people.

In poetry several Oregon residents achieved national acclaim in the 1920s, including, in addition to Davis, Albert Wetjen, Howard McKinley Corning, Borghild Lee, Ada H. Hedges, Mary C. Davies, and Charles O. Olsen, who found outlets for their work in such periodicals as *Poetry,* the *Nation,* the *New Republic,* and the *American Mercury.* Although sometimes known as the "Portland Poets," their identification as a group came from their geographic location (the Northwest Poetry Society was organized in 1924) rather than their subject matter. Neither they nor other gifted successors were "regional" poets.

The development of modern painting and architecture is a somewhat different story, for in these arts the regional influences have struggled with national and international forces. Ironically, one architect who built upon the regional foundations laid by A. E. Doyle was not an Oregonian, not even an American, but an Italian, Pietro Belluschi, born in Ancona in 1899.

After study at Cornell, Belluschi moved to Portland by way of Idaho and practiced in the state from 1930 to 1950, then served as dean of architecture at the Massachusetts Institute of Technology for fifteen years before returning to Portland.

Unlike most in the history of Oregon's formal culture, Belluschi was an innovator of international reputation, an artist who shook off the eclectic classicism of contemporaries to open himself to the functional and organic influences of Frank Lloyd Wright, but clearly one who continued to be governed by local setting. As he himself wrote in 1941: "we may deduce that a region with similar natural and human attributes may have an architecture harmonious to them. The people are neighbors, their interests are alike, they respond the same way to life, they have the same materials at hand, they have similar landscape, the same climate." [4] From this regional consciousness, the influences of his partner Doyle, another brilliant architect, and also John Yeon and Harry Wentz, Belluschi's genius was reflected in a variety of buildings that made him internationally famous. He designed the building of the Portland Art Museum in 1930 and a wing of the structure in 1936, residences like the Jennings Sutor house, and churches, such as Saint Thomas More Chapel and Zion Lutheran Church. Both Belluschi and Yeon did award-winning designs for commercial buildings also.

For John Yeon, the other prominent member of the "Northwest School," fame first came in the design of the Aubrey Watzek House in 1936, a regional scheme that soon became a classic. Although Yeon did other residences in this vein, he also was a pioneer in experimenting with materials like plywood both before and after the Second World War. The influence of Belluschi, Yeon, and many others continues to the present in the "Northwest Style" with its "concern for the setting and integration of landscaping, the open functional plan, the broad sheltering pitched roof, and the use of naturally finished native woods." Their style is the most distinctive Oregon contribution to modern American culture, although in the fifties and sixties it

---

4. George McMath, "Buildings and Gardens," in Thomas Vaughan and Virginia Guest Ferriday, eds., *Space, Style and Structure: Building in Northwest America,* 2 vols. (Portland: Oregon Historical Society, 1974), 2:479.

lost ground to the "international style," a mark of the greater integration of the Pacific Northwest into the national and world culture. But for a short time at least, in this one discipline, Oregon stood apart, confidently asserting the integrity of its culture in the face of pressures to conform to the East Coast, California, or Europe.[5]

Oregon painters, too, have been torn between the region and the world in the last half-century. Certainly their knowledge of international currents was far greater than that of the pre-First World War artists. Equally certainly their work was widely appreciated in the region, and the institutions of the art world— galleries, university departments of fine arts, museums— increased in both quality and quantity. In the twenties and thirties, the Runquist brothers, Arthur and Albert, and Clayton S. Price, Harry Wentz, and David McCosh were among the best-known Oregon artists. They experimented with various styles as the region became less insular, but the Oregon landscape furnished them the subject matter for their best work, even when it was not representational. Price, for example, who developed an interest in Eastern religions and the holistic view of nature, was deeply affected by his local landscape.

In the forties and fifties Oregon artists reached out even more to the world. Carl Morris, Louis Bunce, and Michele Russo arrived in the 1940s. These artists, too, were painters of nature, although not representationally, but they and their colleagues in Oregon painting "were not much affected by abstract art before the 1950s, nor by social consciousness art. They painted in response to what they saw—very often the natural environment—according to the art tradition they were exploring at the time or had adopted." The younger artists who succeeded them, influenced by abstract expressionism or by the mélange of styles of the 1960s which broke down the divisions among the arts, have for the most part abandoned regional influences, as have the architects, for international directions.[6]

Probably the most fervent defender of Oregon culture would

5. McMath, "Buildings and Gardens," 2:476.

6. Rachel Griffin, "Portland and Its Environs," in *Art of the Pacific Northwest from the 1930s to the Present* (Washington: Smithsonian Institution Press, 1974), p. 18.

not assert that the state is in the front rank of American commonwealths. Although there have been men and women of distinction, and more of them with the passing years, such as Tom Hardy in sculpture, Ursula K. LeGuin in fiction, and William Stafford in poetry, and although there has been increasing support for cultural institutions, especially since the close of the Second World War, the people have created only a handful of institutions that are, measured against national standards, of the very top rank. Among these the oldest, founded in the nineteenth century, is the Oregon Historical Society. Although always a solid institution, the OHS underwent a renaissance with the coming of Thomas J. Vaughan as director in 1954. Under his leadership the society has become a distinguished institution with a manuscripts collection containing far more than Oregon history holdings, the only flourishing scholarly press in the state, a historical quarterly, and quarters that, in the testimony of Walter Muir Whitehill of the Boston Athenaeum, "for commodity, firmness, and delight, surpass anything we now have in the United States." [7] Many years ago Angus Bowmer, a young instructor at Southern Oregon Normal, planned at Ashland a Shakespeare festival. Since 1934, this institution in the foothills of the Siskiyous has overcome enormous handicaps to develop a reputation for its productions and physical plant, including a replica of the Globe Theater, that places it as a premiere Shakespearean institution. In the 1920s Mary V. Dodge and Jacques Gershkovitch conceived a plan for an orchestra of young musicians, the Portland Junior Symphony, that has now flourished for half a century. And Reed College almost since its founding has been regarded as a first-rate academic institution.

Yet in spite of these highly ranked institutions Oregonians for some time have self-consciously debated their cultural record. Most agree that their achievements have not been of the first order, some condemning, some exonerating the state for this condition but without providing a consensus to explain it. Some argue that the region is too new and thus lacking in historical as-

7. Walter Muir Whitehill, "Oregon Historical Center Dedication Address, September 23, 1966," *Oregon Historical Quarterly* 67 (September 1966): 199.

sociations, the Indians being conveniently discounted. Newness also means poverty, others maintain, for there has not been sufficient time to develop a leisured class to patronize artists, to endow museums or symphonies, and to support generously the opera or the symphony. Still others assert that the people have stultified the artist, citing the departures of Wood and Reed, and the later self-imposed exile of H. L. Davis and others. Davis himself, and Stevens, made this one of their principal charges against regional culture in their diatribe, *Status Rerum.*

Yet many of these explanations, or excuses, are unsatisfying, for the South and the Great Plains are poor and the plains, the Southwest, and California are as newly settled as Oregon; ethnic composition is about the same on the Great Plains as in Oregon. Perhaps an additional explanation of the condition of Oregon cultural life may be offered to supplement the others. When historian Dorothy Johansen assessed Oregon's first century of independence in 1949, she pointed out that the state's citizens have pursued "an unusually even tenor of existence. In fact, I would say our history is a recapitulation of the middle way, the historical norm, if there is such a thing, of our national history." [8] It could well be, however, that the lack of conflict, which is the essence of art, is the Oregon heritage that makes the formal cultural life so derivative and lacking in outstanding works of art. Oregonians have been homogeneous in values, ethnicity, and religion; with a small proportion of minority groups, racial conflicts in Oregon have been short-lived or forgotten. In a colonial state the extremes of wealth and the diversity of occupations are slight compared to most states, and class conflict has been muted. Although the semiarid environment of eastern Oregon was as strange to the people of the humid lands as the western regions of Kansas, Nebraska, or the Dakotas, it was settled later after earlier experiences on the Great Plains or California had been assimilated. In any case, most Oregonians lived, throughout their history, in a natural environment familiar not only to American migrants but to those

8. Dorothy O. Johansen, "Oregon's Role in American History: An Old Theme Recast," *PNQ* 40 (April 1949): 92.

from the agricultural and forested regions of northern Europe. There have been sectional struggles between east and west, but the weight of numbers has been on those west of the Cascades, and the clashes have been unspectacular. Within the great population center of the state, the Willamette Valley, the rural-urban rivalry, because of the rapid communications between town and country, has paled into insignificance beside the upstate-downstate rivalry in New York or Illinois or the north-south rivalry in California. All of this is not to say that there is no higher culture in Oregon, or that there never will be great art or cultural institutions, but the historical record reveals that the people have been satisfied with the competent, not the distinguished.

Epilogue: Oregon at the Bicentennial

*T*O many Americans of the bicentennial years Oregon seems a fruitful garden, a sort of "chlorophyll commonwealth," set amidst the dessicated wilderness of contemporary urban pollution, violence, crime, and alienation. They read of the state's "livability" or of its "quality of life" as measured by a host of quantitative indices compiled by government researchers, scholars, and journalists. They know of the bottle deposit bill, of the Scenic Rivers Act, and the aerosol spray can statute. Oregonians themselves reinforce the Edenic images and underscore the data by guarding the state against incipient encroachers. A governor urges visitors "to come but not stay"; bumper stickers exhort potential tourists to "visit Colorado"; "ungreeting cards" tell of Oregon's single day of summer. More positively, what Oregonians see themselves as representing, what has been their success in not only drawing but holding people, what they fear they have made too appealing, is a commonwealth in which common decency has been exalted to a way of life, in which there has been a paucity of charismatic figures, where quiet competence, not the pursuit of excellence, is virtuous. This vision disappoints some, who go away, reviling the state as they depart: "Somehow I believe," wrote one disenchanted young person, "that the future of American life is not being decided in the Willamette Valley, but in the chaotic, violent, corrupt and thoroughly exciting urban places in America."

229

This criticism, although heartfelt, misses the mark, for Oregonians have never envisioned themselves as settling the future of the nation. What they have tried to do is to retain the past, and to a large extent they have succeeded in this quest. Oregon has always been like an eighteenth-century club whose members value highly the qualities of self-restraint, cohesion, loyalty, trust, and exclusiveness. Yet the club will admit new members to replenish its ranks and also, although grudgingly, to introduce new ideas, at least those that will enable it to adjust old values to present pressures. Oregon's uniqueness lies in its success in retaining the commonplace and its adventuresomeness in pursuit of the ordinary. The state is, paradoxically, a progressive anachronism, and the story of its dogged resistance yet successful accommodation to the forces of national development furnishes the central theme of its history and remains the state's principal legacy to the American experiment. Oregon's appeal to the nation at the time of the bicentennial lies in this conservatism as well as in its resemblance to the Thirteen Colonies on the eve of the Revolution.

For there are several similarities between the old colonies and the contemporary state. Both have been in many respects appendages of a "mother country." Producer of raw materials, market for manufactured goods, an insignificant political unit, both have been true colonial regions. Culturally, both have been inferior to their metropolitan mentors. Yet in spite of their impotence and backwardness, which they candidly acknowledge, they have had an influence on those who ostensibly control them. Britons feared as well as scorned the American colonists for the explosiveness of their political theory and for their example of a socially and economically fluid commonwealth. So, too, do modern Americans, with nostalgia or with anticipation, look to Oregon for inspiration in responsible government, civil personal relationships, and respect for the natural world. Oregon's experience proclaims, as does that of the Founding Fathers, that the heritage of the Enlightenment, the belief that men and women by the application of reason can shape their destiny, individually and collectively, is neither chimera nor delusion, but a promise and a hope.

Suggestions for Further Reading

Although there is no one-volume history of Oregon in print, sub-stantial portions of three excellent works dealing with larger areas sur-vey the history of the state. The best interpretation of the Pacific Northwest is Dorothy O. Johansen and Charles Gates, *Empire of the Columbia: A History of the Pacific Northwest* (2d ed. New York: Harper and Row, 1967), a work that integrates regional, national, and international developments. Earl S. Pomeroy, *The Pacific Slope: A History of California, Oregon, Washington, Idaho, Utah, and Nevada* (New York: Alfred A. Knopf, 1965), is brilliant and well-written. David S. Lavender, in *Land of Giants: The Drive to the Pacific Northwest, 1750–1950* (Garden City, N.Y.: Doubleday, 1958), em-phasizes heroic deeds and great men and women, particularly those of the nineteenth century.

For the Indians, Ella E. Clark, *Indian Legends of the Pacific North-west* (Berkeley and Los Angeles: University of California Press, 1953), is a compilation of the Indians' views of men and nature. In the splen-did novel *Trask* (New York: Viking Press, 1960), Don Berry deals with many of the same themes and their conflict with the values of the Caucasians. A superb account of an important tribe from the precon-tact era to the 1960s is Theodore Stern, *The Klamath Tribe: A People and Their Reservation* (Seattle: University of Washington Press, 1965), which traces the impact of white attitudes and policies upon the Indian culture.

Among the host of works on the period of exploration and the fur trade are Lavender's *Land of Giants* (cited above) and three other works. Stewart H. Holbrook in his smoothly written work, *The Co-lumbia* (New York: Rinehart, 1956), talks of the explorers in a color-ful vein. John E. Bakeless is equally interesting in his dual biography, *Lewis and Clark, Partners in Discovery* (New York: Morrow, 1947). Warren L. Cook's magisterial *Flood Tide of Empire: Spain and the Pacific Northwest, 1543–1819* (New Haven: Yale University Press,

1973) also gives detailed treatment of the Russian, British, and American interests in the region. The most interesting account of Astor's venture is Gabriel Franchére, *Journal of a Voyage on the North West Coast of North America,* ed. W. Kaye Lamb (Toronto: The Champlain Society, 1969), written by a participant in the events who wrote clearly and vividly.

The life of the American pioneers is captured in A. B. Guthrie, *The Way West* (New York: Sloane, 1949), a fictional account of the settlers' reasons for going to Oregon and their adventures on the trail. Antebellum politics is the theme of Robert Johannsen's detailed *Frontier Politics and the Sectional Conflict: The Pacific Northwest on the Eve of the Civil War* (Seattle: University of Washington, 1955). Economic life of the times is carefully described in Arthur L. Throckmorton's *Oregon Argonauts: Merchant Adventurers on the Western Frontier* (Portland: Oregon Historical Society, 1961).

For post–Civil War cultural and economic life there are several outstanding works. James B. Hedges makes clear the intricacies of railroad building in his *Henry Villard and the Railways of the Northwest* (New Haven: Yale University Press, 1930). Donald W. Meinig deals lucidly with the central and eastern sections of Oregon (and Washington) in their changing patterns of land use in *The Great Columbia Plain: A Historical Geography, 1805–1910* (Seattle: University of Washington Press, 1968). Malcolm Clark has provided a portrait of several features of Oregon's society, especially that of Portland, in his annotated edition of Judge Deady's diaries, *Pharisee Among Philistines: The Diary of Judge Matthew P. Deady, 1871–1892,* 2 vols. (Portland: Oregon Historical Society, 1975). Harold L. Davis's picaresque novel, *Honey in the Horn* (New York: Harper, 1935), which won the Pulitzer Prize in 1936, describes Oregon's economy and society in the early years of the twentieth century.

On more specialized topics, a splendid anthology is Thomas Vaughan and Virginia Guest Ferriday, eds., *Space, Style and Structure: Building in Northwest America,* 2 vols. (Portland: Oregon Historical Society, 1974), which goes beyond architecture to encompass many aspects of the daily life of the people. Twentieth-century politics is lucidly treated in Robert E. Burton, *Democrats of Oregon: The Pattern of Minority Politics, 1900–1956* (Eugene: University of Oregon Press, 1970). A brief, recent, and interesting history of Portland is

Thomas Vaughan and Terrence O'Donnell, *Portland: A Historical Sketch and Guide* (Portland: Oregon Historical Society, 1976). Ken Kesey in *Sometimes a Great Notion* (New York: Viking, 1964) has given first-rate fictional treatment of a "gyppo" logging family in southwestern Oregon. A modern collection of essays on various aspects of Oregon history is Thomas Vaughan, ed., *The Western Shore: Oregon Country Essays Honoring the American Revolution* (Portland: Oregon Historical Society, 1975).

Index